Shakespeare

Hamlet

EDITED BY HUW GRIFFITHS

Consultant Editor: Nicolas Tredell

First published 2005 by
PALGRAVE MACMILLAN
Houndmills, Basingstoke, Hampshire RG21 6XS and
175 Fifth Avenue, New York, N.Y. 10010
Companies and representatives throughout the world.

PALGRAVE MACMILLAN is the global academic imprint of the Palgrave
Macmillan division of St. Martin's Press, LLC and of Palgrave Macmillan Ltd.
Macmillan® is a registered trademark in the United States, United Kingdom
and other countries. Palgrave is a registered trademark in the European
Union and other countries.

ISBN 1–4039–4006–1 hardback
ISBN 1–4039–1136–3 paperback

This book is printed on paper suitable for recycling and made from fully
managed and sustained forest sources.

A catalogue record for this book is available from the British Library

A catalog record for this book is available from the Library of Congress

10 9 8 7 6 5 4 3 2 1
14 13 12 11 10 09 08 07 06 05

Printed in China.

CONTENTS

Contains important information about how the extracts used in the Guide
have been reprinted and what versions of Hamlet have been used when
quoting from the play.

Introduces the key concepts that will be a feature of the Guide.

Neoclassical Approaches to *Hamlet* or 'Does
Ophelia's breath smell?'

This chapter discusses the reactions to Hamlet from the period of the
Restoration of the monarchy in 1660 through to the mid-eighteenth century. This period was the first to get to grips with Shakespeare's work as
coming from a world that was no longer familiar to the critic. Criticism
from this time is dominated by the demands of neoclassicism which
sought, with varying degrees of exactitude, to judge drama by the standards of unity laid out by Aristotle in the Poetics. This chapter examines
these neoclassical 'rules' and considers the extent to which they were
successfully applied to Hamlet as well as some of the ways that critics,
such as James Drake and Samuel Johnson, whilst operating within the
neoclassical paradigm, sought to explain Shakespeare's diversion from
its tenets.

From Sensibility to Romanticism: 'the majesty of melancholy'

In the later eighteenth century, Hamlet came to the attention of two Scottish
academics, William Richardson and Henry Mackenzie, both of them associated with what has been called the 'cult of sensibility'. Their writing shifted
attention away from the neoclassical concern with the decorum of the

play's narrative towards an investigation into the workings of Hamlet's character. Their idea of Hamlet as an isolated figure, too virtuous for the corrupt world in which he found himself, was picked up on by the next literary generation, the Romantics, who delivered a Hamlet who was too philosophical for the world of politics in which he was caught up. This chapter will trace the ways in which Romantic writers – from the German novelist, Goethe, through to the English poets, Coleridge and Keats – produced a Hamlet in their own image – thoughtful, melancholic and isolated. Their version of Hamlet reveals some of their own attitudes towards the creative process.

Psychoanalytic Approaches: Oedipus and After

In this chapter we will see how the work of the Romantics in the early nineteenth century to uncover Hamlet's inner motivations comes to fruition in the ways that he is treated in the early twentieth-century discipline of psychoanalysis. Psychoanalytic readings of Hamlet have often been dominant in the popular understanding of the play. Elements that were previously seen as flaws in the plot or in Hamlet's character are now seen, by Freud and his pupil, Ernest Jones, as symptoms of psychosis. Freud's famous analysis of the Oedipus complex is seen in operation in Hamlet's apparent delay in exacting revenge on his father. Later critics, influenced by Freudian psychoanalysis, will be seen to react against the master. Some attempt to rewrite the family drama that Freud described. Others refute the gender bias that is inherent to his system.

The Early Twentieth Century

The study of English literature as a university discipline emerged in the early part of the twentieth century. An important influence on the study of Shakespeare from this time, and the dominant presence in this chapter, was A.C. Bradley and his book, Shakespearean Tragedy. This chapter shows how he develops his idea of 'action issuing from character, or in character issuing in action' and how this results in a character-based type of criticism. Subsequent critics, such as Dover Wilson and L.C. Knights, however much they reject some of Bradley's work, are shown to be operating in his shadow. This chapter also presents T.S. Eliot's notion of the 'objective correlative' as he developed it in his reading of Hamlet.

CHAPTER FIVE   105

Contemporary Interpretations: Historicist *Hamlet*

In the last twenty years, work on the English Renaissance has been
governed by an overriding interest in the historical contexts of literary
production. Critics, such as Barker and Belsey, have seen, in Hamlet, the
formation of a modern idea of what it means to be human. Where
earlier critics were interested in 'character', more recent critics will be
interested in the 'subject'. They argue that Hamlet's 'interiority' is not
essential and timeless, but part of a historical development. Following this
insight, other critics have further elaborated on the historical contexts
which have produced this kind of subjectivity. Others, here represented by
Harold Bloom, have resented these developments as counter-intuitive and
anti-humanist.

CHAPTER SIX   146

Contemporary Interpretations: Feminism

Much of the criticism we will have looked at in the previous chapters will
have attached great importance to the relationships between Hamlet and
either his mother or Ophelia. However, rarely will the figure of the woman
in the plays have been given great consideration. In this chapter, we will
see how some recent critics have sought to redress the balance of our
interest in Hamlet, interrogating the position of women both in the play
and in the historical contexts of its production as well as addressing the
perceived gender bias of previous critics.

CHAPTER SEVEN   159

Derrida and Lévinas

As well as providing a brief summary of the history of Hamlet criticism as it
has been outlined in the Guide, this chapter looks at possible futures by
examining the position of the play in the work of two important theorists of
the twentieth century. Both offer a way out of the sometimes tautological
approaches to the play that have been seen in earlier generations –
Derrida by helping us rethink the way in which narrative relates to political
consequences, through the figure of the ghost and Lévinas by reintroducing
ethical considerations into our account of literature.

ACKNOWLEDGEMENTS

The editor and publishers wish to thank the following for permission to use copyright material:

Janet Adelman, for material from *Suffocating Mothers: Fantasies of Maternal Origin in Shakespeare's Plays, Hamlet to The Tempest*, Routledge (1992) pp. 10, 11, 12–13, 15–16, 20, 24–5, by permission of Taylor & Francis Books, Inc.

Francis Barker, for material from *The Tremulous Private Body: Essays on Subjection*, Routledge (1984) pp. 27–8, 28–9, 36–7, 37, 38, by permission of Taylor & Francis Books Ltd.

Catherine Belsey, for material from *The Subject of Tragedy: Identity and Difference in Renaissance Drama*, Routledge (1985) pp. ix–x, 27–8, 40–1, 115–16, by permission of Taylor & Francis Books Ltd; and *Shakespeare and Loss of Eden: the Construction of Family Values in Early Modern Culture*, (2001) pp. 139, 158–61, 172–3, by permission of Palgrave Macmillan.

Harold Bloom, for material from *Shakespeare: The Invention of the Human*, Fourth Estate (1998) pp. 383–4, 385–6, 400–1, 405, 408, 408–9. Copyright © 1998 by Harold Bloom, by permission of Riverhead Books, an imprint of Penguin Group (USA) Inc.

A.C. Bradley, for material from *Shakespearean Tragedy* (1904) Penguin edition (1991) pp. 29–30, 35, 108–9, 110, 117–18. 119–20, by permission of Royal Holloway, University of London.

Avi Erlich, for material from *Hamlet's Absent Father* (1977) pp. 25, 28–31, 32–3, 51, 192–8, 249–52, 260–1. Copyright © 1977, renewed, Princeton University Press, by permission of Princeton University Press.

Sigmund Freud, for material from *The Interpretation of Dreams*, ed. J Crick (1999) pp. 201–3, 204, by permission of Oxford University Press.

Jonathan Goldberg, for material from 'Hamlet's Hand', *Shakespeare Quarterly*, 39:3 (1988) pp. 311–13, 321–2, 323–6. Copyright © 1988 Folger Shakespeare Library, by permission of The Johns Hopkins University Press.

Samuel Johnson, for material from *The Yale Edition of the Works of Samuel Johnson Vol. VII*, ed. A Sherbo (1968) pp. 973–4, 981, 1010–11, by permission of Yale University Press.

Ernest Jones, for material from *Hamlet and Oedipus* (1949) pp. 45, 50–1, 60–1, 69–70, 80, 81–2, 82–3, 88. Copyright © 1949 by Ernest Jones, renewed © 1982 by Merwyn Jones, by permission of W W Norton & Company, Inc.

G. Wilson Knight, for material from *The Wheel of Fire: Interpretations of Shakespearean Tragedy*, Routledge (1949) pp. 3, 27–8, 32, 38–9, 40, 45–6 by permission of Taylor & Francis Books Ltd.

L.C. Knights, for material from *Hamlet and Other Shakespearean Essays* (1979) pp. 55–9, by permission of Cambridge University Press.

Ronald Knowles, for material from 'Hamlet and Counter Humanism', *Renaissance Quarterly*, 52 (1999) pp. 1048, 1048–9, 1052, 1058–60, 1061–2, 1063–4, by permission of Renaissance Society of America.

Patricia Parker, for material from, 'Othello and Hamlet: Dilation, Spying, and the "Secret Place" of Women', *Representations*, 0:44 (1993) pp. 76–8, 79–81, 86. Copyright © 1993 The Regents of the University of California, by permission of University of California Press.

Alan Sinfield, for material from *Faultlines: Cultural Materialism and the Politics of Dissident Reading* (1992) pp. 222–3, 227–8, 229, 230. Copyright © 1992 The Regents of the University of California, by permission of University of California Press and Oxford University Press.

Leonard Tennenhouse, for material from *Power on Display: The Politics of Shakespeare's Forms*, Routledge (1986) pp. 85, 87, 88–90, 93, by permission of Taylor & Francis Books Ltd.

J. Dover Wilson, for material from *what Happens in Hamlet* (1951) pp. 16, 39, 43, 46–7, 49–50, 228–9, by permission of Cambridge University Press.

Every effort has been made to trace the copyright holders but if any have been inadvertently overlooked the publishers will be pleased to make the necessary arrangement at the first opportunity.

NOTES ON THE TEXTS USED

When a passage has been taken from an older text, the spelling has been silently modernised. I have also done this with longer, indented quotations from *Hamlet* itself, all of which I have silently replaced with the relevant passage from Harold Jenkins' Arden second edition.[1] The text of the play, *Hamlet*, as it is arrived at in this and other modern editions is a composite text derived from different early printings of the play, most usually the Second Quarto of 1605 and the Folio text from 1623. When modern editions of early modern dramas are produced, their main task is to tackle the inevitable divergences that will be found between different early printings of the text, all in the absence of an authoritative manuscript or authorised edition. The textual history of *Hamlet* is particularly vexed for two reasons. First, there exists a critical controversy over whether the whole play is a substantive revision of a pre-existing play which may or may not be by either Shakespeare or Thomas Kyd. Second, there is a continuing debate over the status of the first printing of *Hamlet* proper, the First Quarto of 1603. Although textual matters are necessarily an essential part of any literary criticism, dealing as they do with important questions of context and intention, they will be seen to have had little direct impact on the content of this book. Most critics have operated, however blindly, from an assumption that a single text called *Hamlet* does exist or, at least, that it did exist at some point. When editorial concerns do impinge on the criticism that is represented here – in Dr Johnson's notes to *his* edition of *Hamlet* or in Harold Bloom's argument about *Hamlet* as a play that is, itself about 'revision' – then these will be seen as part of an argument that extends beyond the immediate controversies of textual scholarship.

Nevertheless, it must be admitted that in recent years there has emerged a more sensitive approach to the relationship between textual matters and literary criticism, as it is normally understood. Since the 1980s, an overtly historicist paradigm has emerged as *the* key approach to literature in general, and to early modern literature in particular. With the variety of different historicisms on offer there has arrived a greater sensitivity to the contexts of production for the literary text. Debates over the supposed authenticity of any given text, judged on an understanding of its supposed proximity to authorial intention have largely been replaced by more nuanced discussions of the precise relevance of the different early editions. The *Hamlet* first quarto has traditionally been though of as a 'Bad Quarto', a text that has been assembled not from any written copy of the play (either the author's 'foul papers' or a prompt copy) but from the flawed memory of one of the actors. Although this idea cannot be wholly dispensed with, some more recent readings have seen the First Quarto as representing a specific performance of the play, aimed at a different effect and a different audience from the other two versions that we have. It appears, for example, to be much more religiously orthodox in its approach to questions about the afterlife.

For the large part, the play *Hamlet* does not exist as a single identity other than in the imagination of its readers and audience. However, the text *Hamlet* is just as much produced by its various critics asking and responding to the same questions over the centuries. If *Hamlet*, the single play, does not really exist, it does not necessarily detract from the interest of the accumulated debate over this fiction, a debate represented in the extracts reprinted in the Guide.

All Act, scene and line references to *Hamlet* are given in Arabic rather than Roman numerals, e.g. 3.1.58–92 rather than III.i.58–92.

Where a writer, critic or other significant figure is mentioned for the first time in the Guide, birth and, where appropriate, death dates have been provided wherever possible, but in some cases these were not available.

Introduction

> We have been so used to this tragedy that we hardly know how to criticize it any more than we should know how to describe our own faces.
>
> (William Hazlitt)

> He hadn't heard of Shakespeare, but Hamlet sounded familiar.
> (Jonathan Safran Foer, *Everything is Illuminated*)

*H*amlet is the most familiar piece of literature in Western culture, and Hamlet, the character, the most enduring figure from the English Renaissance. As the statement above by William Hazlitt (1778–1830) suggests, a writer who begins to analyse *Hamlet* must also embark upon a process of self-discovery. As a text, it is already so well known that it can act a little like a mirror. Harold Bloom writes of the experience of reading *Hamlet* that, 'we seem to have read it before, even when we encounter it for the first time'.[1] This is, I think, true. When you watch the film *Casablanca* (1942) for the first time, there is always that reaction of 'That's where that line comes from!' With *Hamlet*, it is something more. Even without recognising the famous speeches and lines, we would recognise the play as being fundamentally entrenched in our collective psyche.

It might also be said that it seems as if *Hamlet* has been read for us before. Our reception of the play is bound up in the many readings that have preceded us and that have entered, with varying degrees of impact, into the public perception of this play. The way that we think of *Hamlet* would not be the same without Samuel Johnson (1709–84), Samuel Taylor Coleridge (1772–1834), Sigmund Freud (1856–1939), T.S. Eliot (1888–1965) or A.C. Bradley (1851–1935) – all of whose work will be looked at in this Guide.[2] The story of the criticism of *Hamlet* is, therefore, a history of criticism itself and sometimes could even be seen as the story of Western thought more generally. To trace the reactions of writers to this particular play from the early days of neoclassicism in the late seventeenth century, through to the developments of Romanticism in the late eighteenth and early nineteenth centuries and then through to the psychoanalytic, materialist and historicist literary criticisms of the twentieth century is not only to follow the various ways in which people have responded to *this* play, but also to track the various assumptions that people have brought to Shakespeare, and the questions they have asked of literature in general.

The purpose of this Guide is to help students of *Hamlet* find their way through the sometimes bewildering array of material relating to the play. There are a number of critical questions that have been applied specifically to *Hamlet* over time, and this Guide will follow the various responses that critics have had to these in particular. They include a perception that the play is in some way an artistic failure and that its enigmatic nature is partly the result of its not being fully formed. What constitutes a literary failure for these writers is frequently just as illuminating as what they consider successful. There is also an ongoing concern in many of these writers with the idea that Hamlet delays in carrying out his father's instructions in the play. However much the idea that this play is concerned with delay might be denied, the idea is still central to our understanding of its structure and the actions of its main protagonist. It is returned to time and again by writers responding to this play, and the answers they give or even the way that they phrase the question, reveal the nature of their approach to the play as a whole.

The first two chapters of the book will look at some criticism from earlier periods – from the years of the Restoration (the 1660s) through to the early years of the nineteenth century. The specific focus of these chapters will be the development away from the early concentration on 'plot' as the single most important feature of a successful play to the Romantics' concern with character. The basis of neoclassicism in Aristotle's *Poetics* will be explored and we will see the ways in which Aristotelian principles come to work in the criticism of the late seventeenth and early eighteenth centuries. Students will be able to read extracts of neoclassical *Hamlet* criticism, presented in such a way as to reveal the principles and assumptions that are at work in them. The same is true of the criticism of the late eighteenth and early nineteenth centuries which came to reject neoclassical principles as inappropriate ways of approaching a dramatist like Shakespeare, who was not himself interested in the classical unities. In the extracts reprinted here, students will see the revolutionary character of much of this criticism in its reaction to previous assumptions about the way that we should approach the play. At the same time, they will be able to appreciate the contexts of this new approach in the philosophies of the Romantic movement.

The chief focus of the next two chapters will be the important developments of the early twentieth century. In popular opinion, Hamlet is often thought of as having a problem with sex – an obsession with his mother's sexual relations with his uncle, an unhealthy relationship with Ophelia. The analyses of psychoanalysis and their subsequent influence on cinema depictions of the prince have been chiefly responsible for this popular image. The chapter on psychoanalysis will situate Freud's analysis of Hamlet within the context of his advance of the Oedipus complex as an important stage in our sexual development, enabling the student to see from where this impression of Hamlet has come. Subsequent psychoanalytic writers will be seen either developing Freud's rather sketchy reading of *Hamlet* in more detail, or reacting against him by shifting the emphases of his analysis. Chapter 4 in the Guide will present the reader with key extracts from important writers on *Hamlet* from the early years of English literature as an academic discipline. The dominating influence here will be A.C. Bradley. This will enable students to see how their subject developed in its early years and provide them with a background to understand the reactions and developments of later criticism.

The final chapters will look at more contemporary readings of *Hamlet*, showing how the debates of recent critics have developed, and moved on, from the earlier accounts of the play. Chapter 5 will show how the greater interest in historical contexts of literary production have affected readings of Hamlet's 'subjectivity' in particular, placing these readings within the context of 'new historicism' as the leading force in criticism of Renaissance literature. Chapter 6 will look at how feminist analyses of the play have provided still more nuanced historicised readings of *Hamlet* as well as reacting against the gender bias of much older criticism. The final Chapter 7 offers a summary of much of what has been covered in the Guide as well as suggestions about possible routes forward in the story of *Hamlet*.

It is hoped that as well as introducing the reader to a variety of different interpretations of *Hamlet*, this Guide will also serve as a way into various different periods in the history of literature and of literary criticism. The choices made in the selection of specific periods are clearly not the only possible ones. The wealth of material on *Hamlet* means that certain developments and periods have to be excluded. I have tried, however, to isolate periods and movements that seem to be of particular consequence and to demonstrate clear divergence of approach as well as links in areas of concern. With the aid of these extracts, readers should be able to compare the responses of different periods' critics, both to the same critical problems and to each other.

CHAPTER ONE

Neoclassical Approaches to *Hamlet* or 'Does Ophelia's breath smell?'

I t is a little disconcerting to discover that one of the focuses of debate, in the early days of *Hamlet*'s critical reception and in the early days of literary criticism, was the state of Ophelia's breath. Was it, or was it not, 'rank'? However, it was precisely this delicate matter that appeared at the centre of critical interest at the origins of modern English literary criticism.

Whilst determining the moment of origin for English literary criticism might be considered an impossible task, it is nevertheless true to say that the late seventeenth and early eighteenth centuries witnessed a boom in the amount of writing devoted to the critical analysis of literary texts. This period is of added interest to those of us who are concerned with the development of Shakespeare criticism because it is the period which immediately follows the age of Shakespearean theatre. This enables us to see for the first time that writers are attempting to come to terms with literature that does not quite fit their own cultural parameters. The social and cultural contexts that fostered the public theatre of the late sixteenth and early seventeenth centuries were no longer in place. The civil wars of the 1630s and 1640s, the Commonwealth years of the 1650s and the subsequent restoration of the monarchy in 1660 had all made sure that there was, at least, a decisive political break from the years of the Tudors and early Stuarts. Such seismic shifts in the political structures of the country were reflected in societal and cultural changes. It is in this struggle to understand what was, by now, an alien literature and to translate it into current language for a new audience, that literary criticism is born. In this period Shakespeare begins to solidify his reputation as England's greatest writer. And yet, there is also a failure fully to understand, or even necessarily to approve of, the way in which he wrote. In the attempt to bring these two contradictory ideas together, a discourse of literary criticism is born.

It is precisely in this opening between the Shakespearean stage and later seventeenth-century culture that a critical concern emerged over the state of Ophelia's breath. At least, it did on the part of the writer,

Jeremy Collier (1650–1726). This turned into the first critical contro-versy over *Hamlet* when, in a response to Jeremy Collier's *A Short View of the Immorality and Profaneness of the English Stage* (1698), James Drake (1667–1707) writes that Collier's allegation that Ophelia has rank-smelling breath was, in fact, misguided.

■ His [Shakespeare's] *Hamlet*, a play of the first rate, has the misfortune to fall under Mr. Collier's displeasure, and Ophelia, who has had the luck hitherto to keep her reputation, is at last censured for lightness in her frenzy. Nay, Mr. Collier is so familiar with her as to make an unkind discov-ery of the unsavouriness of her breath, which no body suspected before. But it may be this is a groundless surmise, and Mr. Collier is deceived by a bad nose, or a rotten tooth of his own; and then he is obliged to beg the Poet's and the Lady's pardon for the wrong he has done 'em.[1] □

Drake is responding to Collier's allegations, which were made a year earlier, where Collier criticises Shakespeare for what he sees as an indecorous representation of a young woman in the person of Ophelia. One twentieth-century commentator, Paul Conklin, has called this interchange between Collier and Drake, 'the nearest approach to a for-mal *Hamlet* criticism in the seventeenth century'.[2] Collier, in *A Short View*, is arguing against what he considers 'the immodesty of the stage', and particularly of the modern stage. He claims that ancient dramatists, and Euripides in particular, fared much better. Collier's particular com-plaint is against the presentation of women on stage without proper regard for what he considers their 'natural' modesty.

■ Obscenity in any Company is a rustic uncreditable Talent; but among women 'tis particularly rude. Such talk would be very affrontive in conver-sation, and not endured by any lady of reputation. Whence then comes it to pass that those liberties which disoblige so much in conversation, should entertain upon the stage? Do the women leave all the regards to decency and conscience behind them when they come to the play-house? Or does the place transform their inclinations, and turn their former aversions into pleasure? Or were their pretences to sobriety elsewhere nothing but hypocrisy and grimace? Such suppositions as these are all satyr and invective: they are rude imputations upon the whole sex. To treat the ladies with such stuff is no better than taking their money to abuse them. It sup-poses their imagination vicious, and their memories ill-furnished: that they are practised in the language of the stews, and pleased with the scenes of brutishness. [...] Now to bring women under such misbehaviour is violence to their native modesty, and a misrepresentation of their sex. For modesty, as Mr. Rapin observes, is the character of women. To represent them without this quality is to make monsters of them, and throw them out of their kind.[3] □

Collier argues that representing women on stage as immodest is inappropriate, monstrous even. It misrepresents the true nature of women which is, rather, to be modest. That is, even as particular female characters need, as a contingency of the plot, to turn mad, a good playwright would still contain their behaviour and language within the bounds of decency and a sense of the polite. The 'Mr. Rapin' to whom he refers is the contemporary French critic, René Rapin (1621–87), who shared Collier's concern with the decorum of neoclassicism. His *Reflexions sur la Poétique d'Aristotle* had been translated into English by the critic, Thomas Rymer (1641–1713), in 1674. Much of this concern for decorum in drama entered into English dramatic criticism through contact with French conventions for the theatre. Collier believes Shakespeare falls down on this when he is compared to classical writers of tragedy, such as Euripides (c.480–406 BC) who, with the character Phaedra, from his play *Hippolytus*, stretches the representation of women to its limits whilst always maintaining decorum.

■ Euripides, who was no negligent observer of human nature, is always careful of this decorum. Thus Phaedra when possessed with an infamous passion, takes all imaginable pains to conceal it. She is as regular and reserved in her language as the most virtuous matron. 'Tis true, the force of shame and desire, the scandal of satisfying, and the difficulty of parting with her inclinations, disorder her to distraction. However, her frenzy is not lewd; she keeps her modesty even after she has lost her wits. Had Shakespeare secured this point for his young virgin Ophelia, the play had been better contrived. Since he was resolved to drown the lady like a kitten, he should have set her a-swimming a little sooner. To keep her alive only to sully her reputation, and discover the rankness of her breath, was very cruel. But it may be said the freedoms of distraction go for nothing, a fever has no faults, and a man *non compos* [not in his right mind], may kill without murder. It may be so: but then such people ought to be kept in dark rooms and without company. To show them, or let them loose, is somewhat unreasonable. But after all, the modern stage seems to depend upon this expedient. Women are sometimes represented silly, and sometimes mad, to enlarge their liberty; and screen their impudence from Censure: ... [4] □

These objections to *Hamlet* are not necessarily uncharacteristic of a certain kind of late seventeenth-century reaction to plays by Shakespeare and his contemporaries. Part of the reason for these objections was what has been seen as the rise in 'politeness' during this period. After the Restoration of the Stuart monarchy, there began the long rise in influence of the English middle classes.[5] With this rise in prominence, or at least influence, of the middle classes, came a change of ethos relating to behaviour in public. At the end of the seventeenth century, the old social mores that favoured the behaviour patterns of the courtly aristocracy began to disappear. The theatre became a focus for debate in this rapidly changing social and cultural climate. That this should be the case is perhaps obvious as the English stage inherited a repertoire from a previous age. It was where Restoration society confronted its past and the behaviour that was acceptable in its past. The plays of Shakespeare continued to be performed. And yet, in some ways, the audience for these plays defined their own civility *against* what they saw as the uncivilised behaviour of the previous age from which some of their favourite drama emerged. People tended to see the age before the civil wars as barbaric compared to their attempts at civility. Criticism sought to deal with this disjunction in taste and reception. A twenty-first century commentator makes this connection between theatre attendance, politeness and the beginnings of literary criticism in discussing the motivation behind a key text in the early history of English literary criticism, the *Essay of Dramatic Poesy* (1668) by John Dryden (1631–1700).

■ Dryden's first extended work of criticism appeared in 1667 as *The Essay of Dramatick Poesie*. It was the immediate result of his direct engagement in the Restoration theatre as well as a first effort to come to grips with the problem of the rival claims of ancients and moderns. In the years immediately following the Restoration the young author had successfully launched his career as poet and playwright. The time was ripe for experiment; civil war and Interregnum [a term used to describe the period in which there was no King] had virtually closed the theatres and interrupted the cultural life of the court. When Charles II returned from exile, he brought the foreign mode and encouraged French fashions. Elizabethan [and Jacobean] plays were revived, it is true, and were popular, but the long hiatus and changed audience opened the way for innovation. As John Evelyn (1620–1706) noted after a performance of *Hamlet* in 1661, 'now the old plays begin to disgust this refined age, since his majesty's being so long abroad'.[6] □

John Evelyn's impatience with the play seems to provide evidence for the shift in taste that underpins Jeremy Collier's later, more thorough condemnation. This is the only occasion that Evelyn refers to Shakespeare in his diary, but he makes his fears about the theatre in general known in another, later entry.

■ This night was acted my Lord Brahal's tragedy called *Mustapha* before their Majesties &c: at Court: at which I was present, very seldom at any time, going to the public theatres, for many reasons, now as they were abused, to an atheistical liberty, foul and undecent; Women now (and never 'til now) permitted to appear and act, which inflaming several young noble-men and gallants, become their whores, and to some their wives, witness the Earle of Oxford, Sir R: Howard, Pr. Rupert, the E: of Dorset, and another greater person than any of these, who fell into their snares, to the reproach of their noble families, and ruin both of their body and soul: I was invited to see this tragedy, exceedingly well writ, by my Lord Chamberlain, though in my mind, I did not approve of any such pastime, in a season of such judgments and calamity.[7] □

Evelyn's contempt for theatre going merges with his contempt for the court of Charles II, which he sees as debauched. The phrase, 'another greater person than any of these' undoubtedly refers to King Charles II himself. The other great diarist of the Restoration, Samuel Pepys (1633–1703), also displayed the anxieties of his age in the attitude he takes towards his own theatre going. His diary is littered with pledges to himself not to attend the theatre anymore. A few months later, you can read his account of the latest play. The debate, then, is over what is *appropriate* and that is the concern of Jeremy Collier.

■ Obscenity in any company is a rustic uncreditable talent; but among women 'tis particularly rude. Such talk would be very affrontive in conversation, and not endured by any lady of reputation. Whence then comes it to pass that those liberties which disoblige so much in conversation, should entertain upon the stage. Do the women leave all the regards to decency and conscience behind them when they come to the playhouse?[8] □

Collier refuses to acknowledge what we would now think of as the license of art, that it allows you to do and say things that are not necessarily considered appropriate to polite, everyday conversation. He seems to see the stage as an extension of the Restoration drawing room, a forum in which the boundaries of good taste are to be both observed and policed. James Drake's rebuff to Collier does not really move beyond arguing on the basis of language's 'appropriateness', its 'propriety' within a given context. But he does make the argument, more familiar to us, that a stage character's language is judged, not by its appropriateness to its actual social setting, the playhouse, but by its appropriateness to its fictional setting – in this case, Elsinore.

■ ... Shakespeare's Ophelia comes first under his [Collier's] lash for not keeping her mouth clean under her distraction. He is so very nice [particular] that her breath, which for so many years has stood the test of the most critical Noses, smells rank to him. It may therefore be worthwhile to enquire whether the fault lies in her mouth, or his nose.

Ophelia was a modest young virgin, beloved by Hamlet, and in love with him. Her passion was approved and directed by her father, and her pretensions to a match with Hamlet, the heir apparent to the crown of Denmark, encouraged and supported by the countenance and assistance of the King and Queen. A warrantable [allowable] love, so naturally planted in so tender a breast, so carefully nursed, so artfully manured, and so strongly forced up, must needs take very deep root and bear a very great head. Love, even in the most difficult circumstances, is the passion naturally most predominant in young breasts, but when it is encouraged and cherished by those of whom they stand in awe it grows masterly and tyrannical, and will admit of no check. This was poor Ophelia's case. Hamlet had sworn, her father had approved, the King and Queen consented to, nay desired the consummation of her wishes. Her hopes were full blown when they were miserably blasted. Hamlet by mistake kills her father and runs mad; or, which is all one to her, counterfeits madness so well that she is cheated into a belief of the reality of it. Here piety and love concur to make her affliction piercing and to impress her sorrow more deep and lasting. To tear up two such passions violently by the roots must needs make horrible convulsions in a mind so tender and a sex so weak. These calamities distract her and she talks incoherently; at which Mr Collier is amazed, he is downright stupefied; and thinks the woman's mad to run out of her wits. But though she talks a little light-headed, and seems to want sleep, I don't find she needed any cashew in her mouth to correct her breath. That's a discovery of Mr. Collier's (like some other of his), who perhaps is of opinion that the breath and the understanding have the same lodging and must needs be vitiated together. However, Shakespeare has drowned her at last, and Mr Collier is angry that he did it no sooner. He is for having execution done upon her seriously, and in sober sadness, without the excuse of madness for self-murder. To kill her is not sufficient with him unless she be damned into the bargain. Allowing the cause of her madness to be *Partie per Pale* [divided in two aspects (from heraldry)], the death of her father and the loss of her love – which is the utmost we can give to the latter – yet her passion is as innocent and inoffensive in her distraction as before, though not so reasonable and well governed. Mr Collier has not told us what he grounds his hard censure upon, but we may guess that if he be so really angry as he pretends 'tis at the mad song which Ophelia sings to the Queen, which I shall venture to transcribe without fear of offending the modesty of the most chaste Ear.

To morrow is Saint Valentine's day,
  All in the morn betimes,
And I a Maid at your window,
  To be your Valentine.
Then up he rose, and donn'd his clo'es,
  And dupp'd the Chamber door,
Let in the maid that out a maid
  Never departed more. [...]

By Gis, and by Saint Charity:
　Alack and fie for shame!
Young men will do't, if they come to't –
　By Cock they are to blame.
Quoth she, 'Before you tumbled me,
　You promis'd me to wed':

He answers,

'So would I a done, by yonder sun,
And thou hadst not come to bed.'
　　　　　　[4.5.48–66]

'Tis strange this stuff should wamble so in Mr Collier's stomach [make Mr Collier nauseous] and put him into such an uproar. 'Tis silly, indeed, but very harmless and inoffensive; and 'tis no great miracle that a woman out of her wits should talk nonsense, who at the soundest of her intellects had no extraordinary talent at speech-making. Sure Mr Collier's concoctive [digestive] faculty's extremely depraved, that mere water-pap turns to such virulent corruption with him.

But children and mad folks tell truth, they say, and he seems to discover through her frenzy what she would be at. She was troubled for the loss of a sweetheart and the breaking off her match, poor soul. Not unlikely. Yet this was no novelty in the days of our forefathers; if he pleases to consult the Records, he will find even in the days of Sophocles, maids had an itching the same way, and longed to know what was what before they died. □
　　　　　(James Drake, *The Ancient and Modern Stages survey'd.*
　　　　Or, Mr. Collier's View of the Immorality of the English Stage
　　　　　　　　　　Set in a True Light, 1699)[9]

Drake argues, then, that even if what Ophelia says might be considered offensive, it is justified through reference to the part that the speech has to play in the development of her character within the plot. It is a matter of decorum. Where Collier saw Ophelia's speech as always indecorous, Drake claims that it *is* decorous in as much as it makes sense within the plot.

Frivolous as these concerns with the breath of Ophelia may seem – and Drake is evidently being flippant, believing that Collier's objections are near-ridiculous – what they partly illustrate are the parameters of neoclassical criticism as it developed in the early days of English literary criticism and the parameters by which the rest of Shakespeare's play, *Hamlet*, comes to be judged. In the account given of Ophelia above, Drake takes great pains to outline the position of Ophelia within the plot of the play as a whole. This is because his criticism of the play is operating within the neoclassical paradigm that insists on the primacy of plot in the evaluation of any literary work. This is especially true of the evaluation of tragedy, directly inherited from Aristotle's (384–22 BC) theories of tragedy in the *Poetics*. This is Aristotle's definition of tragedy:

> ■ Tragedy is an imitation of an action that is admirable, complete and possesses magnitude; in language made pleasurable, each of its species separated in different parts; performed by actors, not through narration; effecting through pity and fear the purification of such emotions.[10] □

It is the fact that the action of a tragedy is 'complete' that comes to be of primary concern to Aristotle in the following more detailed definition of tragedy. He emphasises the importance of plot in the success of a tragedy.

> ■ So tragedy as a whole has six component parts, which determine the tragedy's quality: i.e. plot, character, diction [register; choice of words], reasoning, spectacle and lyric poetry. [...]
> Virtually all tragedians, one might say, use these formal elements; for in fact every drama alike has spectacle, character, plot, diction, song and reasoning. But the most important of them is the structure of events:
>
> (i) Tragedy is not an imitation of persons, but of actions and of life. Well-being and ill-being reside in action, and the goal of life is an activity, not a quality; people possess certain qualities in accordance with their character, but they achieve well-being or its opposite on the basis of how they fare. So the imitation of character is not the purpose of what the agents do; character is included with and on account of the actions. So the events, i.e. the plot, are what tragedy is there for, and that is the most important thing of all.
> (ii) Furthermore, there could not be a tragedy without action, but there could be one without character. [...]
> (iii) Also, if one were to compose a series of speeches expressive of character, however successful they are in terms of diction and reasoning, it will not achieve the stated function of a tragedy; a tragedy which, though it uses these elements less adequately, has a plot and a structure of events will do so more effectively.
> (iv) Additionally, the most important devices by which tragedy sways emotion are parts of the plot, i.e. reversals and recognitions [i.e. *peripeteia* and *anagnorisis* in the Greek terms usually used in analysing the narratives of tragedy]. □
>
> (Aristotle, *Poetics*, *c*.350BC)[11]

What later literary critics take from Aristotle is this understanding that character is secondary to plot, and this is what lies behind Drake's justification of Ophelia. Her madness *is* decorous if it is to be understood as appropriate to the narrative, rather than in Collier's judgement, socially inappropriate.

> ■ Her hopes were full blown when they were miserably blasted. Hamlet by mistake kills her Father and runs mad; or, which is all one to her, counterfeits madness so well that she is cheated into a belief of the reality of it. Here Piety and Love concur to make her Affliction piercing and to impress her Sorrow more deep and lasting. To tear up two such passions violently by the roots must needs make horrible Convulsions in a Mind so tender and a Sex so weak. These Calamities distract her and she talks incoherently.[12] □

The pathos of Shakespeare's representation of Ophelia lies in the ways in which her character is produced by the narrative in which she is placed.

Neoclassical criticism concerned itself, then, with the appropriateness of the drama, the represented action, to the plot that the drama is supposed to represent. It also concerns itself with the 'completeness' of the plot. Some seventeenth-century critics felt that modern English drama fell down in this regard, when compared to the ancients. This is behind the famous objections to *Othello* given by Thomas Rymer.

> ■ I have chiefly considered the fable or plot, [as opposed to unities and to language] which all conclude to be the soul of a tragedy; which, with the ancients, is always to be a reasonable soul; but with us, for the most part, a brutish, and often worse than brutish.[13] □

For Aristotle, the 'fable' or 'plot' was what gave tragedy its required cathartic effect. Aristotle viewed 'katharsis', literally 'cleansing', as the effect of 'release' generated by the experience of watching tragedy. Whilst we often understand this in personal, psychological terms, in Aristotle, it refers instead to a wider process, where society's tendency to violence can be deflected through art. Although plot is always given primary consideration in his account of drama, the parameters which he sets out for tragic plot do have a necessary connection to character as well. This occurs through the idea that comes to be known, later, as 'poetic justice'.

> ■ The construction of the best tragedy should be complex rather than simple; and it should also be an imitation of events that evoke fear and pity; since that is the distinctive feature of this kind of imitation. So it is clear first of all that decent men should not be seen undergoing a change from good fortune to bad fortune – this does not evoke fear or pity, but disgust. Nor should depraved people be seen undergoing a change from bad fortune to good fortune – this is the least tragic of all: it has none of the right effects, since it is neither agreeable, nor does it evoke pity or fear.

Nor again should a very wicked person fall from good fortune to bad fortune – that kind of structure would be agreeable, but would not excite pity or fear, since the one has to do with someone who is suffering undeservedly, the other with someone who is like ourselves (I mean, pity has to do with the undeserving sufferer, fear with the person like us); so what happens will evoke neither pity nor fear

We are left, therefore, with the person intermediate between these. This is the sort of person who is not outstanding in moral excellence or justice; on the other hand, the change to bad fortune which he undergoes is not due to any moral defect or depravity, but to an error [*hamartia*] of some kind. He is one of those people who are held in great esteem and enjoy great good fortune, like Oedipus, Thyestes, and distinguished men from that kind of family. □   (Aristotle, *Poetics*, *c.*450BC)[14]

As critics respond to *Hamlet*, in the late seventeenth and early eighteenth centuries, they attempt to judge whether or not it fulfils these demands, to find out whether the structure of the plot conforms to Aristotle's demands for justice, tempered with his demands that the story also provoke pity and fear in the minds of the audience. However, in neoclassical criticism, influenced by a Christianisation of Aristotelian theory, there comes to be a much greater emphasis on structuring the narrative around a demand for 'poetic justice' than on the cathartic experience of feeling pity and fear. Divine judgement is given a moral structure that is missing from Aristotle. That is, Aristotle does not work from the premise that divine judgment is necessarily a moral truth whereas a Christian writer has to assume that God's judgement is moral truth. Charles Gildon (1665–1734) believed that Shakespeare was particularly good at writing plots which provided the moral lessons of a poetic justice.

■ Whereas the morals of *Hamlet*, *Macbeth*, and most of Shakespeare's plays prove a lesson of mightier consequence than any in Sophocles except the *Electra*, *viz.* that Usurpation, though it thrive a while, will at last be punished, *&c.* besides. The worst and most irregular of Shakespeare's plays contain two or three such fables as that of Philoctetes, which answers not one of the ends of poetry. For it neither pleases nor profits, it moves neither terror nor compassion, [...][15] □

Different critics of the period tended to disagree on the extent to which *Hamlet* meets the demands of 'poetic justice'. At the later end of this period, Samuel Johnson, whilst seeming to respond positively to the play as a whole, does feel that it falls short in terms of the ways in which the plot allocates justice at the end. In his 1765 edition of Shakespeare, he gave introductions to the individual plays as well as providing glosses on textual details and localised matters of interpretation. This is from the introduction to *Hamlet*.

■ If the dramas of Shakespeare were to be characterised, each by the particular excellence which distinguishes it from the rest, we must allow to the tragedy of *Hamlet* the praise of variety. The incidents are so numerous, that the argument of the play would make a long tale. The scenes are interchangeably diversified with merriment and solemnity; with merriment that includes judicious and instructive observations, and solemnity, not strained by poetical violence above the natural sentiments of man. New characters appear from time to time in continual succession, exhibiting various forms of life and particular modes of conversation. The pretended madness of Hamlet causes much mirth, the mournful distraction of Ophelia fills the heart with tenderness, and every personage produces the effect intended, from the apparition that in the first act chills the blood with horror, to the fop in the last, that exposes affectation to just contempt.

The conduct is perhaps not wholly secure against objections. The action is indeed for the most part in continual progression, but there are some scenes which neither forward nor retard it. Of the feigned madness of Hamlet there appears no adequate cause, for he does nothing which he might not have done with the reputation of sanity. He plays the madman most, when he treats Ophelia with so much rudeness, which seems to be a useless and wanton cruelty.

Hamlet is, through the whole play, rather an instrument than an agent. After he has, by the stratagem of the play, convicted the King, he makes no attempt to punish him, and his death is at last effected by an incident which Hamlet has no part in producing.

The catastrophe is not very happily produced; the exchange of weapons is rather an expedient of necessity, than a stroke of art. A scheme might easily have been formed, to kill Hamlet with the dagger, and Laertes with the bowl.

The poet is accused of having shewn little regard to poetical justice, and may be charged with equal neglect of poetical probability. The apparition left the regions of the dead to little purpose; the revenge which he demands is not obtained but by the death of him that was required to take it; and the gratification which would arise from the destruction of an usurper and a murderer, is abated by the untimely death of Ophelia, the young, the beautiful, the harmless and the pious. □

(Samuel Johnson, *The Plays of William Shakespeare*, 1765)[16]

Johnson starts this account with praise for Shakespeare's capacities as a dramatist, but it turns out that the things that he is good at are not at all to be valued. He begins by praising the apparent decorum of *Hamlet*'s mix of merriment and solemnity, a mix that in the hands of other critics had come to signal the play's failure of decorum. Each part of the play produces the effect which Shakespeare intended. This, though, is not good enough. For, while Johnson believes that Hamlet's feigned madness was intended as humorous by Shakespeare, and that it is successful in producing this result, it is also the case that Johnson sees this part of the plot to be completely spurious.

■ The pretended madness of Hamlet causes much mirth [...]
Of the feigned madness of Hamlet there appears no adequate cause, for he does nothing which he might not have done with the reputation of sanity. □

Johnson is inheriting an idea of Shakespeare's particular talent that had been developing throughout the period – that he was good at delineating character, but not so good at what was considered the more important skill for writing drama – the construction of plot. This judgment of Johnson's is also evident in some of the individual glosses he provides on the text in his edition. Johnson's edition came out in 1765 and is based on an earlier edition by William Warburton (1698–1779). What Johnson tends to do with Warburton's 1747 text is to restore many of the original readings from the First Folio or from earlier quartos that Warburton had emended when he had failed to make sense of them. Johnson sometimes argues that Warburton did not try sufficiently hard to construe the originals and sometimes that it is Shakespeare's style to be difficult and opaque. Although it is not the purpose of this Guide to trace editorial trends, it is interesting here to note that Johnson's approach is surely paradoxical. He both insists on the primacy of the original texts *and* seeks to explain them as making sense. In this move he unwittingly appeals to *two* authorities – Shakespeare *and* common sense. Johnson is important in the history of Shakespeare editing for his insistence on a much more careful return to original texts, a task that he did not complete himself but one that was fulfilled much more thoroughly by the next important editor of Shakespeare, Edward Cappell (1713–81) who really takes the early texts as authoritative and, as such, marks the beginning of modern editorial approaches.

That Johnson retained the neoclassical bias towards rendering the text 'commonsensical' can be seen, not only in his glosses on individual words but also in the way that he treats 'character'. In his note to 2.2.86ff, part of Polonius' conversation with Gertrude and Claudius, Warburton had argued that this had demonstrated Polonius' weak, pedantic nature. Johnson, with his own brand of pedantry, takes issue with this.

■ POLONIUS: My liege and madam, to expostulate
What majesty should be, what duty is,
Why day is day, night night, and time is time,
Were nothing but to waste night, day and time.
(2.2.86–9)

This account [Warburton's] of the character of Polonius, though it sufficiently reconciles the seeming inconsisteny of so much wisdom with so much folly, does not correspond exactly to the ideas of our author. The commentator makes the character of Polonius, a character only of manners, discriminated by properties superficial, accidental, and acquired. The poet intended a nobler delineation of a mixed character of manners and of nature. Polonius is a man bred in courts, exercised in business, stored with observation, confident of his knowledge, proud of his eloquence, and declining into dotage. His mode of oratory is truly represented as designed to ridicule the practice of those times, of prefaces that made no introduction, and of method that embarrassed rather than explained. This part of his character is accidental, the rest is natural. Such a man is positive and confident, because he knows that his mind was once strong, and knows not that it is become weak. Such a man excels in general principles, but fails in the particular application. He is knowing in retrospect, and ignorant in foresight. While he depends upon his memory, and can draw from his repositories of knowledge, he utters weighty sentences, and gives useful counsel; but as the mind in its enfeebled state cannot be kept long busy and intent, the old man is subject to sudden dereiliction of his faculties, he loses the order of his ideas, and entangles himself in his own thoughts, till he recovers the leading principle, and falls again into his former train. This idea of dotage encroaching upon wisdom, will solve all the phenomena of the character of Polonius.[17] □

This last remark is particularly telling. In outlining the character of Polonius, what Johnson seeks to do is to explain all the varying 'phenomena' that contribute to its development in terms of a unified narrative – a wise man that is getting old and yet is unaware of a loss of faculties. Polonius' various utterances and actions are a kind of puzzle from which we can deduce a solution: 'the character of Polonius'. Johnson allies his understanding that Shakespeare's particular strength lies in the delineation of character with the traditionally neoclassical concern for unity. However, at times, and particularly when discussing Hamlet, Johnson cannot quite square some of the 'phenomena' with the unified character, try as he might. He makes an attempt to do this with the 'To be or not to be' soliloquy, insisting on a conjectural unity despite the apparent disorderliness of the speech. He does this by filling in the syntactical gaps in the speech.

■ Of this celebrated soliloquy, which bursting from a man distracted with contrariety of desires, and overwhelmed with the magnitude of his own purposes, is connected rather in the speaker's mind than on his tongue, I shall endeavour to discover the train, and to show how one sentiment produces another.

Hamlet, knowing himself injured in the most enormous and atrocious degree, and seeing no means of redress, but such as must expose him to the extremity of hazard, meditates on his situation in this manner: 'Before I can form any rational scheme of action under this pressure of distress', it is necessary to decide, whether, 'after our present state, we are *to be or not to be*'. That is the question, which, as it shall be answered will determine, 'whether 'tis nobler', and more suitable to the dignity of reason, 'to suffer the outrages of fortune' patiently, or to take arms against 'them', and by opposing them, 'though perhaps' with the loss of life. If 'to die', were 'to sleep, no more, and by a sleep to end' the miseries of our nature, such a sleep were 'devoutly to be wished'; but if 'to sleep' in death, be 'to dream', to retain our powers of sensibility, we must 'pause' to consider, 'in that sleep of death what dreams may come'. This consideration 'makes calamity' so long endured; for 'who would bear' the vexations of life, which might be ended 'by a bare bodkin', but that he is afraid of something in unknown futurity? This fear it is that gives efficacy to conscience, which, by turning the mind 'upon this regard', chills the ardour of 'resolution', checks the vigour of 'enterprise', and makes the 'current' of desire stagnate in inactivity.

We may suppose that he would have applied these general observations to his own case, but that he discovered Ophelia. □
(Samuel Johnson, *The Plays of William Shakespeare*, 1765)[18]

In his account of the speech, Johnson supplies what he sees as missing in order to make the sentences coherent. He then assigns Hamlet a motive in making these observations – that he would apply them to himself given time. Although Johnson often seeks to retain the original text, his explanatory notes sometimes, like this, attempt to give them a logic and a unity which they do not necessarily possess. For Johnson, this breaks down when Hamlet is understood to have said something that is indecorous. Johnson famously objects to Hamlet's desire to pursue his revenge against Claudius, not only in this world, but in the next as well.

■ This speech [3.3.93–5], in which Hamlet, represented as a virtuous character is not content with taking blood for blood, but contrives damnation for the man that he would punish is too horrible to be read or to be uttered.[19] □

Johnson's squeamishness here is as much to do with the sentiment generally being inadmissible as with it being inappropriate for Hamlet. Elsewhere, he is much more explicitly concerned with the sentiments assigned to Hamlet in the script not being easily reconciled to a unified view of his character. When Hamlet shakes hands with Laertes at the start of the duel and begs his pardon, Johnson does not believe that Hamlet is truly sorry or, at least, he believes him not to be telling the full truth. Johnson seems to miss the point that both Hamlet and Laertes appear to be fulfilling the polite role of the dueller to their own ends.

> ■ I wish Hamlet had made some other defence; it is unsuitable to the character of a good or brave man, to shelter himself in falsehood.[20] □

The decorum being breached here is not a general sense of what is *always* inappropriate but what is specifically inappropriate to the delineation of Hamlet's character as a good or brave hero. Johnson wishes to correct this because he assumes that Shakespeare in generally very good at maintaining a consistency in his characterisation. What we see in Johnson, then, is a dependence on the traditional parameters of neoclassical criticism – a concern for decorum and unity – but with an increased emphasis on Shakespeare as a talented, but unbridled, genius whose real strengths lay in the imitation of nature through the depiction of human character.

This view had been most comprehensively developed by George Stubbes (active 1697–1737), in his 1736 account of the play, *Some Remarks on the Tragedy of Hamlet*.

> ■ He [Shakespeare] had beyond doubt a most unbounded genius, very little regulated by art.
>
> His particular excellency consists in the variety and singularity of his characters, and in the constant conformity of each character to itself from its very first setting out in the play quite to the end. And, still further, no Poet ever came up to him in the nobleness and sublimity of Thought so frequent in his Tragedies, and all express'd with the most energick [sic.] comprehensiveness of Diction.
>
> [...] Before I proceed to the particular parts of this tragedy I must premise that the admirers of our poet cannot be offended if I point out some of his imperfections, since they will find that they are very few in proportion to his beauties.
>
> [...] I shall have occasion to remark in the sequel that in one particular he has follow'd the plan so closely as to produce an absurdity in his plot. And I must premise also this, that in my examination of the whole conduct of the play the reader must not be surprised if I censure any part of it, although it be entirely in conformity to the plan the author has chosen; because it is easy to conceive that a poet's Judgement is particularly shown in choosing the proper circumstances, and rejecting the improper ones of the ground-work which he raises his play upon. In general we are to take notice that as history ran very low in his days most of his plays are

founded upon some old wretched chronicler, or some empty Italian novelist; but the more base and mean were his materials so much more ought
we to admire his skill, who has been able to work up his pieces to such
sublimity from such low originals. □
(George Stubbes, *Some Remarks on the Tragedy of Hamlet*, 1736)[21]

Stubbes writes from a position which presumes that he is living in a
uniquely enlightened time and that from this position he is able to look
back and evaluate the position of Shakespearean drama in relation,
both to the work of his own day and to the work of the Ancients. It is
interesting, though, that even in a lengthy and detailed account like
this, the writer is concerned with a decorum that extends beyond the
stage. He, too, finds Ophelia's behaviour a little too much to take.

■ The scenes of Ophelia's madness are to me very shocking, in so noble a
piece as this. I am not against her having been represented mad; but surely
it might have been done with less levity and more decency. Mistakes are less
tolerable from such a genius as Shakespeare's, and especially in the very
pieces which give us such strong proofs of his exalted capacity.[22] □

This neoclassical squeamishness extends to some episodes involving
Hamlet himself.

■ Hamlet's speech upon seeing the King at prayers has always given me
great offence. There is something so very bloody in it, so inhuman, so
unworthy of a hero that I wish our poet had omitted it. To desire to destroy
a man's soul, to make him eternally miserable by cutting him off from all
hopes of repentance; this surely, in a Christian prince, is such a piece of
revenge as no tenderness for any parent can justify. To put the usurper to
death, to deprive him of the fruits of his vile crime, and to rescue the
throne of Denmark from pollution, was highly requisite. But there our young
Prince's desire should have stopped, nor should he have wished to pursue
the criminal in the other world, but rather have hoped for his conversion
before his putting him to death; for even with his repentance there was at
least purgatory for him to pass through, as we find even in a virtuous
Prince, the father of Hamlet.[23] □

We can see how neoclassical assumptions promote the tendency to view
tragedy almost as a judicial proceeding whose purpose is to dispense
admonitory justice. Anything that detracts from this purpose is seen,
not only as pointless, but also as potentially immoral. We can see,
then, that the neoclassical criticism of the late seventeenth and early
eighteenth centuries took Aristotle's concern for a complete plot and
moralised it. Decorum is not just a matter of good or bad art, or achieving, or failing to achieve the desired effect in the audience; proper
decorum also corresponds to proper morality.

■ Hamlet's whole conduct during the play [the 'Mousetrap' incident] which is acted before the King has, in my opinion, too much levity in it. His madness is of too light a kind, although I know he says he must be idle; but among other things, his pun to Polonius is not tolerable. I might also justly find fault with the want of decency in his discourses to Ophelia, without being thought too severe. [...]

Hamlet's pleasantry upon his being certified that his uncle is guilty is not *a-propos* in my opinion. We are to take notice that the poet has mixed a vein of humour in the Prince's character which is to be seen in many places of this play. What was his reason for his so doing I cannot say, unless it was to follow his favourite foible, viz. that of raising a laugh.[24] □

These apparent inconsistencies in Hamlet's 'character' come to be the major concern of *Hamlet* criticism of later years, and different critics attempt to explain them away in different ways. Here, Stubbes sees the question, but refuses to answer it with any seriousness. He resolves it as an idiosyncrasy peculiar to Shakespeare that only detracts from the more important business of constructing a coherent plot which presents a particular view of the way in which the world works – that, ultimately, the bad get punished and those that are wronged are revenged. That those that have been wronged – Hamlet, Laertes – have, themselves, to be destroyed for this to work out, is of course, the sticking point.

As criticism moves away from neoclassical paradigms, this apparent inconsistency in the deployment of tragic plot comes to seem less and less important. Different explanatory frameworks come to be employed to make sense of the play's difficulties and what have been seen as its inconsistencies. Narrative takes a back seat and the changeability of Hamlet's behaviour is not explained through reference to its success or failure in forwarding the narrative, but through reference to character itself. It is in this period, the late eighteenth and early nineteenth centuries, that the archetypal Hamlet of popular culture – a moody, melancholy, poetically suicidal young man – is born. The writers of the Romantic period inherit this view of Hamlet from their immediate predecessors – those involved in developing what became known as 'the cult of sensibility'.

CHAPTER TWO

From Sensibility to Romanticism: 'the majesty of melancholy'

T he neoclassical criticism of the late seventeenth and eighteenth centuries followed Aristotle in making narrative or plot the primary focus of their dramatic criticism. The following centuries of *Hamlet* criticism saw that priority completely changed. Critics still saw inconsistencies in the play, but these inconsistencies were not explained in terms of a falling short in the play's adherence to the classical unities, or as infelicities of decorum, but as being determined by the character of Hamlet himself. Hamlet came to be seen as a more and more complex character, rather than as a straightforward revenge hero, some of whose speeches were rather inappropriate. Some writers, emerging within the late eighteenth-century 'cult of sensibility', initially saw these apparent inconsistencies as moral flaws in the delineation of Hamlet's character; other, later critics who are associated with the mainstream of Romanticism came to resolve these inconsistencies in an enduring image of the character of Hamlet as a noble outsider. This Hamlet, that critics from the last twenty years or so might rightly view as anachronistic, has nevertheless been remarkably influential and endures in countless modern productions of the play.

From the early nineteenth century onwards, there has rarely been a time in which our view of Hamlet has not reflected what it means to be a modern man. More than this, at times our view of what it means to be Hamlet has come to define what it means to be human. Recent criticism, particularly criticism with a materialist influence, has come to see the links between Hamlet, Shakespeare, the business of literary criticism and the definition of human subjectivity as pernicious and self-serving. It is not really the job of this Guide to re-iterate these particular arguments in relation to the nineteenth-century developments, but rather to show some, at least, of the processes that helped to bring the situation about in which these terms come to be so powerfully linked in our culture. It is in this period, which witnessed the emergence of Romanticism, that the popular view of Hamlet was consolidated.

The character of Hamlet today is a powerful cultural icon, instantly recognisable. A handsome, but melancholy young man, clad in black and holding a skull is perhaps the most familiar Shakespearean image. The connotations that this image conjures up are those of the romantic outsider, a young man whose sensitivities have ill-equipped him for the harsh realities of this world. There is also something self-servingly narcissistic about this popular version of Hamlet. On his early 1980s 'Serious Moonlight' tour, the rock star David Bowie epitomised this Hamlet, at one point on stage taking up a skull and staring at it as if it were a mirror, while also wearing sunglasses through which he, presumably, could barely see. It is evident from this kind of easily read shorthand – a black costume and a skull – how much a part of our culture this particular image of Hamlet is.

We have, though, inherited this Hamlet from a specific period in the development of Hamlet criticism – the end of the eighteenth and the beginning of the nineteenth centuries. William Hazlitt typifies this Romantic view of Hamlet when he writes:

■ He is full of weakness and melancholy, but there is no harshness in his nature. He is the most amiable of misanthropes.[1] □

This view of the character of Hamlet, given by Romantic critics, is partly an inheritance from critics that immediately preceded them, partly the result of seeing their own ideal of the artist/philosopher in Hamlet himself, and partly a reaction to what they regarded as the misunderstandings of those critics that we have been calling neoclassical. This reaction against the values of neoclassicism is evident in Hazlitt's denunciation of Dr Johnson's abilities as a literary critic. Even though, as shown in the last chapter, Johnson's work marks a certain break from the rigidities of the neoclassical critics who preceded him, for Hazlitt, Johnson is representative of neoclassical writing as a whole.

■ We have a high respect for Dr. Johnson's character and understanding, mixed with something like personal attachment: but he was neither a poet nor a judge of poetry. He might in one sense be a judge of poetry as it falls within the limits and rules of prose, but not as it is poetry. [...] He reduced everything to the common standard of conventional propriety; and the most exquisite refinement or sublimity produced an effect on his mind, only as they could be translated into the language of measured prose. To him an excess of beauty was a fault; for it appeared to him like an excrescence; and his imagination was dazzled by the blaze of light. His writings neither shone with the beams of native genius, nor reflected them. The shifting shapes of fancy, the rainbow hues of things, made no impression on him: he seized only on the permanent and the tangible. [...] He was a man of strong common sense and practical wisdom, rather than of genius or feeling. [...] Common sense sympathises with the impressions of things on ordinary minds in ordinary circumstances; genius catches the glancing combinations presented to the eye of fancy, under the influence of passion. □

(William Hazlitt, Characters of Shakespeare's Plays, 1838)[2]

For Hazlitt, and, I would suggest Romanticism in general, Johnson was too rigid in his responses to imaginative literature. He had 'common sense' where he needed sensibility. The responses of the critics of the later eighteenth and early nineteenth centuries to *Hamlet* involved a gradual rejection of the rigidities of neoclassicism in favour of a more flexible and intuitive approach to Shakespeare that saw him as one of their own, given a hard deal by eighteenth-century pedants.

THE CULT OF SENSIBILITY

If Romantic critics, like Hazlitt and Coleridge, come to re-model Hamlet in the idealised image of the Romantic poet, their account of the prince is, in part, preceded by the writers of the late eighteenth century who placed Hamlet at the heart of a 'cult of sensibility'. 'Sensibility', in the late eighteenth and early nineteenth centuries means something like 'moral sensitivity'. Hamlet, here, comes to represent the sensitive soul who, though born into this world, was always too good for it. The narrative inconsistencies of the plot are not explained within the parameters of the Aristotelian unities, or even by reference to their Christianised counterpart, the idea of 'poetic justice'; rather they are explained as being produced by a character unable to square his own exemplary virtue with the task that has been laid out for him, both by the ghost of his father and by the definition of his role as revenge hero in a Revenge Tragedy. Hamlet's 'character' becomes the interpretive framework rather than the plot. As William Richardson (1743–1814) puts it:

■ He is moved by finer principles, by an exquisite sense of virtue, of moral beauty and turpitude. The impropriety of Gertrude's behaviour, her ingratitude to the memory of her former husband, and the depravity she discovers in the choice of a successor, afflict his soul, and cast him into utter agony. Here then is the principle and spring of all his actions.

The man whose sense of moral excellence is uncommonly exquisite, will find it a source of pleasure and of pain in his commerce with mankind. Susceptible of every moral impression, the display of virtuous actions will yield him delight, and the contrary action excite uneasiness. □

(William Richardson, A Philosophical Analysis of Some
of Shakespeare's Characters, 1774)[3]

William Richardson was the Professor of Humanity at the University of Glasgow, appointed in 1772. His account of some of Shakespeare's characters was published in 1774 as *A Philosophical Analysis of Some of Shakespeare's Remarkable Characters*. Announced in its title, Richardson's approach to the plays through the idea of 'character' revolutionised the ways in which Shakespeare was written about, and particularly the way that *Hamlet* was written about. Even in the short opening passage given above, it is possible to see this new move in the understanding of Hamlet. If we take the phrase, 'all his actions' to refer to the narrative of the play, then we see here that Richardson locates the explanation for this in the 'principle and spring' of Hamlet's character, his 'exquisite sense of virtue'. Richardson develops this basic idea in more detail throughout his account of the play.

■ The triumph and inward joy of a son, on account of the fame and the high desert of a parent, is of a nature very sublime and tender. His sorrow is no less acute and overwhelming, if those, united to him by a connection so intimate, have acted unbecomingly, and have incurred disgrace. Such is the condition of Hamlet. Exquisitely sensible of moral beauty and deformity, he discerns turpitude [wickedness; depravity] in a parent. Surprise, on a discovery so painful and unexpected, adds bitterness to his sorrow; and led, by the same moral principle to admire and glory in the high desert of his father, even this admiration contributes to his uneasiness. Aversion to his uncle, arising from the same origin, has a similar tendency, and augments his anguish. All these feelings and emotions uniting together, are rendered still more violent, exasperated by his recent interview with the Queen, struggling for utterance, but restrained. Agitated and overwhelmed with afflicting images, no soothing, no exhilarating affection can have admission to his heart. His imagination is visited by no vision of happiness; and he wishes for deliverance from his affliction, by being delivered from a painful existence.[4] □

Richardson, here, confronts a problem that will haunt commentators on *Hamlet* throughout the play's critical history – the question of Hamlet's desire to kill himself. This is, of course, the most extreme example of Hamlet's apparent refusal to execute the demands placed upon him as a revenge hero. For Richardson, though, both his respect for his father and his inability to fulfil the demands made on him originate from the same source – his innate virtue. Also interesting to note, here, is the way in which Richardson identifies the conflict between Hamlet's parents as the main motivating force behind his moral confusion. This clearly anticipates the family drama of Freudian and post-Freudian psychoanalytic readings of the play that will be the subject of the Chapter 3. It is also of interest to note that, at the very moment that Hamlet is inaugurated as a modern man, a character with his own interior life, an assumption is made about the necessary depravity of his mother. Although Richardson is not addressing the position of women in the play, this use of women in *Hamlet* criticism will become an important focus of attention for feminist critics in the twentieth century interested in the relationship between the supposed birth of a modern subjectivity in the character of Hamlet and the denigration of women, both in the play and in the critical response.

The elements of Richardson's analysis that come to fruition in Romantic versions of the prince are the ways in which Richardson resolves any apparent contradictions within Hamlet's behaviour, or within the narrative, as part of Hamlet's psyche. *Hamlet* becomes a solipsistic play about a solipsistic prince. Criticism increasingly sees the prince and the play as inward-looking. Contradictions no longer signal inconsistency of narrative, but consistency and, particularly, complexity of character. The solipsistic nature of this kind of analysis is brought out more fully in the following passage, which discusses the ways in which Richardson sees Hamlet, himself, feeding off, and, at the same time, increasing his fraught emotional state.

■ By giving vent to any passion, its violence at the time increases. Those, for instance, who express their sorrow by shedding tears, find themselves at the instant of weeping more excessively affected than persons of a more reserved and inflexible constitution. Yet, by thus giving vent to their inquietude, they find relief, while those of a taciturn humour are the victims of painful and unabating anxiety: And, the reason is, that the emotion fed to its highest extreme can no longer continue equally violent, and so subsides. In cases of this nature, that is, when emotions, by being expressed, become excessive, the mind passes from general reflections to minute and particular circumstances: and imagination, the pliant flatterer of the passion in power, renders these circumstances still more particular, and better adapted to promote its vehemence. In the foregoing lines the reflections are general; but, in these that follow, they become particular; and the emotion waxing stronger, the imagination, by exhibiting suitable images, and by fitting to its purpose even the time between the death and the marriage, renders it excessive.

> That it should come to this!
> But two months dead – nay, not so much, not two –
> So excellent a king, that was to this
> Hyperion to a satyr, so loving to my mother,
> That he might not beteem the winds of heaven
> Visit her face too roughly.
>
> [1.2.137–42]

The emotion grows still more vehement, and overflows the mind with a tide of corresponding images.

> Heaven and earth,
> Must I remember? Why, she would hang on him,
> As if increase of appetite had grown
> By what it fed on; and yet, within a month □
> [1.2.142–5][5]

In this passage, Richardson inaugurates a tendency that has been at the centre of the subsequent tradition of *Hamlet* criticism. He is searching for traces of a continuous inner life for the Danish prince in the seeming chaos of his verbal utterances. In fact, the more chaotic the development of the dialogue, or of his soliloquies, the more Richardson is able to produce an inner biography for our hero. As Hamlet's dialogue speaks to Richardson of a mind that is falling apart, the more this narrative testifies both to the existence of a single mind which *can* fall apart, and, also, the consistency of Hamlet's character as impossibly virtuous. *Hamlet* criticism from now on will continuously attempt to make this move between outward show and inner story. It is as if, in this play, the narrative of the revenge tragedy has disappeared, has atrophied, in favour of a psychological narrative. The development of character has become narrative in these later versions of Shakespeare's play and *Hamlet* criticism has never really escaped this new paradigm, outlined most fully for the first time by this relatively obscure Scottish academic.

The extent to which Richardson's account of the play privileged character over narrative is evident in the way that, in the final passage of his chapter on *Hamlet*, he dismisses the final part of the play as no longer of interest to him. Although he has claimed character as his particular concern in analysing Shakespeare's plays, here he reveals a tendency to see character, not only as one amongst many approaches but, really, as the only significant way to approach the plays.

■ All the business of this tragedy, in regard to the display of character, is here concluded. Hamlet, having detected the perfidy, and inhumanity of his uncle, and having restored the Queen to a sense of her depravity, ought immediately to have triumphed in the utter ruin of his enemies, or to have fallen a victim to their deceit. The succeeding circumstances of the play are unnecessary; they are not essential to the catastrophe; and, excepting the madness of Ophelia, and the scene of the gravediggers, they exhibit nothing new in the characters. On the contrary, the delay cools our impatience; it diminishes our solicitude for the fate of Hamlet, and almost lessens him in our esteem. Let him perish immediately, since the poet dooms him to perish; yet poetical justice would have it decided otherwise.

On reviewing this analysis, a sense of virtue ... seems to be the ruling principle. In other men, it may appear within the ensigns of high authority: in Hamlet, it possesses absolute power. United with amiable affections, with every graceful accomplishment, and every agreeable quality, it embellishes and exalts them. It rivets their attachment to his friends, when he finds them deserving: it is a source of sorrow, if they appear corrupted. It even sharpens his penetration and, if unexpectedly he discerns turpitude or impropriety in any character, it inclines him to think more deeply of their transgression, than if his sentiments were less refined. It thus induces him to scrutinize their conduct, and may lead him to the discovery of more enormous guilt. As it excites uncommon pain and abhorrence on the appearance of perfidious and inhuman actions, it provokes and stimulates his resentment: yet, attentive to justice, and concerned in the interests of human nature, it governs the impetuosity of that unruly passion: it renders him distrustful of his own judgement, during the ardour and reign of passion; and directs him in the choice of associates, on whose fidelity and judgment he may depend. If softened by a beneficent and gentle temper, he hesitates in the execution of any lawful enterprise, it reproves him. And if there is any hope of restoring those that are fallen, and of renewing in them habits of virtue and of self-command, it renders him assiduous in his endeavours to serve them. Men of other dispositions would think of gratifying their friends by contributing to their affluence, to their amusement, or external honour: but, the acquisitions that Hamlet values, and the happiness he would confer, are a conscience void of offence, the peace and the honour of virtue. Yet, with all this purity of moral sentiment, with eminent abilities, exceedingly cultivated and improved, with manners the most elegant and becoming, with the utmost rectitude of intention, and the most active zeal in the exercise of every duty, he is hated, persecuted and destroyed. □

(William Richardson, *A Philosophical Analysis of Some of Shakespeare's Characters*, 1774)[6]

In this final account of the character, Hamlet, Richardson produces a version of the prince whose melancholy is both self-nurturing and self-serving. His virtue is not the active virtue of the epic hero, but an inner virtue that cannot succeed in a fallen world. He is 'attentive to justice' but sees no way to enact it; he realises his own failings but is unable to rectify them. In the work of Richardson, and many of those that follow him, tragedy, or at least *Hamlet*, ceases to be something to do with the accident of external events and, instead, comes to be played out in the psyche of the central tragic figure. Hamlet, of course, becomes emblematic of this tendency. Shakespeare's play becomes proof that this is the route that tragedy took on the Elizabethan and Jacobean stage. Later critics from the second half of the twentieth century will come, as we shall see, to dispute the validity of this approach to the play, and to early modern drama as a whole. But, for the time being, and throughout the nineteenth century and into the early twentieth century, the supposed inner life of Hamlet, the character, came increasingly to provide the focus for the attentions of literary critics.

If William Richardson fought shy of tracing the development of Hamlet's character through the final stages of the play, a contemporary writer, Henry Mackenzie (1745–1831) did not. Like Richardson, Mackenzie seeks to find a central motivating force behind the apparently contradictory nature of Hamlet's behaviour. And, also like Richardson, he locates it in Hamlet's extreme sensibility and sense of virtue.

■ Of all the characters of Shakespeare, that of Hamlet has been generally thought the most difficult to be reduced to any fixed or settled principle. With the strongest purposes of revenge, he is irresolute and inactive; amidst the gloom of the deepest melancholy, he is gay and jocular; and while he is described as a passionate lover, he seems indifferent about the object of his affections. It may be worth while to enquire whether any leading idea can be found, upon which these apparent contradictions can be reconciled, and a character so pleasing in the closet, and so much applauded on the stage, rendered as unambiguous in the general as it is striking in the detail. I will venture to lay before my readers some observations on this subject, though with the diffidence due to a question of which the public has doubted, and much abler critics have already written.

The basis of Hamlet's character seems to be an extreme sensibility of mind, apt to be strongly impressed by its situation, and overpowered by the feelings which that situation excites. Naturally of the most virtuous and most amiable dispositions, the circumstances in which he was placed unhinged those principles of action, which, in another situation, would have delighted mankind, and made himself happy. That kind of distress that he suffered was, beyond all others, calculated to produce this effect. His misfortunes were not the misfortunes of accident, which, though they overwhelm at first, the mind will soon call up reflections to alleviate, and hopes to cheer: they were such as reflection serves only to irritate, such as rankle in the soul's tenderest part, her sense of virtue and natural affection; they arose from an uncle's villainy, a mother's guilt, a father's murder! – Yet, amidst the gloom of melancholy, and the agitation of passion, in which his calamities involve him, there are occasional breakings-out of a mind richly endowed by nature, and cultivated by education. We perceive gentleness in his demeanour, wit in his conversation, taste in his amusements, and wisdom in his reflections. □

(Henry Mackenzie, 'Criticism on the Character and
Tragedy of Hamlet', 1770)[7]

Mackenzie outlines the plot of the tragedy – 'an uncle's villainy, a mother's guilt, a father's murder' – but these events are not, here, the accidents of fate as one might expect in classically inspired or Aristotelian accounts of tragic action. Rather, they are understood as psychological events in the mind of Hamlet. I am not implying that

Mackenzie believed these events to be figments of Hamlet's imagination, but rather that he sees their importance lying in their status, not as events within a plot, but as events which work on Hamlet's mind. The psyche of Hamlet is becoming the focus of critical attention. These events, Mackenzie tells us, 'were such as reflection serves only to irritate, such as rankle in the soul's tenderest part, her sense of virtue and natural affection'. In the next part of his essay, Mackenzie strengthens this idea that this is a play, not about the accidents of fate, but about the development of a particular character's mind.

■ Had Shakespeare made Hamlet pursue his vengeance with a steady determined purpose, had he led him through difficulties arising from accidental causes, and not from the doubts and hesitation of his own mind, the anxiety of the spectator might have been highly raised; but it would have been anxiety for the event and not the person.[8] □

Hamlet's supposed 'hesitation' in fulfilling his father's request is not necessarily to be judged in terms of tragic plot, but as an effect of character, and the passage above seems, more than any other passage in *Hamlet* criticism from this period, to encapsulate this change of assumptions about the priorities of drama. If Sophocles' *Oedipus Rex*, for example, really was a drama that highlighted, 'difficulties arising from accidental causes', Shakespearian tragedy will, from now on, be distinguished as moving beyond this into the depiction of the 'doubts and hesitations' of particular characters with particular inner lives. Romantic critics, like Coleridge and Hazlitt, will delve further into Hamlet's inner life, preparing the way for Freud's later, full-blown analysis, an analysis that has fixed Hamlet in our culture as *the* subject of psychoanalytic enquiry. The psychoanalytic approach to drama which, initially at least, tends to view events within the narrative as important only in as much as they have an impact on the protagonist's inner life, is inaugurated at the end of the eighteenth century in the work of Richardson and Mackenzie.

ROMANTICISM: GOETHE AND SCHLEGEL

English Romanticism was greatly influenced by German writing, particularly the philosophy of Immanuel Kant (1724–1804) and its refutation in the work of the contemporary German philosopher, Friedrich Schlegel (1774–1829), and the literature of Johann Wolfgang von Goethe (1749–1832). In turn, these German writers were themselves greatly interested in the works of Shakespeare, and *Hamlet* in particular. As Paul Conklin writes, 'it was at the time that when the Germans were throwing off the fetters of [French Enlightenment] rationalism that by some striking intuition they discovered Shakespeare and Hamlet, and found there a most congenial and potent spiritual food'.[9] Although Kant might be seen as the culmination of the Enlightenment in his rationalist approach to philosophy, his grounding of experience in the individual in some way precipitates the rejection of rationalism in Schlegel. Like Hazlitt after them, the German writers of the late eighteenth century were reacting against the dominance of the neoclassical aesthetic associated with the Enlightenment. Many of the ideas developed in Hazlitt and Coleridge's reactions to *Hamlet* can be traced back to their interaction with German writing, and to the lectures of August von Wilhelm Schlegel (1767–1845), Friedrich Schlegel's older brother, in particular.

One of the most influential critical accounts of *Hamlet* in the period came, though, not in literary criticism or in philosophical writings but in Goethe's immense *bildungsroman* (a term for a novel whose main theme is the development and education of a young man), *Wilhelm Meister's Apprenticeship* (English translation 1824). Goethe wrote this novel over a long period of time in the last quarter of the eighteenth century. It explores the development of a young man, Wilhelm Meister as he enters the world of the theatre. It also functions, therefore, as Goethe's own ongoing project of discovery in terms of his own interest in the theatre. Alexander Welsh, in his *Hamlet in His Modern Guises* (2001) has written about the novel's interest in *Hamlet* as that which moves the book away from eighteenth-century Enlightenment towards the Romanticism which it came to influence.

■ Goethe's long *bildungsroman*, composed and refashioned with Hamlet-like deliberation from about 1776 to 1796, is at once a product of the Enlightenment and – implicitly in the life of its hero, explicitly in the hero's interpretation of Hamlet – a Romantic redaction [revision; version] of Shakespeare. By the novel's Enlightenment quality I mean its cool concurrence in the bias of Shakespeare's play toward youth, including the need to be free of parents, and its frank investigation of psychological and social assumptions. The Romantic contribution is more familiar – a warm acceptance of the same bias, an eagerness for development, and a quest for a self; and Goethe's novel also instigates the particular Romantic tradition that conceives of Hamlet as the poet or artist.[10] □

Welsh sees Goethe's novel, then, as an instigator of the Romantic Hamlet. In the following passage from the novel, it can certainly be seen that Goethe's version of Hamlet both echoes, and goes beyond, the concern for Hamlet's individuality that is a feature of the criticism of Mackenzie and Richardson. The hero of the novel is explaining his interest in the play. Reading Shakespeare has had a transformative effect on Wilhelm and he is keen to expand on this to his friend, the actor Serlio, and his sister, Aurelia.

■ Figure to yourselves this youth, ... this son of princes, conceive him vividly, bring his state before your eyes, and then observe him when he learns that his father's spirit walks; stand by him in the terrors of the night, when the venerable ghost itself appears before him. A horrid shudder passes over him; he speaks to the mysterious form; he sees it beckon him; he follows it, and hears. The fearful accusation of his uncle rings in his ears; the summons to revenge, and the piercing oft-repeated prayer. Remember me!

And when the ghost has vanished, who is it that stands before us? A young hero panting for vengeance? A prince by birth, rejoicing to be called to punish the usurper of his crown? No! trouble and astonishment take hold of the solitary young man: he grows bitter about smiling villains, swears that he will not forget the spirit, and concludes with the significant ejaculation:

The time is out of joint: O cursed spite,
That ever I was born to set it right!

In these words, I imagine, will be found the key to Hamlet's whole proce-dure. To me it is clear that Shakespeare meant, in the present case, to rep-resent the effects of a great action laid upon a soul unfit for the performance of it. In this view, the whole piece seems to me to be composed. There is an oak-tree planted in a costly jar, which should have borne only pleasant flowers in its bosom; the roots expand, the jar is shivered.

A lovely, pure, noble, and most moral nature, without the strength of nerve which forms a hero, sinks beneath a burden which it cannot bear and must not cast away. All duties are holy for him; the present is too hard. Impossibilities have been required of him; not in themselves impossibili-ties, but such for him. He winds, and turns, and torments himself; he advances and recoils; is ever put in mind, ever puts himself in mind; at last does all but lose his purpose from his thoughts; yet still without recovering his peace of mind. □

(Wolfgang von Goethe, *Wilhelm Meister's Apprenticeship*, 1824)[11]

Whilst Goethe, like Richardson and Mackenzie, still has Hamlet as 'noble and moral', it is no longer the case that it is just that the world is not good enough to sustain such innate virtue. Rather, there is some-thing in Hamlet, himself, which means that he is unable to stake his claim in the world. The writer and translator of Shakespeare, August von Wilhelm Schlegel, took this even further and it is his work that had a major influence on the writings of Coleridge and Hazlitt.

Schlegel's influential account of the play intensifies the general interest in the character of Hamlet himself, and particularly why it is that he appears to delay in acting on the desires of the ghost of his father. However, unlike Goethe or the English writers of 'sensibility', Schlegel does not locate Hamlet's tendency to prevaricate in his extreme sense of virtue and justice. Here, for the first time, Hamlet is seen, himself, as an inherently flawed and weak character. Early twentieth-century accounts of the play and of the character, both Freudian psychoanalytic accounts and Bradleyan character-based studies, will take this view of the character given by Schlegel as read.

■ The whole [play] is intended to show that a calculating consideration, which exhausts all the relations and possible consequences of a deed, must cripple the power of acting, as Hamlet himself expresses it:

And thus the native hue of resolution
Is sicklied o'er with the pale cast of thought
And enterprises of great pitch and moment
With this regard their currents turn awry,
And lose the name of action.

[3.1.84–8]

With respect to Hamlet's character: I cannot, as I understand the poet's views, pronounce altogether so favourable a sentence upon it as Goethe does. He is, it is true, of a highly cultivated mind, a prince of royal manners, endowed with the finest sense of propriety, susceptible of noble ambition, and open to the highest degree to an enthusiastic admiration of that excellence in others of which he himself is deficient. He acts the part of madness with unrivalled power, convincing the persons who are sent to examine into his supposed loss of reason, merely by telling them unwelcome truths, and rallying them with the most caustic wit. But in the resolutions which he so often embraces and always leaves unexecuted, his weakness is too apparent: he does himself only justice when he implies that there is no greater dissimilarity than between himself and Hercules. He is not solely impelled by necessity to artifice and dissimulation, he has a natural inclination for crooked ways; he is a hypocrite towards himself; his far-fetched scruples are often mere pretexts to cover his want of discrimination: thoughts, as he says on a different occasion, which have

but one part wisdom
And ever three parts coward.

He has been chiefly condemned for his harshness in repulsing the love of Ophelia, which he himself had cherished, and for his insensibility at her death. But he is too much overwhelmed with his own sorrow to have any compassion to spare for others; besides his outward indifference gives us by no means the measure of his internal perturbation. On the other hand,

we evidently perceive in him a malicious joy, when he has succeeded in getting rid of his enemies, more through necessity and accident, which alone
are able to impel him to quick and decisive measures, than by the merit of
his own courage, as he himself confesses after the murder of Polonius,
and with respect to Rosencrantz and Guildenstern. Hamlet has no firm
belief either in himself or in anything else: from expressions of religious
confidence he passes over to sceptical doubts; he believes in the Ghost of
his father as long as he sees it, but as soon as it has disappeared, it
appears to him almost in the light of a deception.[12] He has even gone so
far as to say, 'there is nothing either good or bad, but thinking makes it so';
with him the poet loses himself here in labyrinths of thought, in which neither end nor beginning is discoverable. The stars themselves, from the
course of events, afford no answer to the question so urgently proposed to
them. A voice from another world, commissioned it would appear, by
heaven, demands vengeance for a monstrous enormity, and the demand
remains without effect; the criminals are at last punished, but, as it were,
by an accidental blow, and not in the solemn way requisite to convey to the
world a warning example of justice, irresolute foresight, cunning treachery,
and impetuous rage, hurry on to a common destruction; the less guilty and
the innocent are equally involved in the general ruin. The destiny of humanity is there exhibited as a gigantic Sphinx, which threatens to precipitate
into the abyss of scepticism all who are unable to solve her dreadful
enigmas. □
   (August von Schlegel, *Lectures on Dramatic Art and Literature*, 1808)[13]

In Schlegel's account of the play, and of the character, the sense that
Hamlet is a man too good for this world has disappeared completely.
Rather, his vacillating hypocrisy seems to epitomise a world that has,
itself, lost its way. The intention of the play, Schlegel sees, is not to promote a view of a world organised through moral order, but to present a
more thoroughly tragic view of the world as chaotic and disordered.
Schlegel's Hamlet has no convictions at all, and this is what leads to his
failure to act. If Goethe's Hamlet is epitomised in the sentiment, 'The
time is out of joint ... ', in that it opposes Hamlet to a world that has
gone awry, Schlegel's Hamlet is, himself, 'out of joint' and, in that, a
man *of* his time.
   In looking at the writings of the English writers of sensibility alongside Schlegel, we can see one of the tendencies of this movement
towards taking character as the main focus of critical attention – a tendency to project into the interior space of Hamlet's personality, either
the personality of, or the fantasies of, the critic himself. Richardson and
Schlegel seem to disagree completely. Richardson insists on a Hamlet
that is isolated from the corrupt world around him because of his virtue
and Schlegel sees him as a character that epitomises a society that has
no moral centre and where fate is not guided by a just allocation of

rewards and punishment, but where human destiny is presented as a 'Sphinx', an impenetrable mystery. However, they are both operating within the same critical framework. They are both doing the very opposite of the neoclassicists discussed in the Chapter 1. The neoclassicists saw character as produced by narrative. Schlegel, Richardson, and their contemporaries and followers understood narrative to be produced by character. *Hamlet*, as a play, is seen as peculiarly amenable to this kind of treatment because of the ways in which it focuses on the solitude of its central figure. It is as a result of this that *Hamlet*, from this time onwards, comes to be seen as *the* most important Shakespeare play.

The seventeenth- and eighteenth-century critics had often been uncomfortable with a play that they saw as falling short of Aristotelian ideals. Romantic and proto-Romantic critics, however, disputed the validity of applying such ideals to 'modern' tragedies at the same time as they expanded the sense of what constituted the 'tragic'. In this, the influence of Schlegel on subsequent English criticism of *Hamlet* was crucial.

ROMANTICISM: COLERIDGE AND HAZLITT

Perhaps the most important English Shakespeare critic of the Romantic period, Coleridge, actually published very little of his work on Shakespeare in formal conditions. What we have of Coleridge's version of Shakespeare has come down to us in an amalgamation of the notes prepared for his series of lectures, and the notes of those who attended them. Whilst this might not be the most convenient way in which to access this important moment in the development of *Hamlet* criticism, it does illustrate very well the dissemination of these ideas into wider, more general assumptions about the play. Coleridge was clearly influenced by reading Schlegel, but not to the extent that some people have thought. He takes from Schlegel the need to explain Hamlet's apparent hesitancy and, like Schlegel, he does not explain this in terms of an extreme moral sensibility. On the whole, though, Coleridge, in his comments on the play, seems less likely to condemn Hamlet as inadequate to the task he has to perform. Rather he produces a Hamlet in the image of the Romantic poet. In one of the rare published passages where Coleridge mentions the play, he says, 'I have a smack of Hamlet myself, if I may say so.'[14]

The interior life that Coleridge ascribes to Hamlet is inflected by his account of the creative imagination, an account that is itself profoundly influenced by Kant. Because of this, before we move on to look at what Coleridge says about *Hamlet*, it would be helpful to form an idea of how Coleridge understands the creative imagination of the poet. The clearest account of this is in his *Biographia Literaria*, a book written in 1815–17 in which Coleridge sought to justify his retreat from his earlier associations with radical and revolutionary politics, and to exonerate himself from the charge of being a turncoat levelled at him by Hazlitt, amongst others. In this book, Coleridge grounds the creation of poetry in the search for the absolute, a firm unified basis on which to base his life, away from the contingencies of society and politics. He looks for a philosophical basis for this isolation in German philosophy. And it is also this self-reflective retreat from the world, proper to the life of the Imagination, that Coleridge sees as necessary for the poet and that he identifies in the character of Hamlet.

First, though, this is a passage from the *Biographia Literaria* which goes some way to outlining the ways in which he viewed the process of poetic creation. He divides the act of creation between two faculties – 'Fancy' and 'Imagination' – with precedence being given to the latter as the more important component in the act of producing poetry.

■ The IMAGINATION [Coleridge's capitals] then I consider either as primary, or secondary. The primary IMAGINATION I hold to be the living power and prime agent of all human perception, and as a repetition in the finite mind of the eternal act of creation in the infinite I AM. The secondary I consider as an echo of the former, co-existing with the conscious will, yet still as identical with the primary in the *kind* of its agency, and differing only in the *degree*, and in the *mode* of its operation. It dissolves, diffuses, dissipates, in order to re-create; or where this process is rendered impossible; yet still at all events it struggles to idealize and to unify. It is essentially *vital*, even as all objects (*as* objects) are essentially fixed and dead.

FANCY, on the contrary, had no other counters to play with, but fixities and definites. The Fancy is indeed no other than a mode of memory emancipated from the order of time and space; and blended with, and modified by that empirical phenomenon of the will, which we express by the word CHOICE. But equally with the ordinary memory it must receive all its materials ready made from the law of association. □

(Samuel Taylor Coleridge, *Biographia Literaria*, 1817)[15]

In the accounts that Coleridge gave of *Hamlet* in his lectures, we can see that this view of the life of the Imagination and of the creative process is something that he saw at work in the character of Hamlet. Coleridge's view of Imagination as either primary, that which is beyond the individual, and secondary, the processes of re-creation that an individual goes through in order to make sense of the world, is a more thoroughly thought out version of Wordsworth's explanation of the creative process as 'emotion recollected in tranquillity' in his famous preface to the second edition of their *Lyrical Ballads* (1800) and what, in his most famous poem, 'I wandered lonely as a cloud' he calls, 'that inward eye / Which is the bliss of solitude'. For Coleridge, Hamlet, the man, shares this capacity of the Romantic poet to re-create the world as ideal through personal recollection. Hamlet's world was most clearly available to him 'in the mirror of his mind'.

■ What was the point to which Shakespeare directed himself? He meant to portray a person in whose view the external world and all its incidents and objects were comparatively dim, and of no interest in themselves, and which began to interest only when they were reflected in the mirror of his mind. Hamlet beheld external objects in the same way that a man of vivid imagination who shuts his eyes sees what has previously made an impression upon his organs.

Shakespeare places him in the most stimulating circumstances that a human being can be placed in; he is the heir apparent of the throne; his father dies suspiciously; his mother excludes him from the throne by marrying his uncle. This was not enough, but the Ghost of the murdered father is introduced to assure the son that he was put to death by his own brother. What is the result? Endless reasoning and urging – perpetual solicitation of the mind to act, but as constant an escape from action – ceaseless reproaches of himself for his sloth, while the whole energy of his resolution passes away in those reproaches. This, too, not from cowardice, for he is made one of the bravest of his time – not from want of forethought or quickness of apprehension, for he sees through the very souls of all who surround him; but merely from that aversion to action which prevails among such as have a world within themselves. □

(Samuel Taylor Coleridge, 'Lectures on Shakespeare', 1818)[16]

In this version of Hamlet, he is a man who experiences the world in the same way as a great poet. He does not experience it first hand, however, but rather as a product of his *own* imagination. His understanding of external phenomena is not necessarily one of interacting with the outside world, but the result of self-reflection.

■ How all occasions do inform against me,
And spur my dull revenge. What is a man,
If his chief good and market of his time
Be but to sleep and feed? A beast, no more.
  ... I do not know
Why yet I live to say this thing's to do,
Sith I have cause, and will, and strength, and means
To do't   [4.4.32–46]

Yet with all this sense of duty, this resolution arising out of conviction, nothing is done. This admirable and consistent character, deeply acquainted with his own feelings, painting them with such wonderful power and accuracy, and just as strongly convinced of the fitness of executing the solemn charge committed to him, still yields to the same retiring from all reality which is the result of having what we express by the terms a world within himself.[17] ☐

Coleridge's conception of Hamlet as a Romantic poet in the making, or even as a proto-Coleridgean poet, is what explains his apparent delay. It is because his experience of the world is through his imagination, through the reflection of that world within his own mind, that he cannot act in the real world. At certain times, Coleridge does see this as containing a moral message, but even this quickly turns into a further point about the creative process.

■ Shakespeare's mode of conceiving characters out of his own moral and intellectual faculties, by conceiving any one intellectual or moral faculty in morbid excess, and then placing himself, thus mutilated and diseased, under given circumstances: of this we shall have repeated occasion to restate and enforce. In *Hamlet* I conceive him to have wished to exemplify the moral necessity of a due balance between our attention to outward objectives, and our meditation on inward thoughts – a due balance between the real and the imaginary world. In Hamlet this balance does not exist – his thoughts, images and fancy far more vivid than his perceptions, and his very perceptions instantly passing through the medium of his contemplations, and acquiring as they pass a form and colour not naturally their own. Hence great, enormous, intellectual activity, and a consequent proportionate aversion to real action, with all its symptoms and accompanying qualities.[18] ☐

As well as seeing in Hamlet, the character, an embodiment of the life of the imagination, a life shared by the Romantic poet, Coleridge, at times, extends this view of the character-as-reflection to include the whole of mankind. Here, Hamlet becomes a kind of everyman. It is interesting to note that, like Freud and other psychoanalytic writers on *Hamlet* after him, Coleridge uses the popularity of the play as a justification for this position. It is popular because we all see ourselves in him.

■ The seeming inconsistencies in the conduct and character of Hamlet have long exercised the conjectural ingenuity of critics; and as we are always loath to suppose that the cause of defective apprehension is in ourselves, the mystery has been too commonly explained by the very easy process of supposing that it is, in fact, inexplicable; and by resolving the difficulty into the capricious and irregular genius of Shakespeare.
Mr. Coleridge, in his *third* lecture, has effectually exposed the shallow and stupid arrogance of this vulgar and indolent decision. He has shown

that the intricacies of Hamlet's character may be traced to Shakespeare's deep and accurate science in mental philosophy. That this character must have some common connection with the laws of our nature was assumed by the lecturer from the fact that Hamlet was the darling of every country where literature was fostered. He thought it essential to the understanding of Hamlet's character that we should reflect on the constitution of our own minds. Man was distinguished from the animal in proportion as thought prevailed over sense; but in healthy processes of the mind, a balance was maintained between the impressions of outward objects, and the inward operations of the intellect. If there be an overbalance in the contemplative faculty, man becomes the creature of meditation, and loses the power of action. Shakespeare seems to have conceived a mind in the highest degree of excitement, with this overpowering activity of intellect, and to have placed him in circumstances where he was obliged to act on the spur of the moment. Hamlet, though brave and careless of death, had contracted a morbid sensibility from this overbalance in the mind, producing the lingering and vacillating delays of procrastination; and wasting in the energy of resolving, the energy of acting. [...]

The effect of this overbalance of imagination is beautifully illustrated in the inward brooding of Hamlet, the effect of a superfluous activity of thought. His mind, unseated from its healthy balance, is for ever occupied with the world within him, and abstracted from external things: his words give a substance to shadows, and he is dissatisfied with commonplace realities. It is the nature of thought to be indefinite, while definiteness belongs to reality. The sense of sublimity arises, not from the sight of an outward object, but from the reflection upon it; not from the impression, but from the idea. Few have seen a celebrated waterfall without feeling something of a disappointment; it is only subsequently, by reflection, that the idea of the waterfall comes full into the mind, and brings with it a train of sublime associations. Hamlet felt this: in him we see a mind that keeps itself in a state of abstraction, and beholds external objects as hieroglyphs. His soliloquy, 'O, that this too, too solid flesh would melt' [1.2.129] arises from a craving after the indefinite, a disposition or temper which most easily besets men of genius – a morbid craving for that which is not. The self-delusion common to this temper of mind was finely exemplified in the character which Hamlet gives of himself: ' ... it cannot be / But I am pigeon-liver'd and lack gall / To make oppression bitter' [2.2.572–4]. He mistakes the seeing his chains for the breaking of them, and delays action till action is of no use; and he becomes the victim of circumstances and accident. □

(Samuel Taylor Coleridge, 'Lectures on Shakespeare', 1818)[19]

Hamlet, for Coleridge, is both an example of everyman, someone in whom we must recognise ourselves, but also very particular. And whilst neoclassicists might have seen his particularity as due to the extraordinary circumstances, the plot, in which he found himself, Coleridge sees him as epitomising and overemphasising traits that are within all of us. Hamlet's overactive inner life has both hazards and benefits. It is this that prevents Hamlet from acting on the demands put upon him, but which also allows him an access to the sublime, denied to most.

If what we have of Coleridge's Shakespeare criticism sometimes reads as though he has taken his own advice to 'reflect on the constitution of our own minds', so producing a kind of meditation on Hamlet which does not always appear to constitute a logically progressed argument, William Hazlitt places the Romantic view of *Hamlet* on a more formal and apparently straightforward footing, whilst retaining the focuses of other Romantic writers. More particularly, as we have seen, Hazlitt is much more self-conscious of his position as a critic within a tradition of criticism, addressing himself directly to the neoclassicists and disagreeing with them.

Like Coleridge before him, and the psychoanalysts after him, Hazlitt sees Hamlet as a kind of 'everyman'.

■ Hamlet is a name: his speeches and sayings but the idle coinage of the poet's brain. What then, are they not real? They are as real as our own thoughts. Their reality is in the reader's mind. It is *we* who are Hamlet. This play has a prophetic run, which is above that of history. Whoever has become thoughtful and melancholy through his own mishaps or those of others; whoever has borne about him the clouded brow of reflection, and thought himself 'too much i'th'sun'; whoever has seen the golden lamp of day dimmed by envious mists rising in his own breast, and could find in the world before him only a dull blank with nothing left remarkable in it; whoever has known 'the pangs of despised love, the insolence of office, or the spurns which patient merit of the unworthy takes'; he who has felt his mind sink within him, and sadness cling to his heart like a malady, who has had his hopes blighted and his youth staggered by the apparitions of strange things; who cannot be well at ease while he sees evil hovering near him like a spectre; whose powers of action have been eaten up by thought, he to whom the universe seems infinite, and himself nothing; whose bitterness of soul makes him careless of consequences, and goes to a play as his best resource to shove off, to a second remove, the evils of life by a mock presentation of them – this is the true Hamlet.

We have been so used to this tragedy that we hardly know how to criticize it any more than we should know how to describe our own faces. But we must make such observations as we can. It is the one of Shakespeare's plays that we think of oftenest, because it abounds most in striking reflections on human life, and because the distresses of Hamlet are transferred, by the turn of his mind, to the general account of humanity. Whatever happens to him, we apply to ourselves, because he applies it so himself as a means of general reasoning. He is a great moralizer; and what makes him worth attending to is, that he moralizes on his own feelings and experience. He is not a commonplace pedant. If *Lear* shows the greatest depth of passion, *Hamlet* is the most remarkable for the ingenuity, original- ity, and unstudied development of character. Shakespeare had more mag- nanimity than any other poet, and he has shown more of it in this play than in any other. There is no attempt to force an interest: everything is left for time and circumstances to unfold. The attention is excited without effort, the incidents succeed each other as matters of course, the charac- ters think and speak and act just as they might do, if left entirely to them- selves. There is no set purpose, no standing at a point. The observations are suggested by the passing scene – the gusts of passion come and go like sounds of music borne on the wind. The whole play is an exact tran- script of what might be supposed to have taken place at the court of Denmark, at the remote period of time fixed upon, before the modern refinement in morals and manners were heard of. It would have been inter- esting enough to have been admitted as a bystander in such a scene, at such a time, to have heard and seen something of what was going on. But here we are more than spectators. We have not only 'the outward passions and the signs of grief'; but we have 'that within which passes show'. We read the thoughts of the heart, we catch the passions living as they rise. Other dramatic writers give us very fine versions and paraphrases of nature: but Shakespeare, together with his own comments, gives us the original text that we may judge for ourselves. This is a very great advantage.

The character of Hamlet is itself a pure effusion of genius. It is not a character marked by strength of will or even of passion, but by refinement of thought and sentiment. Hamlet is as little of the hero as a man can well be: but he is a young and princely novice, full of high enthusiasm and quick sensibility – the sport of circumstances, questioning with fortune and refin- ing on his own feelings, and forced from the natural bias of his disposition by the strangeness of his situation. He seems incapable of deliberate action, and is only hurried into extremities on the spur of the occasion, when he has no time to reflect, as in the scene where he kills Polonius, and again, where he alters the letters which Rosencrantz and Guildenstern are taking with them to England, purporting his death. At other times, when he is most bound to act, he remains puzzled, undecided, and sceptical, dallies with his purposes, till the occasion is lost, and always finds some pretence to relapse into indolence and thoughtfulness again. For this rea- son he refuses to kill the King when he is at his prayers, and by a refine- ment in malice, which is in truth only an excuse for his own want of resolution, defers his revenge to some more fatal opportunity, when he shall be engaged in some act 'that has no relish of salvation in it':

> Now might I do it pat, now a is a-praying.,
> And now I'll do't. And so a goes to heaven;
> And so am I reveng'd, *that would be scann'd*:
> A villain kills my father, and for that,

I, his sole son, do this same villain send
To heaven
Why, this is hire and salary, not revenge.
[...]
Up sword, and know thou a more horrid hent,
When he is drunk asleep, or in his rage.
            [3.3.73–9;88–9 Hazlitt's emphases.]

He is the prince of philosophical speculators, and because he cannot have his revenge perfect, according to the most refined idea his wish can form, he misses it altogether. So he scruples to trust the suggestions of the Ghost, contrives the scene of the play to have surer proof of his uncle's guilt, and then rests satisfied with this confirmation of his suspicions, and the success of his experiment, instead of acting upon it. Yet he is sensible of his own weakness, taxes himself with it, and tries to reason himself out of it:

How all occasions do inform against me,
And spur my dull revenge! ...
... O, from this time forth,
My thoughts be bloody or be nothing worth.
            [4.4.32–3;65–6]

Still he does nothing: and this very speculation on his own infirmity only affords him another occasion for indulging it. It is not for any want of attachment to his father or abhorrence of his murder that Hamlet is thus dilatory, but it is more to his taste to indulge his imagination in reflecting upon the enormity of the crime and refining on his schemes of vengeance, than to put them into immediate practice. His ruling passion is to think, not to act: and any vague pretence that flatters this propensity instantly diverts him from his previous purposes. □
            (William Hazlitt, *Characters of Shakespeare's Plays*, 1838)[20]

Hazlitt's account of Hamlet's character largely agrees with Schlegel and Coleridge in insisting on his 'ruling passion' being thought rather than action, but is much more systematic in tracing this through the narrative of the play itself. It is this more considered approach that enables Hazlitt to confront the neoclassicists on their own territory, the morality of both character and play.

■ The moral perfection of this character has been called in question, we think, by those who did not understand it. It is more interesting than according to rules: amiable, though not faultless. The ethical delineations of 'that noble and liberal casuist' (as Shakespeare has been well called) do not exhibit the drab-coloured quakerism of morality. His plays are not copied either from *The Whole Duty of Mankind*, or from *The Academy of*

Compliments! [generic titles for behaviour manuals] We confess, we are a little shocked at the want of refinement in those who are shocked at the want of refinement in Hamlet. The want of punctilious exactness in his behaviour either partakes of the 'license of the time', or else belongs to the very excess of intellectual refinement in the character, which makes the common rules of life, as well as his own purposes, sit loose upon him. He may be said to be amenable only to the tribunal of his own thoughts, and is too much taken up with the airy world of contemplation to lay as much stress as he ought on the practical consequences of things. His habitual principles of action are unhinged and out of joint with the time. His conduct to Ophelia is quite natural in his circumstances. It is that of assumed sever-ity only. It is the effect of disappointed hope, of bitter regrets, of affection suspended, not obliterated, by the distractions of the scenes around him! Amidst the natural and preternatural horrors of his situation, he might be excused in delicacy from carrying on a regular courtship. When 'his father's spirit was in arms', it was not a time for the son to make love in. He could neither marry Ophelia, nor wound her mind by explaining the cause of his alienation, which he durst hardly trust himself to think of. It would have taken him years to have come to a direct explanation on the point. In the harassed state of his mind, he could not have done otherwise than he did. His conduct does not contradict what he says when he sees her funeral:

> I lov'd Ophelia. Forty thousand brothers
> Could not with all their quantity of love
> Make up my sum.
> [5.1.264–6]

Nothing can be more affecting or beautiful than the Queen's apostrophe to Ophelia on throwing flowers into the grave:

> Sweets to the sweet. Farewell.
> I hop'd thou shoudst have been my Hamlet's wife:
> I thought thy bride-bed to have deck'd, sweet maid,
> And not have strew'd thy grave.
> [5.1.236–9]

Shakespeare was thoroughly a master of the mixed motives of human char-acter, and he here shows us the Queen, who was so criminal in some respects, not without sensibility and affection in other relations of life. Ophelia is a character almost too exquisitely touching to be dwelt upon. Oh rose of May, oh flower too soon faded! Her love, her madness, her death, are described with the truest touches of tenderness and pathos. It is a character which nobody but Shakespeare could have drawn in the way that he has done, and to the conception of which there is not even the smallest approach, except in some of the old romantic ballads. Her brother,

Laertes, is a character we do not like so well: he is too hot and choleric, and somewhat rodomontade [boastful]. Polonius is a perfect character in its kind; nor is there any foundation for the objections which have been made to the consistency of this part. It is said that he acts very foolishly and talks very sensibly. There is no inconsistency in that. Again, that he talks wisely at one time and foolishly at another; that his advice to Laertes is very sensible, and his advice to the King and Queen on the subject of Hamlet's madness very ridiculous. But he gives the one as a father, and is sincere in it; he gives the other as a mere courtier, a busy-body, and is accordingly officious, garrulous and impertinent. In short, Shakespeare has been accused of inconsistency in this and other characters, only because he has kept up the distinction which there is in nature, between the understandings and the moral habits of men, between the absurdity of their ideas and the absurdity of their motives. Polonius is not a fool, but he makes himself so. His folly, whether in his actions or speeches, comes under the head of impropriety of intention. □

(William Hazlitt, *Characters of Shakespeare's Plays*, 1838)[21]

In the passage above, we can see the way in which the Romantic view of this play, emerging from its initial concentration on the internal life of Hamlet himself, becomes, in this instance, a criticism of character, not just the central character, but the other characters and their relation to him. In this the Romantics prefigure the work of many early twentieth-century critics, such as A.C. Bradley, who will be one of the subjects of Chapter 4. Although, of course, it may be more accurate to say that the legacy of Romanticism continued in them, in the sometimes watered-down form of 'character-criticism', something that Hazlitt is already doing in the passage above.

One of the characteristics of Romantic criticism that situates it in its age is its reliance on the plays as printed documents rather than as dramatic events. This Guide is not really concerned with the dramatic interpretations of *Hamlet* through time but with critical interpretations. However, it is, I think, important to note that neoclassical criticism, with its important notions of decorum, was, on the whole, imagining the play as acted. Goethe's novel had discussed the difficulties of staging the play and Hazlitt makes a specific point about preferring the play as read, referring to the offences of some of his contemporary actors. In some ways, then, Hazlitt's portrayal of Hamlet is an idealised one; it is a portrayal that can only exist from reading the play rather than seeing it acted. This is not, though, to deny the importance of encountering Hamlet, or *Hamlet*, in this way. Whilst recent criticism might attempt in various ways to reconstruct the material conditions of the production of this character and of this play, it should still be remembered that most people's primary encounter with the play is through the written word.

■ We do not like to see our author's plays acted, and least of all, *Hamlet*. There is no play that suffers so much in being transferred to the stage. Hamlet himself seems hardly capable of being acted. Mr. Kemble unavoidably fails in this character from a want of ease and variety. The character of Hamlet is made up of undulating lines; it has the yielding flexibility of 'a wave o'th'sea'. Mr. Kemble plays it like a man in armour, with a determined inveteracy of purpose, in one undeviating straight line, which is as remote from the natural grace and refined susceptibility of the character as the sharp angles and abrupt starts which Mr. Kean introduces into the part. Mr. Kean's Hamlet is as much too splenetic and rash as Mr. Kemble's is too deliberate and formal. His manner is too strong and pointed. He throws a severity, approaching to virulence, into the common observations and answers. There is nothing of this in Hamlet. He is, as it were, wrapped up in his reflections, and only *thinks aloud*. There should therefore be no attempt to impress what he says upon others by a studied exaggeration of emphasis or manner; no *talking at* his hearers. There should be as much of the gentleman and the scholar as possible infused in the part, and as little of the actor. A pensive air of sadness should sit reluctantly upon his brow, but no appearance of fixed and sullen gloom. He is full of weakness and melancholy, but there is no harshness in his nature. He is the most amiable of misanthropes.[22] □

'The most amiable of misanthropes' is a wonderful paradox to sum up Hamlet. In the letters of John Keats (1795–1821), a contemporary and close friend of Hazlitt, the poet sometimes seems to have taken to heart the image that Hazlitt gives of Hamlet as a misanthropist. Keats was an avid reader of Shakespeare, as can be seen from his own copy of Shakespeare's works which is heavily annotated and underlined. He also refers to Shakespeare in his letters. On two occasions, he makes reference to *Hamlet* and these instances both provide insight into how the Romantic view of the play was received and circulated. On 9 June, 1819, in a letter to Sarah Jeffrey, the daughter of his landlady, he talks about the possibility of his travelling on an Indiaman, a merchant ship bound for either India or the West Indies that would, to increase its profits, occasionally take on passengers. In her letter to him, she has evidently suggested that this kind of isolation from society will have a detrimental effect on his work. He argues that, on the contrary, suffering breeds great literature.

■ One of the great reasons that the English have produced the finest writers in the world is that the English world has ill-treated them during their lives and fostered them after their deaths. They have in general been trampled aside into the bye paths of life and seen the festerings of society. They have not been treated like the Raphaels of Italy. And where is the Englishman and Poet who has given a magnificent Entertainment at the

Christening of one of his hero's horses as Boyardo did? He had a Castle in the Appenine. He was a noble Poet of Romance; not a miserable and mighty Poet of the human heart. The middle age of Shakespeare was all c[l]ouded over; his days were not more happy than Hamlet's who is perhaps more like Shakespeare himself in his common every day life than any other of his characters.[23] ☐

Keats is, of course, projecting his own feelings of rejection onto Shakespeare, but finding a common image for both artists in the Romantic Hamlet. The full weight of the Romantic view of Hamlet lies behind the assumptions that Keats is able to make here – like Richardson and Mackenzie he assumes that he as well as Shakespeare and Hamlet himself are too good for this world. Like Coleridge, he sees that Hamlet is an image of the artist and, like Hazlitt, that he shuns society.

In what turned out to be Keats's last letter to the love of his life, Fanny Brawne, and at an even more traumatic moment, he returned again to the figure of Hamlet. Again, we can see the background of a specifically Romantic reception of Hamlet in the assumptions he makes. Keats has been advised by his doctors to spend the winter in Italy and he feels that he is becoming increasingly isolated from Fanny because of his ill health. In a very moving letter, that demonstrates a deep depression, he tells her that, 'If I cannot live with you I will live alone'.

■ If my health could bear it, I could write a Poem which I have in my head, which would be a consolation for people in such a situation as mine. I would show someone in love as I am, with a person living in liberty as you do. Shakespeare always sums up matters in the most sovereign manner. Hamlet's heart was full of such misery as mine is when he said, 'Go to a nunnery, go, go!' Indeed I should like to give up the matter at once – I should like to die. I am sickened at the brute world which you are smiling with. I hate men and women more. I see nothing but thorns for the future – wherever I be next winter either in Italy or nowhere. Brown will be living near you with his indecencies – I see no prospect of any rest. Suppose me in Rome – well, I should there see you as in a magic glass going to and from town at all hours – I wish you could infuse a little confidence in human nature into my heart. I cannot muster any – the world is too brutal for me – I am glad there is such a thing as the grave I am sure I shall never have any rest till I get there. At any rate I will indulge myself by never seeing any more Dilke or Brown or any of their Friends. I wish I was either in you're a[r]ms full of faith or that a thunder bolt would strike me.[24] ☐

Taking his cue from Hazlitt, Keats imagines Hamlet as a misanthropist, unable to cope with society. This emerges in a bitter irony aimed not only at Fanny herself but also at his friends, Brown and Dilke. Although he refers Fanny to a specific passage, where Ophelia confronts Hamlet on the instructions of her father in order to discover whether love is the origin of his 'madness', his sentiments seem to be drawn from elsewhere in the play, particularly the speech Hamlet makes to Rosencrantz and Guildenstern in Act 2, scene 2, 'I have of late, but wherefore I know not, lost all my mirth ... ', with Keats's 'I hate men and women more' seeming to echo Hamlet's 'Man delights not me – nor woman neither though by your smiling you seem to say so' (2.2.309–10). Keats's suicidal sentiments here also seem to echo some other of Hamlet's early speeches. In imagining himself *as* Hamlet, Keats identifies with what has emerged as *the* Romantic version of Hamlet – isolated, suicidal, sensitive. What he also reveals is a side to this Hamlet that comes to be of specific interest to the next set of *Hamlet* critics that this Guide is going to look at – psychoanalytic readers of the play. Gary Taylor has argued that Keats's apparent assessment of *Hamlet* in the letters differs from that of Coleridge in that it turns Hamlet even more into a private individual, and converts the political dilemma of assassination into a personal obsession with guilt. Whereas Coleridge, the conservative, is keen to stress Hamlet's political indecision as a way of discussing the English response to the French Revolution. Keats takes the indecision and melancholy on board, but ignores the political contexts, both of Hamlet's Denmark and of early nineteenth-century Europe. Importantly, the anxieties that Keats imagines himself sharing with Hamlet circulate around sexual matters. He appears disgusted with his friend's 'indecencies' and, although he never reaches the misogyny of Hamlet's 'nunnery' speech, there is more than a hint of it when he imagines himself stranded in Rome, dwelling on Fanny going amongst London society with ease and pleasure. It is precisely this misanthropy, and misogyny in particular, that has fuelled the development of psychoanalytic interest in the play from the very early twentieth century through to more recent developments in psychoanalysis. Psychoanalytic criticism, in its origins with Freud and Ernest Jones, shares with Romanticism a concern to explain Hamlet's 'character', including the by now all-important delay, in terms of his psyche, but it does so not by relating it to Hamlet's potential creative capabilities but in terms of a general scientific model of the human psyche. We explore some key examples of this kind of criticism in the Chapter 3.

CHAPTER THREE

Psychoanalytic Approaches: Oedipus and After

FREUD AND JONES: OEDIPAL HAMLET

In an essay from 1904, called 'Psychopathic Characters on the Stage', Sigmund Freud made the almost unbelievably bold claim that, 'After all, the conflict in *Hamlet* is so effectively concealed that it was left to me to unearth it.'[1] That is, the mystery of the motivations behind Hamlet's actions in *Hamlet* are, or rather *were*, so obscure that the Danish prince needed to go into Freudian psychoanalysis. As therapy had not yet been invented in the late sixteenth century, he had to wait until the scientific advances of the late nineteenth and early twentieth centuries for a thorough diagnosis. What Freud is, in fact, referring to in the essay is a footnote he had earlier written in his book, *The Interpretation of Dreams* (1899). Ernest Jones (1879–1958), one of Freud's pupils, later expanded this footnote into a full, book-length psychoanalytic account of the play, *Hamlet and Oedipus* (1945). And it is these two texts together that form the basis for the influential psychoanalytic reading of the play that has proved so durable in the twentieth century, both in criticism and in performance.

This is most obviously true in the case of Olivier's 1947 film version of the play. Throughout the film, Hamlet's soliloquies are presented as voiceovers rather than as speeches out loud, intensifying the impression that this is a play about the workings of an individual's psyche, rather than about his interaction with the world. Peter Donaldson has written about the clearly Freudian influence on the film, that extends to its set as well as to its understanding of character.

■ Laurence Olivier's film of *Hamlet* announces itself as a psychoanalytic, Oedipal text. The phallic symbolism of rapier and dagger, the repeated dolly-in down the long corridor to the queen's immense, enigmatic and vaginally hooded bed, the erotic treatment of the scenes between Olivier and Eileen Herlie as Gertrude all bespeak a robust and readily identifiable, if naïve, Freudianism.[2] □

The 1990 Zeffirelli film, starring Mel Gibson as Hamlet and Glenn Close as Gertrude, also encourages a psychoanalytic reading of the play. In this film, the potentially sexual nature of the relationship between the mother and son was emphasised by the performances of these two actors who, by virtue of their status in the film industry, were clearly intended as the lead roles in the play. Glenn Close was also most recently known for her role in Stephen Frears' 1988 film version of *Dangerous Liaisons* in which she had played the sexually predatory Marquise De Merteuil. Of course, Gibson's status as international sex symbol underwrote his appearance as the 'young' Prince. Even the opening scene of Zefferelli's film, in which they meet in public, is charged with a heavily sexual atmosphere between them. That Zefferelli chose to open with this scene rather than the ramparts scene, which places the action of the play within its political contexts, reveals the extent to which the reception of this play has moved away from the active and political and into the introspective and personal. Although the Romantic reception of the play inaugurates this trend, it is consolidated by its position within Freudian psychoanalysis, and by subsequent psychoanalytic readings. These two film versions are in contrast to the two recent and less introspective films, directed by Kenneth Branagh (1996) and Michael Almereyda (2000) which both, in different ways, choose to emphasise the power struggles within which the protagonist is caught.

In claiming that he unearthed the conflict in *Hamlet*, Freud is, in part, mistaken. It is almost impossible to overestimate the importance of Freudian psychoanalysis in all of our subsequent understandings of drama and character, even if we reject the specific ideas contained here. This is doubly the case for *Hamlet*, a play which, in the popular imagination, sometimes seems to represent Freudian theories of sexuality and family relationships, more so, even, than Sophocles' *Oedipus*, the play that Freud himself makes a lot more of. However, in his account of the play he also seems to be responding to a critical question that we have seen at the heart of critical writings on *Hamlet* before, and which becomes a key question in mainstream literary criticism at about the same time as Freud is writing, as we will see in the Chapter 4. The question that he is concerned with is why it is that Hamlet appears to delay in killing his uncle, despite the fact that this is precisely what he appears to want to do. Like some of the Romantic critics before him, notably Schlegel and Coleridge, Freud locates the explanation for this both in the peculiar psyche of Hamlet himself and, more generally, in a trait of the human psyche as a whole. As with Coleridge, it is not easy in Freud either to reconcile or to separate these two strands.[3] This continues to be the case in Ernest Jones' work, even though he is much more clearly involved in literary critical debates than his teacher.

The classic, and highly influential, explanation for the character of Hamlet as a manifestation of the Oedipus complex comes in Freud's *The Interpretation of Dreams*. Freud explains the origins of two common dreams – one in which you kill your father and the other in which you have sex with your mother – as he explains all dreams, which is as a kind of wish-fulfilment. These particular dreams are said, by Freud, to have had their origins in early childhood rivalry with your father for your mother's affections. Although the violent urges towards your father and the sexual feelings towards your mother are repressed as you become socialised, these repressed feelings can emerge as wish-fulfilling dreams or, Freud, seems to argue, as art. His prime example is, as the name of the behaviour pattern might suggest, Sophocles' play, *Oedipus the King* which, he says, is an artistic embodiment of the two common dreams of killing your father and having sex with your mother.

■ I refer to the legend of King Oedipus and the drama of that name by Sophocles. Oedipus, son of Laius, King of Thebes, and Jocasta, is abandoned as an infant because an oracle had proclaimed to his father that his son yet unborn would be his murderer. He is rescued and grows up as a king's son at a foreign court, until he himself consults the oracle about his origins, and receives the counsel that he should flee his home city, because he would perforce become his father's murderer and his mother's spouse. On the road from his supposed home city he encounters King Laius and kills him in a sudden quarrel. Then he arrives before Thebes, where he solves the riddle of the Sphinx as she bars his way, and in gratitude he is chosen by the Thebans to be their king and presented with Jocasta's hand in marriage. He reigns long in peace and dignity, and begets two sons and two daughters with his – unbeknown – mother, until a plague breaks out, occasioning fresh questioning of the oracle by the Thebans. At this point Sophocles' tragedy begins. The messengers bring word that the plague will end when the murderer of Laius is driven from the land. But where is he?

... Where shall we hope to uncover
The faded traces of that far-distant crime?

The action of the play consists now in the gradually intensified and skilfully delayed revelation – comparable to the work of a psychoanalysis – that Oedipus himself is Laius' murderer, but also that he is the son of the murdered king and Jocasta. Shattered by the abomination he has in his ignorance committed, Oedipus blinds himself and leaves his homeland. The oracle is fulfilled.

Oedipus the King is what we call a tragedy of fate; its tragic effect is supposed to depend on the contrast between the all-powerful will of the gods and the vain struggles of men threatened by disaster. What the deeply moved spectator is meant to learn from the tragedy is submission to the will of the divinity and insight into his own powerlessness. Consequently, modern dramatists have tried to achieve a similar tragic effect by weaving the same contrast into a plot of their own invention. But the spectators have looked on unmoved as, despite all the efforts of innocent humans, some curse or oracle is fulfilled. The later tragedies of fate have failed in their effect.

If *Oedipus the King* is able to move modern man no less deeply than the Greeks who were Sophocles' contemporaries, the solution can only be that the effect of Greek tragedy does not depend on the contrast between fate and human will, but is to be sought in the distinctive subject-matter exemplifying this contrast. There must be a voice within us that is ready to acknowledge the compelling force of fate in *Oedipus*, while we are able to reject as arbitrary such disposals as are to be found in *Die Ahnfrau* [*The Ancestress* (1817), a play by Franz Grillparzer (1791–1872)] or other tragedies of fate. And a factor of this kind is indeed contained in the story of King Oedipus. His fate moves us only because it could have been our own as well, because at our birth the oracle pronounced the same curse upon us as it did on him. It was perhaps ordained that we should all of us turn our first sexual impulses towards our mother, our first hatred and violent wishes against our father. Our dreams convince us of it. King Oedipus, who killed his father Laius and married his mother Jocasta, is only the fulfilment of our childhood wish. But, more fortunate than he, we have since succeeded, at least insofar as we have not become psychoneurotics, in detaching our jealousy from our mothers and forgetting our jealousy of our fathers. We recoil from the figure who has fulfilled that ancient childhood wish with the entire sum of repression which these wishes have since undergone with us. As the poet brings Oedipus' guilt to light in the course of his investigation, he compels us to recognize our own inner life, where those impulses, though suppressed, are still present. The contrast with which the chorus takes its leave:

> ... behold: this was Oedipus,
> Greatest of men; he held the key to the deepest mysteries;
> Was envied by all his fellow-men for his great prosperity;
> Behold, what a full tide of misfortune swept over his head.

this admonition refers to us too and our pride, who have grown so wise and powerful in our own estimation since our childish years. Like Oedipus we live in ignorance of those wishes, offensive to morality and forced upon us by Nature, and once they have been revealed, there is little doubt we would all rather turn our gaze away from the scenes of our childhood.

There is an unmistakable indication in the text of Sophocles' tragedy itself that the legend of Oedipus sprang from that ancient dream material which contains the painful disturbance of our relationships with our parents by the first stirrings of our sexuality. Jocasta consoles Oedipus at a stage where he has not yet learned the truth, but is troubled by the memory of what the oracle proclaimed. She refers to a dream which many indeed do dream, but without – or so she thinks – its having any significance:

Nor need this mother-marrying frighten you;
Many a man has dreamt as much. Such things
Must be forgotten, if life is to be endured.

The dream of having sexual intercourse with the mother is dreamed by many today as it was then, and they recount it with indignation and amazement. It is clearly the key to the tragedy and the complement to the dream of the father's death. The Oedipus story is the imagination's reaction to these two typical dreams, and just as the dreams of the adult are filled with feelings of revulsion, the legend too is bound to include the horror and self-punishment in its content. □

(Sigmund Freud, *The Interpretation of Dreams*, 1899)[4]

Freud makes much of the continuing popularity of *Oedipus* and *Hamlet*. He does this in order to justify the generalised claims for the story of human development that he extrapolates from these dramas. It therefore becomes interesting that he seems to undermine this by marking the differences between the two plays as an historical development. This appears to be the result of Freud seeing modern man as yet more repressed than his more primitive ancestors. As a result, the later play also enacts that repression more thoroughly. However these primitive urges are never so thoroughly repressed that, when presented, or even alluded to, in drama they fail to provoke a response. It is, then, these same Oedipal motivations that lie at the at the heart of *Hamlet* as well, only this time, as a result of a modern tendency to further repression, they are not expressed so clearly as in the Sophocles drama.

■ Another great creation of tragic poetry is rooted in the same soil as *Oedipus the King*: Shakespeare's *Hamlet*. But the change in treatment of the same material reveals the difference in the inner life of these two cultural periods so remote from each other: the advance of repression over the centuries in mankind's emotional life. In *Oedipus* the child's wishful fantasy on which it is based is out in the open and realized – as it is in dreams; in *Hamlet* it remains repressed, and we learn of its existence – as we learn of a neurosis – only through the inhibiting effects it produces. Curiously, *Hamlet* has shown that the overwhelming power of modern drama is compatible with the fact that we can remain quite unclear about the hero's character. The play is based upon Hamlet's hesitation in fulfilling the task of revenge laid upon him; what the reasons or motives are for this hesitation the text does not say; the most various attempts at interpretation have not been able to identify them. According to the view argued by Goethe and still dominant today, Hamlet represents the type of human being whose power of action is paralysed by the over-development of the activity of thought ('sicklied o'er with the pale cast of thought'). According to others, the poet has attempted to portray a pathological, irresolute character close to neurasthenia. However, the drama's plot tells us that Hamlet should certainly not appear to be entirely incapable of action. We see him in action twice, once in sudden passion, when he stabs the eavesdropper behind the arras, the second time purposefully, indeed cunningly, when with all the insouciance of a renaissance prince he dispatches two courtiers to the death intended for himself. So what inhibits him from fulfilling the task laid upon him by his father's ghost? Here again we have at our disposal the knowledge that it is the particular nature of this task. Hamlet can do anything – except take revenge on the man who removed his father and took the latter's place beside his mother, the man who shows him his own repressed infant wishes realized. The revulsion that should urge him to revenge is thus replaced by self-recrimination, by the scruples of conscience which accuse him of being, quite literally, no better than the sinner he has to punish. I have translated into conscious terms what is bound to remain unconscious in the hero's psyche; if anyone wants to call Hamlet a hysteric, I can only acknowledge that it is an inference my interpretation admits. The sexual revulsion which Hamlet expresses in the dialogue with Ophelia is congruent with it – the same sexual revulsion which was to take increasing hold of the poet's psyche in the following years, reaching its extreme in *Timon of Athens*. Of course it can only have been the poet's inner life that confronts us in *Hamlet*; I note from the work on Shakespeare by Georg Brandes (1896) that the drama was written immediately after his father's death (1601), that is, when Shakespeare's mourning for his father was still fresh, and when presumably his childhood feelings towards him were revived. It is also known that Shakespeare had a son called Hamnet (identical with Hamlet) who died young. Just as *Hamlet* deals with the relationship of the son to his parents, so *Macbeth*, written in much the same period, deals with the theme of childlessness. Incidentally, just as every neurotic symptom, even the dream, is capable of over-interpretation, indeed demands it, if we are to understand it fully, so every truly poetic creation will have arisen from more than one motive and more than one impulse in the poet's psyche, and will admit of more than one interpretation. What I have attempted here is only an interpretation of the deepest layer of the impulses in the psyche of the creative poet. ☐

(Sigmund Freud, *The Interpretation of Dreams*, 1899)[5]

We can see, here, that Freud is not only attempting a psychoanalytic account of Hamlet's behaviour, but also of his author, Shakespeare, and his motivations in presenting that character. In his book, *Hamlet and Oedipus*, Ernest Jones also has these two strands but separates them out much more clearly. Although Jones does, in fact, write in a particularly dull and unappealing style, he explicates very clearly the narrative of *Hamlet*, the character of Hamlet and their interrelationship in the light of Freud's footnote. Like Freud, and many literary critics before and after, Jones addresses the question of Hamlet's apparent delay in exacting his revenge. In his footnote on *Hamlet*, Freud acknowledged that there had been many attempts to find the cause for the delay, but what had not been seen, he says, are the causes for his delay in performing *this* particular action. Not normally a dilatory sort, it is only when it comes to killing the uncle who has married his mother that he hesitates. Jones develops this suggestion.

■ We are compelled then to take the position that there is some cause for Hamlet's vacillation which has not yet been fathomed. If this lies neither in his incapacity for action in general, nor in the inordinate difficulty of the particular task in question, then it must of necessity lie in the third possibility – namely, in some special feature of the task that renders it repugnant to him. This conclusion, that Hamlet at heart does not want to carry out the task, seems so obvious that it is hard to see how any open-minded reader of the play could avoid making it.⁶ □

And again, after Freud, Jones insists that we all share the psychological conflicts that prevent Hamlet from fulfilling his task and that this explains the play's continuing popularity.

■ But, if the motive of the play is so obscure, to what can we attribute its powerful effect on the audience since, as Kohler asks, 'Who has ever seen Hamlet and not felt the fearful conflict that moves the soul of the hero?' This can only be because the hero's conflict finds its echo in a similar inner conflict in the mind of the hearer, and the more intense is this already present conflict the greater is the effect of the drama. Again, it is certain that the hearer himself does not know the inner cause of the conflict in this own mind, but experiences only the outer manifestations of it. So we reach the apparent paradox that the hero, the poet and the audience are all profoundly moved by feelings due to a conflict of the source of which they are unaware.⁷ □

Jones then examines various possible reasons for Hamlet's delay, including the possibility, which he dismisses, that Hamlet could have had ethical problems with committing murder in the name of revenge.

■ Bearing these considerations in mind, let us return to Hamlet. It should now be evident that the conflict hypotheses discussed above, which see Hamlet's conscious impulse towards revenge inhibited by an unconscious misgiving of a highly ethical kind, are based on ignorance of what actually happens in real life, since misgivings of this order belong in fact to the more conscious layers of the mind rather than to the deeper, unconscious ones. Hamlet's intense self-study would speedily have made him aware of any such misgivings and, although he might subsequently have ignored them, it would almost certainly have been by the aid of some process of rationalization which would have enabled him to deceive himself into believing that they were ill-founded; he would in any case have remained conscious of the nature of them. We have therefore to invert these hypotheses and realize – as his words do often indicate – that the positive striving for vengeance, the pious task laid on him by his father, was to him the moral and social one, the one approved by all his consciousness, and that the 'repressed' inhibiting striving against the act of vengeance arose in some hidden source connected with his more personal, natural instincts. The former striving has already been considered, and indeed is manifest in every speech in which Hamlet debates the matter: the second is, from its nature, more obscure and has next to be investigated.

This is perhaps most easily done by inquiring more intently into Hamlet's precise attitude towards the object of his vengeance, Claudius, and towards the crimes that have to be avenged. These are two: Claudius' incest with the Queen, and his murder of his brother. Now it is of great importance to note the profound difference in Hamlet's attitude towards these two crimes. Intellectually of course he abhors both, but there can be no question as to which arouses in him the deeper loathing. Whereas the murder of his father evokes in him indignation and a plain recognition of his obvious duty to avenge it, his mother's guilty conduct awakes in him the intensest horror. □   (Ernest Jones, *Hamlet and Oedipus*, 1949)[8]

What Jones extrapolates from Freud's footnote, and from the application of the Freudian model of the psyche to the character of Hamlet, is that the discussion of ethics cannot be behind the action (or inaction) of the play. An ethical understanding of the situation would, in the Freudian model, belong to the conscious level of the Ego. Hamlet's objections to acting, if they were ethical, could have been easily discussed in the open. They are not; they are hidden. This locates them in the unconscious and relates, therefore, to Hamlet's (and our) earliest childhood experiences, forgotten in the conscious mind but retained in the unconscious mind – that is, 'repressed'.

■ For some deep-seated reason, which is to him unacceptable, Hamlet is plunged into anguish at the thought of his father being replaced in his mother's affections by someone else. It is as if his devotion to his mother had made him so jealous for her affection that he had found it hard enough to share this even with his father and could not endure to share it with still another man. Against this thought, however, suggestive as it is, may be urged three objections. First, if it were in itself a full statement of the matter, Hamlet would have been aware of that jealousy, whereas we have concluded that the mental process we are seeking is hidden from him. Secondly, we see in it no evidence of the arousing of an old and forgotten memory. And, thirdly, Hamlet is being deprived by Claudius of no greater share in the Queen's affection than he had been by his own father, for the two brothers made exactly similar claims in this respect – namely, those of a loved husband. The last-named objection, however, leads us to the heart of the situation. How if, in fact, Hamlet had in years gone by, as a child, bitterly resented having had to share having had to share his mother's affection with his own father, had regarded him as a rival, and had secretly wished him out of the way so that he might enjoy undisputed and undisturbed the monopoly of that affection? If such thoughts had been present in his mind in childhood days they evidently would have been 'repressed', and all traces of them obliterated, by filial piety and other educative influences. The actual realization of his early wish in the death of his father at the hands of a jealous rival would then have stimulated into activity these 'repressed' memories, which would have produced, in the form of depression and other suffering, an obscure aftermath of his childhood's conflict. This is at all events the mechanism that is actually found in the real Hamlets who are investigated psychologically.

The explanation, therefore, of the delay and self-frustration in the endeavour to fulfil his father's demand for vengeance is that to Hamlet the thought of incest and parricide combined is too intolerable to be borne. One part of him tries to carry out the task, the other flinches inexorably from the thought of it. □   (Ernest Jones, *Hamlet and Oedipus*, 1949)[9]

Jones, then, makes the same claims as Freud for the importance of this play – that it articulates, in the working out of its narrative, a primary Oedipal experience that is common to all, but which comes to seem particular with some – with, that is, 'the real Hamlets who are investigated psychologically'. What Jones adds, though, is a kind of character analysis which, when applied to Gertrude, insists on her 'sensual nature' and her 'passionate fondness'. This, interestingly, seems to prefigure the later psychoanalytic interpretation that Jacques Lacan (1901–81) gives of *Hamlet*, but removes the play from its immediate Freudian Oedipal structure. Lacan, too, makes much of Gertrude's 'desire'. It is the mark of later psychoanalytic accounts, drawing on and offering critiques of the classic Freudian account, that a move is made to look at the women in the play. This concern has its origins in Jones's psychoanalytic explanation of the play, even if it is barely acknowledged.

■ As a child Hamlet had experienced the warmest affection for his mother, and this, as is always so, had contained elements of a disguised erotic quality, still more so in infancy. The presence of two traits in the

Queen's character accord with this assumption, namely her markedly sensual nature and her passionate fondness for her son. The former is indicated in too many places in the play to need specific reference, and is generally recognized. The latter is also manifest: Claudius says, for instance (Act 4, Sc. 7), 'The Queen his mother lives almost by his looks'. Nevertheless Hamlet appears to have with more or less success weaned himself from her and fallen in love with Ophelia. The precise nature of his original feeling for Ophelia is a little obscure. We may assume that at least in part it was composed of a normal love for a prospective bride, though the extravagance of the language used (the passionate need for absolute certainty, etc.) suggests a somewhat morbid state of mind.[10] ☐

It is also in Jones that we get the ongoing interest of psychoanalytic accounts of the play in Ophelia and in Hamlet's relationship with her. What is often perceived as a 'dysfunctional' relationship between the two comes to be as keenly analysed as a symptom as Hamlet's delay. For Jones, Ophelia is a tool in Hamlet's rivalrous relationships with his parents and his stepfather.

■ A case might even be made out for the view that part of his courtship originated not so much in direct attraction for Ophelia as in an unconscious desire to play her off against his mother, just as a disappointed and piqued lover so often has resort to the arms of a more willing rival. It would not be easy otherwise to understand the readiness with which he later throws himself into the part. When, for instance, in the play scene he replies to his mother's request to sit by her with the words 'No, good mother, here's metal more attractive' (3.2.108) and proceeds to lie at Ophelia's feet, we seem to have a direct indication of this attitude; and his coarse familiarity and bandying of ambiguous jests with the woman he has recently so ruthlessly jilted are hardly intelligible unless we bear in mind that they were carried out under the heedful gaze of the Queen. It is as if his unconscious were trying to convey to her the following thought: 'You give yourself to other men whom you prefer to me. Let me assure you that I can dispense with your favours and even prefer those of a woman whom I no longer love.' His extraordinary outburst of bawdiness on this occasion, so unexpected in a man of obviously fine feeling, points unequivocally to the sexual nature of the underlying turmoil.[11] ☐

It is, then, in the relationship between Hamlet and his parents that the psychological 'symptom' of his difficult relationship with Ophelia emerges, as well as his ambivalent reaction to the task of revenge laid upon him by his father's ghost.

■ The long 'repressed' desire to take his father's place in his mother's affection is stimulated to unconscious activity by the sight of someone usurping this place exactly as he himself had once longed to do. More, this someone was a member of the same family, so that the actual usurpation further resembled the imaginary one in being incestuous. Without his being in the least aware of it these ancient desires are ringing in his mind, are once more struggling to find conscious expression, and need such an expenditure of energy again to 'repress' them that he is reduced to the deplorable mental state he himself so vividly depicts.

There follows the Ghost's announcement that the father's death was a willed one, was due to murder. Hamlet, having at the moment his mind filled with natural indignation at the news, answers normally enough with the cry:

> Haste me to know't that I with wings as swift
> As meditation or the thoughts of love
> May sweep to my revenge.
>   [1.5.29–31]

The momentous words follow revealing who was the guilty person, namely a relative who had committed the deed at the bidding of lust. Hamlet's second guilty wish had thus also been realized by his uncle, namely to procure the fulfilment of the first – the possession of the mother – by a personal deed, in fact by murder of the father. The two recent events, the father's death and the mother's second marriage, seemed to the world to have no inner causal relation to each other, but they represented ideas which in Hamlet's unconscious fantasy had always been closely associated. These ideas now in a moment forced their way to conscious recognition in spite of all 'repressing forces', and found immediate expression in his almost reflex cry: 'O my prophetic soul! My uncle?' The frightful truth his unconscious had already intuitively divined, his consciousness had now to assimilate as best it could. For the rest of the interview Hamlet is stunned by the effect of the internal conflict thus re-awakened, which from now on never ceases, and into the essential nature of which he never penetrates. □
                         (Ernest Jones, *Hamlet and Oedipus*, 1949) [12]

Jones's account of the play may, at times, seem like a rather simplistic and inappropriate application of Freudian analysis, a method intended for 'real' people, to a fictional character. It can appear, at times, much too systematic, whilst at the same time unsure of whether it is using *Hamlet* to explain Freud's idea of Oedipal development or *vice versa*. Nevertheless, it does have some interesting insights, one of which is in this final passage from the book. Jones identifies a narcissistic relation between Hamlet and Claudius and indicates that this is at the heart, not only of Hamlet's delay in killing him, but also of his suicide as he eventually does kill him. Hamlet's movement between action and inaction also emerges in the final scene as both his murder and his own death are, and are not, his own responsibility.

■ It will be seen from the foregoing that Hamlet's attitude towards his uncle-father is far more complex than is generally supposed. He of course detests him, but it is the jealous detestation of one evil-doer towards his successful fellow. Much as he hates him, he can never denounce him with the ardent indignation that boils straight from his blood when he reproaches his mother, for the more vigorously he denounces his uncle the more powerfully does he stimulate to activity his own unconscious and 'repressed' complexes. He is therefore in a dilemma between on the one hand allowing his natural detestation of his uncle to have free play, a consummation which would stir still further his own horrible wishes, and on the other hand ignoring the imperative call for vengeance that his obvious duty demands. His own 'evil' prevents him from completely denouncing his uncle's, and in continuing to 'repress' the former he must strive to ignore, to condone, and if possible even to forget the latter; *his moral fate is bound up with his uncle's for good or ill.* In reality his uncle incorporates the deepest and most buried part of his own personality, so that he cannot kill him without also killing himself. This solution, one closely akin to what Freud has shown to be the motive of suicide in melancholia, is actually the one that Hamlet finally adopts. The course of alternate action and inaction that he embarks on, and the provocations he gives to his suspicious uncle, can lead to no other end than to his own ruin and, incidentally, to that of his uncle. Only when he has made the final sacrifice and brought himself to the door of death is he free to fulfil his duty, to avenge his father, and to lay his other self – his uncle.[13] □

AVI ERLICH: ANTI-OEDIPAL

Avi Erlich's book, *Hamlet's Absent Father* (1977) is an important example of a later analysis of the play which has its origins in the clinical practice of psychoanalysis; however Erlich draws on a tradition that diverges from straightforward Freudian analysis. The tradition that he draws on is called 'ego-psychology'; one of its most influential theorists and practitioners was Erik Erikson (1902–94). 'Ego-psychology' tends to reject the Freudian emphasis on an archaeology of neurotic symptoms in individual patients, preferring to emphasise the development of a healthy mental state through the ego's assimilation of the psychic chaos of the drives. Whereas Freud emphasised the working of the unconscious within the conscious and his analyses tended to focus on understanding how the unconscious interrupts normal patterns of behaviour, 'ego-psychology' emphasised the ego's ability to cope with, and absorb, the disturbances of unconscious life. Erlich's analysis of *Hamlet* relates to this in two ways – he sees Hamlet, the character, failing in his attempt to absorb his counter-productive feelings about his childhood, but Shakespeare as using the writing process as his means of gaining a sound mental state, his fantasies being mastered in the creation of a work of art. This approach may seem to repeat many of the problems that are inherent in Freudian analyses of literary texts, and the application of a clinical technique to a fictional text – how can a 'character' be analysed?; how can a dead author be put on the couch? However, Erlich's approach is in some ways more useful for literary criticism, or at least closer to traditional literary criticism. Because he emphasises the processes by which the writer copes with potential disturbances in his psyche, he is much more interested in the conscious artistic process involved in writing a piece of fiction, rather than merely seeing it as a set of symptoms. For Erlich, the play is a play-off between the influence of the unconscious and the controlling work of the conscious mind. He says that he is searching for 'a style of psychoanalytic criticism that can assume that artistic creativity involves the whole mind but that does not presume to have perfect insight into this creativity, conscious or unconscious'.[14]

■ It should be objected that a play is not a dream, that it is no more a spontaneous elaboration on unconscious life than it is a thematic elaboration on conscious life. A play is a crafted ordering of both conscious themes and unconscious fantasies, as well as something more. It is a total experience larger than the words that comprise it or the time it fills on the stage, a whole world of human coping within a controlled framework of technique.[15] □

Starting with this position, Erlich ends up paying much more attention to literary effect than Jones. He discovers patterns of speech, language and imagery that are conscious attempts to control psychic reality as much as they are shown to reveal unconscious motivations.

Importantly, also, he starts out from a position that contradicts Freud's and Jones's central assumptions. Freud and Jones saw the relationship between Hamlet and Claudius as the most important feature of the play. Hamlet sees his own wishes being fulfilled in his uncle's murder of his father and marriage to his mother and so cannot bring himself to kill him. In his analysis of Hamlet's motivations, Erlich does not entirely disagree with this, and is careful always to stress that Freud himself never entered into an extensive analysis of the play, but he chooses to emphasise Hamlet's relationship with his dead father. This is because he sees Jones's application of Freud's Oedipal model of family development as far too simplistic and formulaic.

■ Worse than stressing the wrong aspect (Claudius) of the play, Jones stressed the wrong (because too superficial) way of specifying the play's unconscious fantasies. Oedipus complexes are universal only in the abstract sense; they are as different as plays are different. And, of course, the ways the mind deals with unconscious pressures, including the Oedipus complex, are as various as people. *Hamlet* represents a complicated attempt to deal with a very specific kind of Oedipal crisis, one that has to do with an absent father, a ghostly father.[16] □

Erlich suggests that Hamlet's psychic problems stem from a father whom he wishes were strong but perceives to be weak. The play represents him as attempting to identify strong father figures that then let him down and reveal themselves as no more than fantasy, as too weak or as feminised.

■ King Hamlet was absent on the day his son was born. His ghost is also absent for most of the play, present and yet not present. When the Ghost does appear, he commands with the power of the resurrected, yet supplicates with the impotence of the murdered. Imposing and imposed upon, terrifying yet pitiable, he is an ambiguous figure who both comes to renew his son's sense of purpose and, ultimately, to crush him. Prince Hamlet inherits his father's name as well as his double nature of strength and weakness.[17] □

He summarises his objections to Freud's position and his own position in the conclusion to the book.

■ Freud argued that Hamlet cannot kill Claudius, and hence avenge his father's death, because Claudius has committed just the crimes of patricide and incest that Hamlet himself secretly wished to commit; for Hamlet, killing Claudius would thus be like killing himself, and this he of course does not wish to do. I find this argument suspect even on psychoanalytic grounds, for if Hamlet had identified with Claudius, there are good psychological reasons for him to go straight for Claudius' throat, punishing himself in a projected form for his incest fantasies. [...]

I find that in *Hamlet* Shakespeare deals not with repressed patricidal impulses but with a highly complex search, partially unconscious, for a strong father. Much more than he wants to have killed his father, Hamlet wants his father back, wants a strong man with whom to identify. Shakespeare presents to us one ambivalent father figure after another, each an imitation or a parody of King Hamlet, the seemingly titanic father who proved surprisingly vulnerable and easily forgotten by his doting wife. King Hamlet opens the play as a frightening apparition, a shell of power hiding a ghostly insubstantiality, a weak and impotent prisoner in purgatory who is unable to exact his own revenge, an absent man.

Polonius, Osric, Yorick, the God who could not punish a Claudius murdered while praying, the hopeless Poles, Old Fortinbras, Old Norway, Adam, Priam, Achilles, the First Player, even Horatio, are all versions of the ambivalent father who constitutes part of Hamlet's identity. I see Hamlet struggling with real and imagined weaknesses of his father, vainly wishing these weaknesses away, fearing that he too has been weakened by the same processes that brought King Hamlet unexpectedly to death, unsuccessfully trying to fabricate a strong father, a model of uncompromised strength. □

(Avi Erlich, *Hamlet's Absent Father*, 1977)[18]

It may seem that Erlich's list of potential but failing fathers is too exhaustive to make much sense, but his detailed work on these individual instances can be very persuasive, particularly when he pays close attention to the ways in which words come to be loaded with meaning, both within the play itself and within the language of the English Renaissance. A good example of this would be 'the God who could not punish a Claudius murdered while praying', partly because it is an unexpected instance of a weakened father but also because it engages with the traditional debate over Hamlet's delays. His unwillingness to kill Claudius as he is praying is often thought of as an excuse, and the real reason, for Jones, is because of Hamlet's identification with Claudius. Erlich's detailed account has it very differently.

Now might I do it pat, now a is a-praying.
And now I'll do't.   [*Draws his sword.*]
               And so a goes to heaven;
And so I am reveng'd. That would be scann'd:
A villain kills my father, and for that
I, his sole son, do this same villain send
To heaven.
Why, this is hire and salary, not revenge.
A took my father grossly, full of bread,
With all his crimes broad blown, as flush as May;
And how his audit stands who knows save heaven?
But in our circumstance and course of thought
'Tis heavy with him. And am I then reveng'd,
To take him in the purging of his soul,
When he is fit and season'd for his passage?
No.
Up, sword, and know thou a more horrid hent:
When he is drunk asleep or in his rage,
Or in th'incestuous pleasure of his bed,
At game a-swearing, or about some act
That has no relish of salvation in't,
Then trip him, that his heels may kick at heaven
And that his soul may be as damn'd and black
As hell, whereto it goes.

(3.3.73–95)

■ Here, in the prayer scene Hamlet is, more than anything else, anxious to see Claudius punished, not by himself but by God, the universal father figure. If we take God as a stand-in for King Hamlet, the father figure who concerns Hamlet most in the matter of Claudius' punishment, then we hear Hamlet unconsciously wishing that his father were able to do his own revenging. In this regard, 'hire and salary' deserves more emphasis than it gets. At least two meanings of the phrase are possible. One is supplied by Thomas Caldecott's gloss: killing Claudius would be 'a thing for which from *him* I might claim recompense'. Caldecott's emphasis on 'him' (Claudius) is meant to wrench us from the other possible interpretation of the phrase that Hamlet is thinking of himself as hired and salaried by his father. In this second view, Hamlet would be saying that if he were to kill Claudius and send him to heaven, he would be behaving like a hired assassin who carries out the letter of his commission and is not concerned, as a loving son would be, with the spirit of the commission.

If Hamlet does think of himself as a hired assassin, then it follows that he thinks of his father as a hirer of assassins, as a man who must find a mercenary because he cannot carry out his own dirty work. Since it would be mad for Hamlet to blame his dead father for the inability to act, 'hire and salary' can, on a rational level, mean only what Caldecott says it means. But Shakespeare has not been at pains to make his rational meaning clear ..., nor is Hamlet being particularly rational; thus the possibility of an irrational meaning is left open. Just as Hamlet wants to see God the father as the crucial punisher, he also would like his own father to be able to punish, and he implies that his father has abdicated this responsibility by hiring and salarying his son. This reading becomes all the more probable when we realise that alternative phrases for 'hire and salary' were available to Shakespeare, that both the First Quarto's 'a benefit and not revenge' and the Second Quarto's 'base and silly' would have avoided ambiguity if Shakespeare had wanted to avoid ambiguity.

Most literary and psychoanalytic critics justifiably see Hamlet's reasons for not killing Claudius here mainly as a hastily conceived rationalisation for his inability to act, but I do not think it has been seen how specifically Hamlet betrays the reason for that inability. By deferring the killing of Claudius, Hamlet can fantasise a situation in which the crucial punisher, God the Father, can be counted on; *now* is not a good time because God would be handcuffed by His own rules and, according to Hamlet's tortured theology, He would have to pardon Claudius. Hamlet needs a God and a father who is not so tolerant of incestuous criminals. Nor do I think that the critics have noticed how closely the prayer scene is related to Hamlet's 'let be' attitude at the end of the play. His profession of belief in a 'divinity' that shapes our ends can be a convenient sublimation for someone in desperate need of a strong father. Hamlet does not act in the prayer scene, I think, because he unconsciously wants his father to act. He desperately needs a strong father who, like his putative God, will damn Claudius to hell. □

(Avi Erlich, *Hamlet's Absent Father*, 1977) [19]

■ Perhaps it is King Lear, Shakespeare's most ambivalent father figure, who best expresses this plea for a father or a God who unambiguously punishes incest. What is implicit in *Hamlet* is made explicit in *King Lear*:

> Let the great gods
> That keep this dreadful pudder o'er our heads
> Find out their enemies now. Tremble, thou wretch,
> That hast within thee undivulged crimes
> Unwhipped of justice. Hide thee, thou bloody hand,
> Thou perjured, and thou simular of virtue
> That art incestuous.
>
> (3.2.49–55)

Every boy may wish to kill his father, but, more importantly, every boy needs a strong father to make him give up his incest fantasies and go on to be a strong man like his father.

Freud repeatedly argued that a son's identification with a strong father is necessary for the successful dissolution of the Oedipus complex. Without this identification the son would be doomed to acting out versions of the oedipal triangle in later life. So even if Hamlet's inability to form a moral and rational plan to punish Claudius results from his identification with his incestuous uncle, this signals a primary failure in his ability to identify with an unambiguously strong father. Hamlet thus pleads, as Lear does on the heath, for a great god to punish the 'incestuous' wretch. □

(Avi Erlich, *Hamlet's Absent Father*, 1977)[20]

In his analysis of the prayer scene, then, it is possible not only to see how Erlich adapts and alters the interpretations of Freud and Jones, but also to see how he achieves this through a close reading of the text. He is particularly adept at picking up on small details and uncovering wider contexts for their interpretation. In that, his attention to the details of language seems to prefigure later approaches to Renaissance texts, particularly those influenced by deconstruction and which paid attention to Renaissance rhetorical teaching, such as Jonathan Goldberg (born 1946) and Patricia Parker. In Erlich's work, the meaning of any given word is always deferred and multiple, open to interpretation and never fixed. This can be seen in his detailed examination of the famous 'To be or not to be ...' speech. In this speech, Erlich identifies several strategies whereby Hamlet attempts to resolve his Oedipal conflict and, particularly, his need for a strong father which is contradicted by a knowledge of an overwhelming mother. Erlich sees Hamlet as always having to deal with witnessing the fantasy of the castration of his father at a young age by an overwhelmingly sexual mother and the fact that this fantasy seems to have come true in his new reality.

■ To defend against the deadly oedipal conflict he has been born into, Hamlet can either (1) wish his father strong enough to have avoided castration and to have unambiguously discouraged his son's oedipal desires, or (2) wish that his mother was less seductive and less castrating, or (3) wish, as he does elsewhere, that parental sexuality does not exist and that he was never born, or (4) stop trying to wish away anxiety and sublimate it, weave it into a meditation. As it happens, he tries all these things in the 'To be' soliloquy, none of them successfully:

1. Parallel in construction to the 'slings and arrows of outrageous fortune' is 'the whips and scorns of time'. Just as the 'outrageous fortune' conjures up an image of Hamlet's mother so do the 'scorns of time' conjure up his father.

   For who would bear the whips and scorns of time,
   Th'oppressor's wrong, the proud man's contumely,
   The pangs of despised love, the law's delay,
   The insolence of office, and the spurns
   That patient merit of th'unworthy takes.

   (3.1.70–4)

   Here Hamlet, in rough strokes, shadows forth an imposing authority figure (or composite of figures), an oedipal 'oppressor' who makes his son feel the 'pangs of despised love'. As far as it goes, it represents Hamlet's wish for a father sufficiently strong to make him give up incest once and for all. Unfortunately, this authority figure also manifests weaknesses. He is an oppressor in the 'wrong', with no clear claim to his son's obedience, a 'proud man', 'unworthy' of his arrogance, insolently rejecting the 'patient merit' of his son. He is not strong enough to exact the law; like his son who has incorporated him as a tarnished ideal, he is involved in 'delay', forcing his son to make his own law, his own 'quietus'. Johnson was right in pointing out that these are not ills that would plague a prince, but they are the ills that would unconsciously strike a prince in Hamlet's oedipal situation. Like Hamlet's madness, these 'whips and scorns of time' symbolically represent an ambivalent father who both scorns and is scorned by his son.

2. Hamlet could make do with this ambiguous image of his father if his mother were not so seductively carnal and so potently castrating. Hence he tries to temper the sexual death that the mother can inflict. 'A consummation / Devoutly to be wished' is his almost pathetic attempt to enfold the nightmarish primal-scene mother in the less carnal, less threatening version of marital 'consummation' sanctified by the devout church. In offering this interpretation, I am assuming that the juxtaposition of 'consummation' and 'devoutly' is not accidental and that it suggests marriage. Of course Hamlet is referring to himself, to his death, when he speaks of 'consummation', but it would not be strange to find

Hamlet condensing a reference to his own death with a wish for a more sanctified mother who would free him from his death wishes. Hamlet also may be echoing Christ on the cross ('consummatum est' [it is finished]); if so, he is alluding to another son who condensed birth and death – though Christ of course wishfully managed to turn death into rebirth, thus avoiding Hamlet's fears that birth has been turned into death. But then Christ was the son of the Immaculate Mary. Gertrude (or Fortune), however, with her 'thousand natural shocks', with her ability 'To post/ With such dexterity to incestuous sheets', [1.2.156–7] is too incontestably carnal to wish away successfully.

3. Hamlet, mired in the guilt and shame of inadequacy, trapped with a mother whose carnality cannot be altered even in fantasy and with a father whose weakness was proved by his death and his wife's early remarriage, centers his wishes on the third member of the oedipal triangle: he wishes himself unborn (just after the soliloquy):

I could accuse me of such things that it were better my mother had not borne me: I am very proud, revengeful, ambitious, with more offences at my beck that I have thoughts to put them in, imagination to give them shape, or time to act them in. What should such fellows as I do crawling between earth and heaven? We are arrant knaves all, believe none of us. Go thy ways to a nunnery.   (3.1.123–30)

This is Hamlet describing himself as Laertes described him to Ophelia. But Hamlet cannot be describing his actual behaviour. To some degree, all these 'offences' that this noble philosopher-prince is harping on must refer to 'thoughts' that he has never acted on, that are deeper than imagination and more terrible, to 'proud, revengeful, ambitious' fantasies that sound suspiciously like those which make oedipal sons wish their mothers had never borne them. Psychoanalysis usually identifies such powerful and unnameable 'offences', such exaggerated feelings of sin that appear to have no reference in the manifest world, as derived from incest fantasies. The way to handle incest, Hamlet seems to be saying on an unconscious level, is to banish birth, to banish himself from 'between heaven and earth', and to banish women, the 'breeder[s] of sinners', to an asexual 'nunnery'. Of course 'nunnery', taken as an Elizabethan brothel, undermines the wish. Sexuality cannot be wished away, though this is, I think, what Hamlet tries to do by contemplating making his own 'quietus'. *Quietus* is a legal term for 'full discharge'; it is thus not far, in sound or sense, from *coitus*. In Hamlet's world, however, women will always breed sinners, both biologically and oedipally, and there is no way to expropriate their sexuality by making one's own 'quietus'.

4. His wishes undercutting themselves as they are made, Hamlet must continue his dynamic struggle to manage his troubling fantasies by disguising them. The soliloquy, in its manifest guise as a meditation on suicide, offers him the opportunity to sublimate, and thereby control to

some extent, his worst fears. I have mentioned the feared results of vis-
iting the 'undiscovered country'; but it is important to note that this fear
is sublimated, hidden in the Christian fear of the universe. Fear of castration also seems to be disguised in these lines of rarefied meditation:

> To die, to sleep –
> To sleep, perchance to dream: ay, there's the rub,
> For in that sleep of death what dreams may come
> When we have shuffled off this mortal coil,
> Must give us pause.

(3.64–8)

I think we are again dealing with the nightmares of castration and primal-
scene 'sleep'. We get two images of here that reinforce that interpretation.
The first is the 'rub', 'a term of bowls, meaning a collision hindering the
bowl in its course',[21] and it was probably chosen because it unconsciously
represented to Shakespeare incapacitated phallicism. My evidence for this
assertion goes a little further than the plausibility of phallic symbolism in
the hindered bowl. 'Rub' seems to have been an Elizabethan vulgarism for
sexuality, as in *Troilus and Cressida*, where Pandarus shoos the lovers off
the bed ('so, so; rub on and kiss the mistress'), and in *Love's Labours Lost*
where Maria and Boyet engage in a little bawdy repartee:

Mar:	Come, come, you talk greasily; your lips grow foul.
Costard:	She's too hard for you at pricks, sir. Challenge her to bowl.
Boy:	I fear too much rubbing.

(4.1.139–41)

What Boyet fears is a sexual encounter with the dangerous Maria, and
perhaps something of this nature is in the unconscious content of
Hamlet's fear of his 'rub'. In addition to 'rub' we have 'mortal coil'. In the
course of time the word 'coil' has provoked much emendation because it
does not quite seem to be used in either of the two familiar Elizabethan
senses ('turmoil' and 'looped rope'), but I am going to offer a scintilla of
further evidence for maintaining it as it is. My evidence takes the form of
an etymology possible only in the unconscious, but this is probably
no stranger than the Gaelic derivations that are suggested in the Variorum
Edition. 'Coillen' (the *OED* lists other possible sixteenth-century spellings
under 'cullion') means *testicle* and it seems possible to me that
Shakespeare wrenched 'coil' out of its usual uses because it brought with
it certain appropriate unconscious associations. What Hamlet is unconsciously doing, I think, is trying to diffuse in philosophic speculation the
consequences of the erotic sleep, the 'rub', that shuffles off the most
'mortal' part of man, his 'coillens'.

[...]

This sublimation unfortunately gets Hamlet no further than did his wish making. Contemplating suicide with a 'bare bodkin', he fantasises avoiding castration at the hands of a pernicious woman by turning his phallicism against himself in self-castration. By castrating oneself in fantasy one can avoid the real thing at the hands of Gertrude. However, 'bodkin', besides meaning a small dagger, also means 'a little implement ... with which women separate and twist over their hair'. Hamlet is right back in the primal scene, suffering castration from a woman's 'little implement'. And in the following moments with Ophelia, Hamlet is again outraged by the threat of castration as he re-enacts a primal scene with dotard-castrate Polonius playing Hamlet's role of peeper. [...] Thus all four of Hamlet's unconscious defence strategies fail him, for he must return to the manifest facts of his life, that his father proved to be as weak and castrated as he once imagined him, that Claudius verified Gertrude's castration of King Hamlet, that the fears of childhood are part of his adult reality. □

(Avi Erlich, *Hamlet's Absent Father*, 1977) [22]

One of the problems with Erlich's approach, as the passage above perhaps reveals, is a problem with much psychoanalytic criticism – that it takes Hamlet's status as a 'character' who can be analysed for granted without paying enough attention to artistic process. However, Erlich does attempt to address this by focussing on the play's concern with 'writing' In a chapter headed, 'Managing the unconscious', he details the many instances of writing that occur in the play, from letters to books and play scripts, both literal and metaphorical. He associates this interest with two processes in the play – with the kind of failed attempts at sublimation that Hamlet goes through and which he sees at work in the 'To be ...' speech, as shown above, and with Shakespeare's own successful sublimation of primal trauma in the production of the play itself.

■ For Shakespeare, writing was a successful adaptive mechanism against being overwhelmed by the unconscious; but for Hamlet writing is a defence that fails.[23] □

This is where Erlich's work comes closest to American 'ego-psychology' in which the act of writing, of tracing the dream-like associations of the unconscious as it emerges in the conscious mind, becomes a healing act rather than merely an excavatory process. *Hamlet* is a tragedy because Hamlet is shown to be unsuccessful in this; it is a work of art because Shakespeare *is* successful.

■ Looking back over my mind's stage, I find *Hamlet* one thing with its documents emphatically produced and another with them either expurgated or down-played. In the former case I see the play's most baffling aspects, Hamlet's relationship with the Ghost, his conscience-catching play so frantically interfered with in its presentation, his cruelty to Ophelia, his callousness with Rosencrantz and Guildenstern, all revolving around the meaning of setting things down. In the latter case I see the play from what must be Horatio's point of view, and the 'story' I would tell would be one 'Of accidental judgements, casual slaughters', [5.2.387] thus missing a good part of the play's unity.

The unity I see underlying the play's emphasis on writing is a consistent, though dynamic, attempt to fabricate a father strong enough to punish the oedipal criminal with castration. Since a son is in so many ways only as strong as his incorporated father, we can see that a son who feared he had a weak father would wish things otherwise. We might also expect him to wish for a less seductive mother, thus neutralizing the weak father. Hamlet's matricidal impulses and Ophelia's melting away into the elements perhaps express this corollary wish, but for the most part the play deals with a mother who is irrefutably present and carnal and a father who is literally only as potent as the desperate 'mind's eye' of his son can make him.

When writing is successful, it is a defence against the way things are, as in the sealed compact; when it is not successful, it is merely a restatement of brutal reality, as in the book of 'old men'. To do without writing, to attempt to rearrange reality in life instead of fiction, leads Hamlet to the psychotic situation in which he, no longer able to *imagine* Claudius a woman punished by his father [another of his failed coping fantasies], must literally try to make him one, in 'union' with Gertrude. Writing for Hamlet is a defence that failed, thus making his life a failure.

Shakespeare's father was either dying or just dead when *Hamlet* was being written. This fact from his adult life, coupled with his father's business failures, may have resurrected some of his earliest repression, the fantasised fear that his father was not strong enough to make him give up his (perhaps) oversolicitous mother who had lost two children before William was born. However this may be, *Hamlet* seems to me to embody, among other things, a highly complex fantasy of a strong father who betrays all the weaknesses his son ever imagined him to have. As the father, so too the son's self-image; as King Hamlet, so Prince Hamlet. Our favourite character in Shakespeare's works, the most intelligent, the strongest, the most beautiful, inherits, alas, his poisoned father's failure.

As in the case of the 'To be' soliloquy, I have discovered failure at the heart of the play – King Hamlet's failure to maintain himself as a strong father, Hamlet's failure to fabricate the father he needed, Shakespeare's failure to construct a set of mental strategies that could save his hero. But what about the successes? What about the value of Hamlet's intelligence and beauty in adversity? What about our *enjoyment* of this study in adversity? What about Shakespeare's, not Hamlet's, successful use of writing to turn nightmares into creativity?

[...]

In *Hamlet*, Shakespeare portrays a man, highly gifted like himself, who is largely destroyed by the mental defences he marshals against intrapsychic conflict. Hamlet's tragedy is the failure of his mental defences. Any attempt to make this failure a success for the dramatic character Hamlet seems to me replete with the kind of unfulfillable wishing that I find in the 'To be' passage ... But the portrait of failure *was* a success for Shakespeare – and for us. He was able to watch from a distance Hamlet's self-destruction and thereby gain mastery over it. We too can distance Hamlet's inherited familial vicissitudes, and wish things otherwise for ourselves; we can enshrine his virtues and, in our awe of his conflicted mind, rededicate ourselves to the mental strategies that keep us from failing. By watching tragedy, we can wish, and thereby help create, our own psychic health. It is the miracle of tragedy that failure belongs to the fictitious characters and health to the creators, the artist and his audience. □

(Avi Erlich, *Hamlet's Absent Father*, 1977) [24]

Revealed in this rather optimistic passage is not only Erlich's relationship with the hopeful tenor of 'ego-psychology' but also the extent to which literature is taken out of the social and placed firmly in the personal in psychoanalysis. Aristotle's social 'katharsis' is translated into a personal experience of learning how to cope with private trauma. Such inevitably fictionalised psychoanalytic accounts of authors and their audiences came quickly, however, to seem rather spurious. What Erlich does signal for the future of psychoanalytic and other approaches to literature is both a continuing attempt to confront sexuality and gender in the plays – psychoanalysis was to play a large role in feminist approaches to Shakespeare – and a turn to examine the complexity of language. These twin legacies of psychoanalysis were promoted still further by the work of Jacques Lacan, who has been much more influential than Erlich has been in the field of literary study.

LACAN

After Freud, the most influential psychoanalytic theorist has been Jacques Lacan. In the 1950s and 1960s, Lacan began to rewrite Freudian theory through a careful rereading of Freud's texts. More specifically, Lacan gave psychoanalytic theory a structuralist inflection, foregrounding language as that which structures the unconscious rather than primal experiences. Elizabeth Wright has written that, 'The psychoanalysis of Jacques Lacan could be said to found itself on the failure of language to match the body.'[25] Lacan takes his cue from the insights of post-Saussurean structuralist linguistics. An important insight of structuralist linguistics was that there is no *necessary* relation between a word and the thing it represents, but that any such relationship is only ever a matter of convention. Applying this insight to psychoanalysis, Lacan viewed the subject, or the person, as constantly in search of a language which was always inadequate and yet had already defined the subject him or herself. Like Freud, Lacan often turned to literary examples to illustrate his theories. In doing this, he follows Freud's tendency to use the text as illustrative rather than to assume that the characters within the play are, themselves, case studies, as Ernest Jones does.

In 1958–59, Lacan delivered a series of lectures on *Hamlet*, entitled 'Desire and its interpretation'. A part of these was translated as 'Desire and the Interpretation of Desire in *Hamlet*' in 1977. In this title, and in this essay, Lacan deliberately echoes the title of Freud's famous work, *The Interpretation of Dreams*, and replaces the motivating concept of Freud's book, 'wish-fulfilment' with the idea of desire.[26] In Lacan's account of the formation of the subject, desire plays its part in establishing the subject's relationship to the world. Lacan discards Freud's Oedipal narrative as an explanatory framework for the formation of the subject and replaces it with a process in which the subject comes to realise his/her difference from the world through the 'mirror-phase'. Access to subjectivity, to becoming a speaking subject, is achieved, for Lacan, through identification with the law of the father, under which the subject enters into the symbolic realm of signification, of language. Such entry always entails a feeling of loss, and is indeed predicated on this feeling of loss. This feeling can be identified as 'desire'. In his account of *Hamlet*, Lacan attempts to outline this process at work, but sees in Hamlet, the character, a problem with his object of desire, or rather, a problem with his ability to identify properly with any object of desire. He links this to the seeming hesitation in Hamlet's actions and to the seeming interruptions in the narrative of the play. He calls *Hamlet*, the 'tragedy of desire'. The tragedy that Lacan identifies is that Hamlet is somehow caught up in the desire of his mother. It is not that he *desires* his mother, but that he is unable fully to become a speaking subject, an agent in his own right, because he, like his mother, is caught in an inability to choose between the two father / husband figures with which they are presented. This results in his inability to relate properly to his object of desire, Ophelia. He has, Lacan writes, 'lost the way of his desire'[27] As a result of this, Hamlet is suspended in what Lacan calls 'the time of the other'.

■ ... our friend Hamlet, to whom everyone can attribute at will all the forms of neurotic behaviour, as far as you want to go, i.e., up to character neurosis. The first factor that I indicated to you in Hamlet's structure was his situation of dependence with respect to the desire of the Other, the desire of his mother. Here now is the second factor that I ask you to recognize: Hamlet is constantly suspended in the time of the Other, throughout the entire story until the very end. [...] Whatever Hamlet may do, he will do it only at the hour of the Other.[28] □

So Lacan also links the narrative pattern of the play, with its seeming delays in action, with the psyche of its central character. For Lacan, this is because Hamlet's actions are out of his own control. Lacan's interesting insight is that this does not merely entail Hamlet being apparently behind the time but also peremptory in some of his actions. As well as apparently delaying, he rushes into things too quickly at times.

■ Thus, for Hamlet, the appointment is always too early, and he postpones it. Procrastination is thus one of the essential dimensions of the tragedy.

When, on the contrary, he does act, it is always too soon. When does he act? When all of a sudden something in the realm of events, beyond him and his deciding, calls out to him and seems to offer him some sort of ambiguous opening, which has, in specifically psychoanalytical terms, introduced the perspective we call flight (*fuite*) into the dimension of accomplishment.

Nothing could be clearer on this score than the moment in which Hamlet rushes at whatever it is moving behind the arras and kills Polonius. Or think of him awakening in the dead of night on the storm-tossed ship, going about almost in a daze, breaking the seals of the message borne by Rosencrantz and Guildenstern, substituting almost automatically one message for another, and duplicating the royal seal with his father's ring. He then has the amazing good luck to be carried off by pirates, which enables him to ditch his guards, who will go off unwittingly to their own execution. □

(Jacques Lacan, 'Desire and the Interpretation of Desire in *Hamlet*', 1977) [29]

Being in the 'time of the Other', for Hamlet, eventually leads him towards his death. Death is that which is beyond *all* our controls.

■ Yet the subject's appointment with the hour of his destruction is the common lot of everyone, meaningful in the destiny of every individual. Without some distinguishing sign, Hamlet's fate would not be of such great importance to us. That's the next question: what is the specificity of Hamlet's fate? What makes it so extraordinarily problematic?[30] □

Lacan, then, having established the symptoms within the narrative, seeks the cause of its apparent dislocations, linking them to his (our?) experience of desire. Lacan hints at something more within this lecture though, without resolving the questions that he asks. He notices, and outlines, the relationship between the Hamlet family's scandalous sexuality, the chief concern of post-Freudian criticism, and the 'maimed rites', the disfigured attempts at mourning, that punctuate the play. I think that Lacan is probably right to suggest that very little has been made, in the mainstream of *Hamlet* criticism, of the play's attitudes towards death. Lacan, though, dramatically lists the number of instances in which the normal social function of mourning is interrupted or scandalised within the action of the play. He leaves us, however, with the question about the relationship between the demands of mourning, and the narrative of desire that he has previously delineated.

■ The tragedy *Hamlet* is the tragedy of desire. But as we come to the end of our trajectory it is time to notice what one always takes note of last, i.e. what is most obvious. I know of no commentator who has ever taken the trouble to make this remark, however hard it is to overlook once it has been formulated: from one end of *Hamlet* to the other, all anyone talks about is mourning.

Mourning is what makes the marriage of Hamlet's mother so scandalous. In her eagerness to know the cause of her beloved son's 'distemper', she herself says: 'I doubt it is no other but the main, / His father's death and our o'erhasty marriage' [2.2.56–7]. And there's no need to remind you of what Hamlet says about the leftovers from 'the funeral baked meats' turning up on the 'marriage tables': 'Thrift, thrift, Horatio'. [1.2.180].

This term is a fitting reminder that in the accommodations worked out by modern society between use values and exchange values there is perhaps something that has been overlooked in the Marxian analysis of economy, the dominant one for the thought of our time – something whose force and extent we feel at every moment: ritual values. Even though we note them constantly in our experience, it may be useful to give them special consideration here as essential factors in human economy.

I have already alluded to the function of ritual in mourning. Ritual introduces some mediation of the gap (*béance*) opened up by mourning. More precisely, ritual operates in such a way as to make this gap coincide with that greater *béance*, the point *x*, the symbolic lack. The navel of the dream, to which Freud refers at one point, is perhaps nothing but the psychological counterpart of this lack.

Nor can we fail to be struck by the fact that in all the instances of mourning in *Hamlet*, one element is always present: the rites have been cut short and performed in secret.

For political reasons, Polonius is buried secretly, without ceremony, posthaste. And you remember the whole business of Ophelia's burial. There is the discussion of how it is that Ophelia, having most probably committed suicide – this is at least the common belief – still is buried on Christian ground. The gravediggers have no doubt that if she had not been of such high social standing she would have been treated differently. Nor is the priest in favor of giving her Christian burial ('She should in ground unsanctified have lodged / Till the last trumpet. For charitable prayers, / Shards, flints, and pebbles should be thrown on her' [Act 5, Sc 1]), and the rites to which he has consented are themselves abbreviated.

We cannot fail to take all these things into account, and there are many others as well.

The ghost of Hamlet's father has an inexpiable grievance. He was, he says, eternally wronged, having been taken unawares – and this is not one of the lesser mysteries as to the meaning of this tragedy – 'in the blossoms of [his (translator's interpolation)] sin'. He had no time before his death to summon up the composure or whatever that would have prepared him to go before the throne of judgement.

Here we have a number of 'clues', as they say in English, which converge in a most significant way – and where do they point? To the relationship of the drama of desire to mourning and its demands. □

(Jacques Lacan, 'Desire and the Interpretation of Desire
in *Hamlet*', 1977) [31]

JANET ADELMAN

One of the main ways in which psychoanalytic literary criticism has developed since the early twentieth century has been through feminist interventions. The central concern with sexuality that has been a feature of the psychoanalytic interest in the play was bound to attract the interest of feminist critics, particularly the extent to which the sexuality of women in the play is assumed to take the burden of Hamlet's damaged psyche. In her book, *Suffocating Mothers: Fantasies of Maternal Origin in Shakespeare's Plays* (1992), Janet Adelman, as her title suggests, turns her attention to the position mothers play in narratives of psychological development. Even though Lacan obviously afforded Hamlet's mother a larger role than Freud or Jones could within their Oedipal framework, his model of psychological development still insists on the primacy of the father, or 'the law of the father' in the important childhood conflicts that go towards the foundation of adult identity, and Erlich's analysis shifts attention almost exclusively onto Hamlet's relationship with his dead, biological father. Adelman takes her cue from the psychoanalyst, Nancy Chodorow, who saw the Freudian narrative in which the infant learns to reject the primary relationship with the mother, as a cultural development rather than an essential part of being human. Through this, Adelman situates Shakespeare's plays within particular forms of motherhood that were available in the early modern period. She argues that the trauma inherent in the separation from the maternal body was doubly felt in early modern England due to the extended period in which children were closer to their mothers, a period considerably longer than we would now consider usual. Cultural anxieties develop around the undue influence that this early feminine influence, whether from mothers or, even more so, from wet nurses, might have on the child. In the earlier plays, this results in the absence of mothers from the narrative but, for Adelman, *Hamlet* marks the return of the mother into Shakespeare's drama, and an attempt to come to terms with the difficult relationship with the mother that is the result of this traumatic early split. For Adelman, *Hamlet* is not the 'tragedy of desire' but rather the tragedy of contaminating maternal power.

■ But the mother occluded in these plays [*Julius Caesar* and the English history plays] returns with a vengeance in *Hamlet*; and it is the thesis of this book that the plays from *Hamlet* on all follow from her return. For the masculine selfhood discovered and deflected in *Richard III* – selfhood grounded in paternal absence and in the fantasy of overwhelming contamination at the site of origin – becomes the tragic burden of Hamlet and the men who come after him. And they do not bear the burden alone: again and again, it is passed on to the women, who must pay the price for the fantasies of maternal power invested in them.[32] □

The chronicle history plays and the early comedies were able to hold the figure of the mother at arm's length, but *Hamlet* as tragedy confronts the potential horror of the contaminating mother head-on. Adelman had traced a structuring narrative in the earlier plays in which a 'son' figure is required to choose and to emulate a 'father' figure. This narrative of choosing the right father, and attempting to act out the role which that choice involves, is disturbed by the presence of the mother in *Hamlet*. If Lacan saw Hamlet as psychologically held back through his identification with the desire of his mother, Adelman sees the mother in *Hamlet* as a figure who comes between the son and his father or potential fathers.

■ In *Hamlet*, the figure of the mother returns to Shakespeare's dramatic world, and her presence causes the collapse of the fragile compact that had allowed Shakespeare to explore familial and sexual relationships in the histories and romantic comedies without devastating conflict; this collapse is the point of origin of the great tragic period. The son's acting out of the role of the father, his need to make his own identity in relationship to his conception of his father – the stuff of *1 and 2 Henry IV* and *Julius Caesar* – becomes deeply problematic in the presence of the wife/mother: for her presence makes the father's sexual role a disabling crux in the son's relationship with his father. At the same time, the relations between the sexes that had been imagined in the comedies without any serious confrontation with the power of female sexuality suddenly are located in the context of the mother's power to contaminate, with the result that they can never again be imagined in purely holiday terms. Here again, *Hamlet* stands as a kind of watershed, subjecting to maternal presence the relationships previously exempted from that presence.[33] □

After Lacan, Adelman attributes part of the family crisis in *Hamlet* to Hamlet's difficulty in deciding between his two fathers, and finds that this difficulty arises through the desire of (but not for) his mother. And, again like Lacan, Adelman links this lack of proper differentiation between paternal figures to a failure in the proper processes of mourning and remembrance.

■ The triangulated choice between two fathers that is characteristic of these plays is at the center of *Hamlet*; here, as in the earlier plays, assuming masculine identity means taking on the qualities of the father's name – becoming a Henry, Brutus, or a Hamlet – by killing off a false father. Moreover, the whole weight of the play now manifestly creates one father true and the other false. Nonetheless, the choice in immeasurably more difficult for Hamlet than for his predecessors; for despite their manifest differences, the fathers in *Hamlet* keep threatening to collapse into one another, annihilating in their collapse the son's easy assumption of his father's identity. The initiating cause of this collapse is Hamlet's mother: her failure to serve her son as the repository of his father's ideal image by mourning him appropriately is the symptom of her deeper failure to distinguish properly between his father and his father's brother. Even at the start of the play, before the ghost's crucial revelation, Gertrude's failure to differentiate has put an intolerable strain on Hamlet by making him the only repository of his father's image, the only agent of differentiation in a court that seems all too willing to accept the new king in place of the old. Her failure of memory – registered in her undiscriminating sexuality – in effect defines Hamlet's task in relation to his father as a task of memory: as she forgets, he inherits the burden of differentiating, of idealizing and making static the past; hence the ghost's insistence on remembering (1.5.33, 91) and the degree to which Hamlet registers his failure as a failure of memory (4.4.40). Hamlet had promised the ghost to remember him in effect by becoming him, letting his father's commandment live all alone within his brain; but the intensity of Hamlet's need to idealize in the face of his mother's failure makes his father inaccessible to him as a model, hence disrupts the identification from which he could accomplish his vengeance. As his memory of his father pushes increasingly in the direction of idealization, Hamlet becomes more acutely aware of his own distance from that idealization and hence of his likeness to Claudius, who is defined chiefly by his difference from his father. Difference from the heroic ideal represented in Old Hamlet becomes the defining term common to Claudius and Hamlet; the very act of distinguishing Claudius from his father – 'no more like my father / Than I to Hercules' (1.2.152–3) – forces Hamlet into imaginative identification with Claudius. The intensity of Hamlet's need to differentiate

between true father and false thus confounds itself, disabling his identification with his father and hence his secure identity as son. □
(Janet Adelman, Suffocating Mothers: Fantasies of Maternal
Origin in Shakespeare's Plays, 1992) [34]

A problem for Adelman's reading of the play is the weight that she
comes to give to the character of Gertrude. Unlike Lacan, she does not
see the problems in the relationship between Hamlet and Gertrude as
transferring themselves onto Hamlet's relationship with Ophelia and,
hence, into the narrative of the play as a whole. One of the analytical
methods that psychoanalysis is particularly adept at deploying is based
on the notion that ideas can be transferred from one object to another.
The absolutely central position afforded Gertrude as the mother does
not allow Adelman to do this. She associates this disjunction in the play –
between the psychological weight attached to the position of Gertrude
and her relative lack of characterisation – as linked to T.S. Eliot's argument about the play's lack of an 'objective correlative',[35] but also as
something which illustrates her argument. The essay by Eliot in question will be treated in the next chapter.

This disjunction in the play reveals the fantasies of maternal power,
harboured both by Hamlet, the character and by *Hamlet*, the play as precisely that – fantastic projections. Whilst this may be a reasonable argument applied to the play as case study, it seriously diminishes its impact
as drama. It might be possible to translate the first sentence in the
following passage as follows: 'Given her centrality in Adelman's argument, it is surprising how little of Gertrude there is on which to base this
argument.' This is, though, a little unfair, as Hamlet's relationship with
his mother has been the focus of many performances of the play since
Freud.

■ Given her centrality in the play, it is striking how little we know about
Gertrude; even the extent of her involvement in the murder of her first husband is left unclear. We may want to hear her shock at Hamlet's accusation
of murder – 'Almost as bad, good mother, / As kill a king and marry with
his brother' (3.4.28–9) – as evidence of her innocence; but the text permits us alternatively to hear it as shock either at being found out or at
Hamlet's rudeness. The ghost accuses her at least indirectly of adultery
and incest – Claudius is 'that incestuous, that adulterate beast' (1.5.42) –
but he neither accuses her of nor exonerates her from the murder. For the
ghost, as for Hamlet, her chief crime is her uncontrolled sexuality; that is
the object of their moral revulsion, revulsion as intense as anything
directed toward the murderer Claudius. But the Gertrude we see is not
quite the Gertrude they see. And when we see her in herself, apart from
the characterizations of her, we tend to see a woman more muddled than
actively wicked; even her famous sensuality is less apparent than her

conflicted solicitude both for her new husband and for her son. She is capable from the beginning of a certain guilty insight into Hamlet's suffering ('I doubt it is no other but the main, / His father's death and our o'erhasty marriage' [2.2.56–7]). Insofar as she follows Hamlet's instructions in reporting his madness to Claudius (3.4.189–90; 4.1.7), she seems to enact every son's scenario for the good mother, choosing his interests over her husband's. But she may of course believe that he is mad and think that she is reporting accurately to her husband; certainly her courageous defence of her husband in their next appearance together – where she bodily restrains Laertes, as 4.5.122 specifies – suggests that she has not wholly adopted Hamlet's view of Claudius. Here, as elsewhere, the text leaves crucial aspects of her action and motivation open. Even her death is not quite her own to define. Is it a suicide designed to keep Hamlet from danger by dying in his place? She knows that Claudius has prepared the cup for Hamlet, and she shows unusual determination in disobeying Claudius's command not to drink it ('Gertrude, do not drink. / I will, my Lord' [5.2.294–5]). In her last moment, her thoughts seem to be all for Hamlet; she cannot spare Claudius even the attention it would take to blame him ('O my dear Hamlet! / The drink! The drink! I am poison'd' [5.2.315–16].) Muddled, fallible, fully human, she seems ultimately to make the choice that Hamlet would have her make. But even here she does not speak clearly; her character remains relatively closed to us.

The lack of clarity in our impression of Gertrude contributes, I think, to the sense that the play lacks, in Eliot's famous phrase, an 'objective correlative'. For the character of Gertrude as we see it becomes for Hamlet – and for *Hamlet* – the ground for fantasies quite incongruent with it; although she is much less purely innocent than Richard III's mother, like that mother she becomes the carrier of a nightmare that is disjunct from her characterization as a specific figure. This disjunction is, I think, the key to her role in the play and hence to her psychic power: her frailty unleashes for Hamlet, and for Shakespeare, fantasies of maternal malevolence, of maternal spoiling, that are compelling exactly as they are out of proportion to the character we know, exactly as they seem to reiterate infantile fears and desires rather than an adult apprehension of the mother as a separate person. □

(Janet Adelman, *Suffocating Mothers: Fantasies of Maternal Origin in Shakespeare's Plays*, 1992) [36]

Adelman's psychoanalytic reading of the text is at its best when it leaves behind the Jones-ian tendency to treat the characters as patients and instead treats the text as the analysand (the object of psychoanalytic treatment). In this way, the text itself is seen to have an unconscious:

■ Literalized in the plot, the splitting of the father thus evokes the ordinary psychological crisis in which the son discovers the sexuality of his parents, but with the blame handily shifted from father onto another man as unlike father as possible – and yet as like, hence his brother; in effect, the plot itself serves as a cover-up, legitimising disgust at paternal sexuality without implicating the idealized father. But thus arbitrarily separated, these fathers are always prone to collapse back into one another. The failure to differentiate between Old Hamlet and Claudius is not only Gertrude's: the play frequently insists on their likeness even while positing their absolute difference; for the sexual guilt of the father – his implication in the mother's body – is its premise, its unacknowledged danger. Even Hamlet's attempt to imagine a protective father in the soliloquy returns him to this danger:

> So excellent a king, that was to this
> Hyperion to a satyr, so loving to my mother
> That he might not beteem the winds of heaven
> Visit her face too roughly. Heaven and earth,
> Must I remember? Why, she would hang on him
> As if increase of appetite had grown
> By what it fed on; and yet within a month –
> Let me not think on't ...
>
> [1.2.139–46]

This image of parental love is so satisfying to Hamlet in part because it seems to enfold his mother safely within his father's protective embrace: by protecting her against the winds of heaven, he simultaneously protects against her, limiting and controlling her dangerous appetite. But as soon as that appetite has been invoked, it destabilizes the image of paternal control, returning Hamlet to the fact of his father's loss: for Gertrude's appetite is always inherently frightening, always potentially out of control; as the image of the unweeded garden itself implied, it has always required a weeder to manage its over-luxuriant growth. The existence of Gertrude's appetite itself threatens the image of the father's godlike control; and in his absence, Gertrude's appetite rages, revealing what had been its potential for voraciousness all along. ☐

> (Janet Adelman, *Suffocating Mothers: Fantasies of Maternal Origin in Shakespeare's Plays*, 1992) [37]

In a critical move in which Adelman seems to see the text of *Hamlet* saying things that it might not mean to say, revealing the anxieties that underlie its apparent need to denigrate the maternal, she begins to understand the text itself as having an unconscious. The 'maternal' is the unconscious of Shakespeare's text.

■ This subjection of male to female is, I think, the buried fantasy of *Hamlet*, the submerged story that it partly conceals and partly reveals; in its shift of contaminating agency from Claudius to the female body as the site of origin, Hamlet's meditation seems to me to be diagnostic of this fantasy. The poisoning of Old Hamlet is ostentatiously modelled on Cain's killing of Abel; Claudius cannot allude to his offense without recalling the 'primary eldest curse upon't' (3.3.37). But this version of Cain and Abel turns out in part to be a cover for the even more primary story implicit in the unweeded garden, the prior explanation for the entrance of death into the world: the murder here turns not on the winning of a father's favor but on the body of a woman; and Old Hamlet is poisoned in his orchard-garden (1.5.35; 3.2.255) by the 'serpent' who wears his crown (1.5.39). On the surface of the text, that is, the story of Adam and Eve has been displaced, the horrific female body at its center occluded: Eve is conspicuously absent from the Cain-and-Abel version of the fall. But if the plot rewrites the Fall as a story of fratricidal rivalry, locating literal agency for the murder in Claudius, a whole network of images and associations replaces his literal agency with Gertrude's, replicating Eve in her by making her both the agent and the locus of death. Beneath the story of fratricidal rivalry is the story of the woman who conduces to death, of the father fallen not through his brother's treachery but through his subjection to this woman; and despite Gertrude's conspicuous absence from the scene in the garden, in this psychologized version of the Fall, the vulnerability of the father – and hence of the son – to her poison turns out to be the whole story.

In an astonishing transfer of agency from male to female, malevolent power and blame for the murder tend to transfer from Claudius to Gertrude in the deep fantasy of the play. We can see the beginnings of this shift of blame even in the Ghost's initial account of the murder, in which the emotional weight shifts rapidly from his excoriation of Claudius to his much more powerful condemnation of Gertrude's sexuality. And in 'The Murder of Gonzago', Hamlet's version of his father's tale, the murderer's role is clearly given less emphasis than the Queen's: Lucianus gets a scant six lines, while her protestations of undying love motivate all the preceding dialogue of the playlet. Moreover, while the actual murderer remains a pasteboard villain, the Queen's protestations locate psychic blame for the murder squarely in her. 'None wed the second but who killed the first', she tells us (3.2.175). In her reformulation, remarriage itself is a form of murder: 'A second time I kill my husband dead, / When second husband kisses me in my bed' (3.2.179–80). We know that Hamlet has added some dozen or sixteen lines to the play (2.2.535), and though we cannot specify them, these protestations seem written suspiciously from the point of view of the child, whose mother's remarriage often seems like her murder of the image of his father. When Hamlet confronts his mother in her closet immediately after his playlet, he confirms that he at least has shifted agency from Claudius to her: his own killing of Polonius is, he says, 'A bloody deed. Almost as bad, good Mother, / As kill a king and marry with his brother' (3.4.28–9). Given the parallel with his killing of Polonius, 'as kill a king' first seems to describe Claudius's act; but when the line ends with 'brother' rather than 'queen' or 'wife', the killing attaches itself irrevocably to Gertrude, playing out in miniature the shift of agency from him to her. For Claudius's crime is nearly absent here: in Hamlet's accusation, Claudius becomes the passive victim of Gertrude's sexual will; she becomes the active murderer. □

(Janet Adelman, *Suffocating Mothers: Fantasies of Maternal Origin in Shakespeare's Plays*, 1992)[38]

Adelman's feminist interventions into the apparently masculinist field of psychoanalytic readings of this play are mirrored in other recent developments that will be explored in Chapters 5 and 6. First of all, however, in Chapter 4 we will consider the early twentieth-century developments in *Hamlet* criticism, developments which, in many ways, fed off and mirrored the psychoanalytic interest in Hamlet's inner life.

CHAPTER FOUR

The Early Twentieth Century

A.C. BRADLEY

As we saw in the last chapter, the story of the psychoanalytic criticism of literature, witnessed a tendency to move away from the classic example of someone like Ernest Jones, providing a psychoanalytic account of a character and his motivations, and a move towards a psychoanalytic account of the plays themselves. A similar story has occurred in what might be called the mainstream of literary criticism in the twentieth century. A.C. Bradley was writing at the very beginning of 'English Literature' as a University discipline, and yet he discusses the plays in a way that is the culmination of previous traditions of literary criticism. He amalgamates the neoclassicist concern with unified narrative and the Romantic concern with character. As the twentieth century moved on, this kind of 'character criticism', which in many ways echoes early psychoanalytic criticism's focus on internal character, was increasingly seen as fallacious and misleading. At the time, however, Bradley was highly influential and he continues to be reprinted and read with interest. Even though the adjective 'Bradleyan' came to represent all that was wrong with earlier modes of literary criticism, it would be a misrepresentation to describe Bradleyan criticism as nothing more than 'character criticism'.[1] His concern for the unity, or at least the 'appropriateness' of the plot is almost neoclassical. This joint concern for both character and action led him to the famous formulation, 'The centre of the tragedy, therefore, may be said with equal truth to lie in action issuing from character, or in character issuing in action.'[2] For Bradley, then, Shakespearean tragedy focuses on the story of the central individual, and this story, in turn, defines their character, a character expressed in the actions that are specific to them.

■ What we do feel strongly, as a tragedy advances to its close, is that the calamities and catastrophe follow inevitably from the deeds of men, and that the main source of these deeds is character. The dictum that, with Shakespeare, 'character is destiny' is no doubt an exaggeration, and one that may mislead (for many of his tragic personages, if they had not met with peculiar circumstances, would have escaped a tragic end, and might even have lived fairly untroubled lives); but it is the exaggeration of a vital truth.[3] ☐

Bradley, often conceived of as nothing more than a naïve follower of a post-Romantic view of drama as all about character, is in fact attempting something quite challenging in his accounts of Shakespearean tragedy, even if we eventually disagree with his premises. He adapts Aristotelian notions of the tragic to a drama that seems, to him, to foreground character over action. He retains, from Aristotle, the idea that the tragic experience of life is based on irreconcilable conflict. He locates this conflict, neither purely in the action as Aristotle and neoclassical critics might have, nor in a conflict between the world and a poorly adapted character as the Romantic and Freudian critics might, but rather as an 'inward struggle'.

■ ... the notion of tragedy as a conflict emphasizes the fact that action is the centre of the story, while the concentration of interest, in the greater plays, on the inward struggle emphasizes the fact that this action is essentially the expression of character.[4] ☐

In *Shakespearean Tragedy*, Bradley argues, then, that the innovation Shakespeare brings to the genre of tragedy is that the central character or characters are not, necessarily, caught up in a fate which is beyond their control, but rather in something which emerges from their specific character. His concern for unity is Aristotelian in its demands, but his location of this in 'character' is post-Romantic. What this starting point produces in Bradley's analyses of texts is a tendency to view them almost as nineteenth-century realist novels, and his approach has often been seen as anachronistic, ignorant of the way in which the early modern stage might have worked. He, himself, preferred not to theorise his approach, depending instead on its apparent 'common-sense'. He said that he relied on, ' ... that habit of reading with an eager mind, which may make many an unscholarly lover of Shakespeare a far better critic than many a Shakespeare scholar'.[5] For this reason, he has often been seen as blind to his own faults, and to the possibility that his approach to Shakespearean drama is rather limiting. Its concern with an 'inner conflict' seems to ignore, for example, the possibility that social or political confrontations might be the source of tragic action. Having said that, this approach does result in very careful readings of the plays which follow the narrative thoroughly. It is, perhaps, this aspect of his work that guarantees his enduring popularity with undergraduate students. Bradley's approach is also of interest as the culmination of a long tradition of humanist criticism which was to become increasingly questioned as the twentieth century went on.

Bradley's analysis of the character and action of *Hamlet* leads him, necessarily, to the conflict between the demands put on Hamlet as the agent in a Revenge tragedy, and his apparent unwillingness to fulfil that role. He engages directly with the tradition that has already concerned itself with this question, and aims to contradict Coleridge's characterisation of Hamlet as a man unable to act through excessive thought, thus placing himself both within and outside Romantic criticism of the play. Bradley disagrees with Coleridge, and sees this inaction only as a feature of Hamlet's character issuing out of the peculiar circumstances of the action of *this* play. Without these circumstances, Hamlet would not have presented himself in such a disengaged light.

■ Hamlet's irresolution, or his aversion to real action, is, according to the theory, the *direct* result of 'an almost enormous intellectual activity' in the way of 'a calculating consideration which attempts to exhaust all the relations and possible consequences of a deed'. And this again proceeds from an original one-sidedness of nature, strengthened by habit, and, perhaps, by years of speculative inaction. The theory describes, therefore, a man in certain aspects like Coleridge himself, on one side a man of genius, on the other side, the side of will, deplorably weak, always procrastinating and avoiding unpleasant duties, and often reproaching himself in vain; a man, observe, who at *any* time and in *any* circumstances would be unequal to the task assigned to Hamlet. And thus, I must maintain, it degrades Hamlet and travesties the play. For Hamlet, according to all the indications in the text, was not naturally or normally such a man, but rather, I venture to affirm, a man who at any *other* time and in any *other* circumstances than those presented would have been perfectly equal to his task; and it is, in fact, the very cruelty of his fate that the crisis of his life comes on him at the one moment when he cannot meet it, and when his highest gifts, instead of helping him, conspire to paralyse him. This aspect of the tragedy the theory quite misses; and it does so because it misconceives the cause of that irresolution which, on the whole, it truly describes. For the cause was not directly or mainly an habitual excess of reflectiveness. The direct cause was a state of mind quite abnormal and induced by special circumstances – a state of profound melancholy. □

(A.C. Bradley, *Shakespearean Tragedy*, 1904)[6]

The narrative of the play, in this version, contrives to produce a character who is unequal to the demands laid on him during the course of the remains of the plot, rather than a character who would *always* be unequal to any task. Bradley has, then, to prove Hamlet's abilities as 'action man'. In this, he is not unlike early psychoanalytic criticism in identifying family trauma rather than a general disposition as the cause of Hamlet's supposed character failings.

■ ... it is downright impossible that the man we see rushing after the Ghost, killing Polonius, dealing with the King's commission on the ship, boarding the pirate, leaping into the grave, executing his final vengeance, could *ever* have been shrinking or slow in an emergency. Imagine Coleridge doing any of these things![7] □

As Bradley goes on to outline the particular circumstances that have unnerved this ordinarily well-balanced young man, it comes, perhaps, as no shock to discover that it is his mother who has to shoulder the burden of his trauma, or rather the 'sudden ghastly disclosure of his mother's true nature'. Again, in this, Bradley seems to be mirroring developments in psychoanalytic readings of the play, but without the sophisticated theories of developmental psychology that locate that disclosure within the fantasies of the child. For all Bradley's attempts to locate tragic conflict within Hamlet's interior life, without a working model for the human psyche his analysis of the play sometimes reads too much as though Shakespeare really has depicted a monstrous mother in Gertrude.

■ Now this is what actually happens in the play. Turn to the first words Hamlet utters when he is alone; turn, that is to say, to the place where the author is likely to indicate his meaning most plainly. What do you hear?

O that this too too sullied flesh would melt,
Thaw and resolve itself into a dew,
                    Or that the Everlasting had not fix'd
His canon 'gainst self-slaughter. O God! God!
How weary, stale, flat and unprofitable
Seem to me all the uses of this world!
Fie on't! ah fie! 'tis an unweeded garden,
That grows to seed; things rank and gross in nature
Possess it merely.

[1.2.129–37]

Here are a sickness of life, and even a longing for death, so intense that nothing stands between Hamlet and suicide except religious awe. And what has caused them? The rest of the soliloquy so thrusts the answer upon us that it might seem impossible to miss it. It was not his father's death; that doubtless brought deep grief, but mere grief for someone loved and lost does not make a noble spirit loathe the world as a place full only of things rank and gross. It was not the vague suspicion that we know Hamlet felt. Still less was it the loss of the crown; for though the subserviency of the electors might well disgust him, there is not a reference to the subject in the soliloquy, nor any sign elsewhere that it greatly occupied his mind. It was the moral shock of the sudden ghastly disclosure of his mother's true nature, falling on him when his heart was aching with love, and his body doubtless was weakened by sorrow. And it is essential, however disagreeable, to realize the nature of this shock. It matters little here whether Hamlet's age was twenty or thirty: in either case his mother was a matron of mature years. All his life he had believed in her, we may be sure, as such a son would. He had seen her not merely devoted to his father, but hanging on him like a newly wedded bride, hanging on him,

> As if increase of appetite had grown
> By what it fed on
>   [1.2.144–5]

He had seen her following his body 'like Niobe, all tears'. And then within a month – 'O God! a beast [...] would have mourned longer' [1.2.150–1] – she married again, and married Hamlet's uncle, a man utterly contemptible and loathsome in his eyes; married him in what to Hamlet was incestuous wedlock; married not for any reason of state, nor even out of old family affection, but in such a way that her son was forced to see in her action not only an astounding shallowness of feeling but an eruption of coarse sensuality, 'rank and gross', speeding post-haste to its horrible delight. Is it possible to conceive an experience more desolating to a man such as we have seen Hamlet to be; and is its result anything but perfectly natural? It brings bewildered horror, then loathing, then despair of human nature. His whole mind is poisoned. He can never see Ophelia in the same light again; she is a woman, and his mother is a woman; if she mentions the word 'brief' to him, the answer drops from his lips like venom, 'as woman's love'. The last words of the soliloquy, which is *wholly* concerned with this subject, are,

> But break, my heart, for I must hold my tongue.
>   [1.2.159]

He can do nothing. He must lock in his heart, not any suspicion of his uncle that moves obscurely there, but that horror and loathing; and if his heart ever found relief, it was when those feelings, mingled with the love that never died out in him, poured themselves forth in a flood as he stood in his mother's chamber beside his father's marriage-bed. □

(A.C. Bradley, *Shakespearean Tragedy*, 1904)[8]

These are the events, then, that Bradley sees as formative of Hamlet's 'character' within the action of the play. The tragic action of the play, from this point on, is, for Bradley, informed by the effect of these revelations on Hamlet. For all his disavowal of a Coleridgean view of the play and of Hamlet himself, the resulting analysis is very reminiscent of Romantic versions of the play.

■ If we still wonder, and ask why the effect of this shock should be so tremendous, let us observe that *now* the conditions have arisen under which Hamlet's highest endowments, his moral sensibility and his genius, become his enemies. A nature morally blunter would have felt even so dreadful a revelation less keenly. A slower and more limited and positive mind might not have extended so widely through its world the disgust and disbelief that have entered it. But Hamlet has the imagination which for evil as well as good, feels and sees all things in one. Thought is the element of his life, and his thought is infected. He cannot prevent himself from probing and lacerating the wound in his soul. One idea, full of peril, holds him fast, and he cries out in agony at it, but is impotent to free himself ('Must I remember?' 'Let me not think on't'). And when, with the fading of his passion, the vividness of this idea abates, it does so only to leave behind a boundless weariness and a sick longing for death.

And this is the time which his fate chooses. In this hour of uttermost weakness, this sinking of his whole being towards annihilation, there comes on him, bursting the bounds of the natural world with a shock of astonishment and terror, the revelation of his mother's adultery and his father's murder, and, with this, the demand on him, in the name of everything dearest and most sacred, to arise and act. And for a moment, though his brain reels and totters, his soul leaps up in passion to answer his demand. But it comes too late. It does but strike home the last rivet in the melancholy which holds him bound.

The time is out of joint. O cursed spite,
That ever I was born to set it right.
[1.5.196–7]

So he mutters within an hour of the moment when he vowed to give his life to the duty of revenge; and the rest of the story exhibits his vain efforts to fulfil this duty, his unconscious self-excuses and unavailing self-reproaches, and the tragic results of his delay. □
(A.C. Bradley, *Shakespearean Tragedy*, 1904)[9]

Bradley sees, then, the action of the play as forged within the first act when Hamlet realises both his duty of revenge and what he (and Bradley?) sees as the truth about his mother. From that moment on the tragic action of the play 'issues' from his character, just as his character has been forged by this potentially tragic situation.

T.S. ELIOT

For Bradley, then, the age-old question of Hamlet's apparent delay comes to be the perfect peg on which to hang his theory of 'character-in-action', 'action-in-character'. His delay constitutes both his character, and the source of the tragedy within the action of the play. For the modernist poet, T.S. Eliot, another important figure at the birth of English literature as a serious academic discipline, the disjunctions in the play reveal it as a flawed piece of art where other critics had sought to resolve these apparent contradictions as part of their excavation of Hamlet's character. It is in his essay on *Hamlet* (1919), here taken from his collection of essays, *The Sacred Wood* (1920), that Eliot develops his famous concept of the 'objective correlative'. In some ways, Eliot is reacting against Bradleyan criticism, although he is still writing within humanist terms. Bradley, as L.C. Knights (1906–97) point out in his famous essay, 'How Many Children Had Lady Macbeth?', relies quite heavily on the assumption of things which are not strictly available in the text of the play itself. Eliot is not so much concerned with the unity of the character of Hamlet, as the unity of the play as it might be sustained by the interaction of the characters. In this, he too seems to hark back to Aristotle but, like Bradley, he is not quite able to shake off Romanticism and its focus on character.

He begins, though, with the idea that this play is not fully formed and that even its language is inconsistent. This, for Eliot, denies the play its by now customary position as Shakespeare's true 'masterpiece'.

■ So far from being Shakespeare's masterpiece, the play is most certainly an artistic failure. In several ways, the play is puzzling, and disquieting as is none of the others. Of all the plays it is the longest and is possibly the one on which Shakespeare spent most pains; and yet he has left in it superfluous and inconsistent scenes which even hasty revision should have noticed. The versification is variable. Lines like

> Look, the morn, in russet mantle clad,
> Walks o'er the dew of yon high eastern hill,

are of the Shakespeare of *Romeo and Juliet*. The lines in Act 5, sc. 2.,

> Sir, in my heart there was a kind of fighting
> That would not let me sleep ...
> Up from my cabin,
> My sea-gown scarf'd about me, in the dark
> Grop'd I to find out them: had my desire;
> Finger'd their packet;

are of his quite mature. Both workmanship and thought are in an unstable condition. We are surely justified in attributing the play, with that other profoundly interesting play of 'intractable' material and astonishing versification, *Measure for Measure*, to a period of crisis, after which follow the tragic successes which culminate in *Coriolanus*. *Coriolanus* may not be as 'interesting' as *Hamlet*, but it is, with *Antony and Cleopatra*, Shakespeare's most assured artistic success. And probably more people have thought *Hamlet* a work of art because they found it interesting, than have found it interesting because it is a work of art. It is the 'Mona Lisa' of literature. ☐ (T.S. Eliot, 'Hamlet and His Problems', 1919)[10]

Jacqueline Rose famously took Eliot up on this statement, that *Hamlet* is the 'Mona Lisa' of literature, to reveal the anti-feminist bias in Eliot's aesthetics, and extracts from that essay are printed in Chapter 6 of this Guide. Her chief concern is the burden that Gertrude is expected to bear in this account of the play's artistic weakness. It is, indeed, Gertrude who fails to be *Hamlet*'s 'objective correlative', as the extract below explains. If, for Bradley, Gertrude is the root of Hamlet's problems, for Eliot, she is the root of *Hamlet*'s problems.

■ The only way of expressing emotion in the form of art is by finding an 'objective correlative'; in other words, a set of objects, a situation, a chain of events which shall be the formula of that *particular* emotion; such that when the external facts, which must terminate in sensory experience, are given, the emotion is immediately evoked. If you examine any of Shakespeare's more successful tragedies, you will find this exact equivalence; you will find that the state of mind of Lady Macbeth walking in her sleep has been communicated to you by a skilful accumulation of imagined sensory impressions; the words of Macbeth on hearing of his wife's death strike us as if, given the sequence of events, these words were automatically released by the last event in the series. The artistic 'inevitability' lies in this complete adequacy of the external to the emotion; and this is precisely what is deficient in *Hamlet*. Hamlet (the man) is dominated by an emotion which is inexpressible, because it is in *excess* of the facts as they appear. And the supposed identity of Hamlet with his author is genuine to this point: that Hamlet's bafflement at the absence of objective equivalent to his feelings is a prolongation of the bafflement of his creator in the face of his artistic problem. Hamlet is up against the difficulty that his disgust is occasioned by his mother, but that his mother is not an adequate equivalent for it; his disgust envelops and exceeds her. It is thus a feeling which he cannot understand; he cannot objectify it, and it therefore remains to poison life and obstruct action. None of the possible actions can satisfy it; and nothing that Shakespeare can do with the plot can express Hamlet for him. And it must be noticed that the very nature of the *données* [the given facts] of the problem precludes objective equivalence. To have heightened the criminality of Gertrude would have been to provide the formula for a totally different emotion in Hamlet; it is just *because* her character is so negative and insignificant that she arouses in Hamlet the feeling which she is incapable of representing.

The 'madness' of Hamlet lay to Shakespeare's hand; in the earlier play [Eliot refers to the idea that *Hamlet* is an adaptation of an earlier play by either Shakespeare or Thomas Kyd (1558–94) that is now lost] a simple ruse, and to the end, we may presume, understood as a ruse by the audience. For Shakespeare it is less than madness and more than feigned. The levity of Hamlet, his repetition of phrase, his puns, are not part of a deliberate plan of dissimulation, but a form of emotional relief. In the character Hamlet it is the buffoonery of an emotion which he cannot express in art. The intense feeling, ecstatic or terrible, without an object or exceeding its object, is something every person of sensibility has known; it is doubtless a study to pathologists. It often occurs in adolescence: the ordinary person puts these feelings to sleep, or trims down his feelings to fit the business world; the artist keeps it alive by his ability to intensify the world to his emotions. The Hamlet of Laforgue is an adolescent; the Hamlet of Shakespeare is not, he has not that explanation and excuse.[11] We must simply admit that here Shakespeare tackled a problem which proved too much for him. Why he attempted it at all is an insoluble puzzle; under what compulsion of experience he attempted to express the inexpressibly horrible, we cannot ever know. We need a great many facts in his biography; and we should like to know whether, and when, and after or at the same time as what personal experience, he read Montaigne, 2. xii., *Apologie de Raimond Sebond*.[12] We should have, finally, to know something which is by hypothesis unknowable, for we assume it to be an experience which, in the manner indicated, exceeded the facts. We should have to understand things which Shakespeare did not understand himself. □

(T.S. Eliot, 'Hamlet and His Problems', 1919)[13]

To an extent, Eliot seems to be repeating certain assumptions about Shakespeare that were popular amongst the neoclassicists of the late seventeenth century – that he was adept at representing something like 'life' but not so good, at least in this play, of converting that into a successful and balanced work of art. Where I think that Eliot is most interesting is in the revelation that the character of Gertrude is too flimsy a base on which to define Hamlet's character. Eliot is accusing Shakespeare of doing this, but it could equally be a criticism levelled at the literary critics themselves – particularly Bradley and Ernest Jones, but perhaps also, Eliot himself. Later twentieth-century critics will respond to this in a different way, seeing the problems that Hamlet has with the women in his life, not as symptoms of his psyche, his dramatic character or the play's failed aesthetics, but in relation to wider social problems with gender.

J. DOVER WILSON

The most sustained investigation of *Hamlet* undertaken in the first half of the twentieth century, indeed of the twentieth century as a whole, was that of John Dover Wilson (1881–1969). From 1917 onwards until 1935 he produced a number of articles culminating in the book, *What Happens in Hamlet* (1935). Dover Wilson was also a member of the school of new textual critics in the early part of the twentieth century who sought to put the editing of early modern texts on a more scientific footing. They eschewed subjective opinion about the efficacy of textual variants in making their selection, preferring to depend on historical knowledge of early modern printing procedures to arrive at the text. The aim, though, as it still remains today to some extent, was to produce a text that some-how represented the best intentions of the author, Shakespeare himself. We might now see this aim as being at odds with the supposed methods. We are more likely, perhaps, to view the textual variants that are avail-able to us as the product of the collective nature of early modern theatre production, rather than as a disastrous degradation of the author's origi-nal intention. Dover Wilson's edition of *Hamlet* came out in 1934 and the book, he claims, details the work of explanation that was necessary to him in producing the edition. In *What Happens in Hamlet*, he sets out to recover 'Shakespeare's purposes' guided by a belief that these can be recovered if sufficient attention is paid to the play's original contexts. He outlines some of the processes he embarked on with this end in mind in a charming introduction to the book which takes the form of an 'epistle dedicatory' to W.W. Greg, a fellow literary critic. He explains that he was spurred on to his efforts in investigating the play by his initial objection to Greg's theory that Shakespeare can never have intended us to believe that the ghost was in any way 'real', and that we are therefore to under-stand it as the figment of Hamlet's imagination. This judgement Dover Wilson rightfully sees as anachronistic.

■ The difficulties I shall be mainly concerned with are dramatic problems, which have arisen through forgetfulness of Shakespeare's purposes; for-getfulness due to textual corruption, to our ignorance of Elizabethan stage-effects, to the break in the theatrical tradition at the Puritan Revolution [A loaded term for the Civil Wars (1642–9) that assumes that Religious Puritanism was its major impetus], and above all to the change in social customs and in the ordinary man's assumptions about the universe and politics which three centuries have brought with them. In brief, I shall try to show that parts of the plot have fallen into disuse through 'bestial obliv-ion'. Fortunately, there is nothing, I think, lost beyond recovery, nothing that care cannot restore to its pristine beauty and its original function.

[...] *Hamlet* and the audience for which it was written belong to the beginning of the seventeenth century, and to a given moment of its author's development: and these considerations must be allowed due weight. □
(J. Dover Wilson, *What Happens in Hamlet*, 1935)[14]

Despite his obvious sensitivity to the historical context of the play, Dover Wilson objects to what he calls 'members of the historical school' who are too keen to relegate the play to a state of being beyond recovery, 'fond of referring to the Elizabethans as barbarous and to their drama as crude'.[15] He refuses to believe that the text of *Hamlet* as we have it cannot ultimately be explained as an artistic unity given enough patience and research. His belief in Shakespeare's achievement in *Hamlet* also leads him to disagree with T.S. Eliot's judgement of the play as an artistic failure. He explains that Eliot's feeling that Hamlet's emotions are in excess of the facts can be put aside when it is realised to what extent incest is a matter of both political and emotional horror in the period during which *Hamlet* was written and performed.

■ This incest-business is so important that is scarcely possible to make too much of it. Shakespeare places it in the very forefront of the play, he devotes a whole soliloquy to it, he shows us Hamlet's mind filled with the fumes of its poison, writhing in anguish, longing for death as an escape.[16] □

The prominence that Dover Wilson affords the play's concern with incest is not, however, necessarily part of a psychological explanation. Indeed, he specifically attempts to show that a psychological explanation for a fictional character is totally anachronistic and inappropriate. Rather, the idea of incest is given weight by considering its contemporary political and social importance and it is this importance which explains Hamlet's reaction.

■ His mother is a criminal, has been guilty of a sin which blots out the stars for him, makes life a bestial thing, and even infects his very blood. She has committed incest. Modern readers, living in an age when marriage laws are the subject of free discussion and with a deceased wife's sister act upon the statute book [An Act of Parliament, for Dover Wilson recently passed, that allowed, for the first time, a man to marry the sister of his dead wife], can hardly be expected to enter fully into Hamlet's feelings on this matter.[17] □

Dover Wilson further explains the historical contexts of incest, as treated in *Hamlet,* in his discussion of the way in which the revenge task is set out for Hamlet by his father.

■ At their private conference together the Ghost speaks some eighty lines to Hamlet, and of these a dozen at most are concerned with the commission he has come to give his son:

If thou didst ever thy dear father love,
[...]
Revenge his foul and most unnatural murder.
>   [1.5.23–5]

that is the gist of it. Revenge, but how? On this point the Ghost gives no help at all:

But howsomever thou pursuest this act,
>   [1.5.84]

is all he says. Yet, at the same time, he attaches certain conditions, which so far from simplifying the problem, make it more complicated:

If thou hast nature in thee, bear it not,
Let not the royal bed of Denmark be
A couch for luxury and damned incest.
But howsomever thou pursuest this act,
Taint not thy mind nor let thy soul contrive
Against thy mother aught. Leave her to heaven,
And to those thorns that in her bosom lodge
To prick and sting her.
>   [1.5.81–8]

First there is to be an end to 'luxury and damned incest'. That royal couch! The thought of it ... had begun to 'taint' Hamlet's mind before he sees the Ghost, and that it continues to do so to the end of the play is partly due to the fact that he might at any moment stop the 'luxury' by a single thrust with his right arm. Thus the second injunction comes too late. Hamlet's mind is already tainted; and that in turn is partly the reason why he cannot act. 'Taint not thy mind' is an ominous command.

The third condition presents practical difficulties, which would I think be obvious to Elizabethan courtiers and statesmen, who thought in dynastic terms, though easily overlooked by moderns living in a different political atmosphere. Hamlet was to avenge his father without in any way injuring the woman who shared the murderer's crown and his incestuous bed. The salvation of his Queen by the rescuing of her from the seductions of her paramour is as strong a motive with the Ghost as the vengeance itself, which is after all the only means of rehabilitating the family honour. This loyalty to Gertrude, revealed, we shall find, in the bedroom scene as a loving tenderness which blinds him to the real weakness of her character, is a touching trait in the spirit of King Hamlet; but it does not make his son's task any easier. How can he, Gertrude's son, kill Claudius without contriving against her? □ (J. Dover Wilson, *What Happens in Hamlet*, 1935)[18]

Dover Wilson argues that Hamlet's task is nearly impossible given this demand that the family name is not to be smeared in the process. It is this near-impossibility that is seen to be behind Hamlet's prevarications, his 'antic disposition', feigned or otherwise, as well as his attempts to bring things to a head in the Mousetrap scene, which Dover Wilson regards as central to the whole play. In the process, he rejects the Romantic view of Hamlet as predisposed to inaction and madness.

■ At the end of the first act, the back upon which the tragic load rests begins to show signs of breaking. Not because, in Goethe's words, 'a beautiful, pure, noble and most moral nature, without the strength of nerve which makes a hero, sinks beneath a burden which it can neither bear nor throw off'. Nor yet because, as Coleridge diagnosed, he is endowed with 'a great, an almost enormous, intellectual activity, and a proportionate aversion to real action consequent upon it'. But simply because of the sheer weight of the load. So great is Hamlet's moral stature, so tough is his nerve, that the back does *not* break. But he is crippled, and the arm which should perform the Ghosts' command is paralysed. Thus he continues to support the burden, but is unable to discharge it. That, in a sentence, is 'the tragical history of Hamlet, the prince of Denmark'.[19] □

Dover Wilson seeks to answer a series of riddles that he sees as being presented by the reception in the twentieth century of a older text: why does the Ghost place certain conditions on the execution of revenge? Why do the various characters react to the Ghost in different ways? Why does Hamlet talk to Ophelia and Polonius in the ways that he does? These are, for him, dramatic questions that have historical answers. That is, he seeks to explain how a contemporary audience might have reacted to a performance of Hamlet, given what we know about their systems of belief, their superstitions, their more general immersion in the world of the 'supernatural' and their supposed political values, including a conservative conviction of the justice of a divine monarchy . Thus he is less interested in clearing up the finer points of the Danish constitution in his explanation of the political contexts of the play, than in a more general reaction to the notion of usurpation on the part of a London audience. This is not done in a piecemeal way, however, but in the service of establishing that the play, when 'recovered' in this way, would have been a total achievement. We might, these days, be less concerned with establishing the aesthetic integrity of an early modern piece of drama, and certainly less optimistic about resurrecting the lost intentions of an author through guesswork about how a contemporary audience might, or might not, be expected to react to any given theatrical event. However, I do not think that Dover Wilson's attempts should be dismissed because of what we now see as a spurious attempt to recover an artistic unity that can never really have been there, given the collaborative nature of early modern drama productions. They must, rather, be seen in context, as well as being a contribution to a tradition of Hamlet criticism that we have been exploring. He is responding to, and rejecting, two kinds of anachronism, as he views it – both the lazy anachronisms of traditional literary criticism which too often assumes that, as Shakespeare appears to write as a man 'for all time', his beliefs can be separated from those of his audiences, and the more difficult anachronisms of a psychological approach which Dover Wilson sees as forgetting not only the historical context of Shakespeare's writings but also their status as fiction.

What is interesting about Dover Wilson's approach is that, when it comes to what he calls the 'heart of the mystery' of the play – Hamlet himself – he finds almost nothing there. For all his exuberant confidence in the possibility of restoring a 'pristine' seventeenth-century Hamlet to us, in the centre of the play there remains for him the essential experience of theatre as illusion. This, despite an attempt to align Shakespeare's Hamlet with a very real historical figure, the Earl of Essex (1566–1601).

■ I believe, as many other have believed, that this conception first came to Shakespeare from the career and personality of his patron's [Henry Wriothesley, Earl of Southampton (1573–1624)] hero, the brilliant, melancholy and ill-fated Earl of Essex, who met his death upon the scaffold some six to twelve months before *Hamlet*, as we now have it, appeared upon the stage. Apart from the question of its probability [...] the theory has the merit of explaining why Shakespeare set out to surround his Prince with an atmosphere of mystery. The character of Essex was also a mystery, the most baffling and widely discussed of the age, and if audiences at the beginning of the seventeenth century saw the features of the Earl in those of Shakespeare's Hamlet, so far from worrying about the mystery as modern critics do, they would expect it and accept it as a matter of course. But, while the theory explains the historical origin of Hamlet's mystery, it does nothing to reveal its true nature. If Shakespeare made Hamlet mysterious partly in order to increase his likeness to Essex, he secured the effect not by psychological analysis but through dramatic illusion. Even if the historians could recapture for us the very soul of Essex and hand it over for examination to psychologists endowed with finer instruments than have yet been or are ever likely to be fashioned, the diagnosis would not help us a whit with Hamlet. For Hamlet is not Essex; he is not even Essex as reflected in the mind of Shakespeare; he is that reflection, sufficiently life-like to be recognisable by Shakespeare's contemporaries, but moulded, adapted and remade for the purposes of dramatic art.

In fine, we were never intended to reach the heart of the mystery. That it has a heart is an illusion; the mystery itself is an illusion; Hamlet is an illusion. The secret that lies behind it all is not Hamlet's, but Shakespeare's: the technical devices he employed to create this supreme illusion of a great and mysterious character, who is at once mad and the sanest of geniuses, at once a procrastinator and a vigorous man of action, at once a miserable failure and the most adorable of heroes. The character of Hamlet, like the appearance of his successive impersonators on the stage, is a matter of 'make-up'. □

(J. Dover Wilson, *What Happens in Hamlet*, 1935)[20]

To a large extent, Dover Wilson seems trapped within an almost neoclassical demand for unity in his attempt to fend off those whom he sees as attacking the artistic integrity of the play. However, the continuing strength of his criticism does not really lie here, but rather in the compellingly paradoxical nature of the work that he undertakes. Dover Wilson seeks unflinchingly to situate the play in its historical context, but refuses to admit that the past is lost to us; he reveals the motivations of Hamlet as a contemporary might have seen them, but continues to insist on their inevitable inaccessibility. What is invigorating about this approach is its commitment to facing up to problems that we have in reading early texts, realising that it is the business of literary criticism to attempt to provide solutions for the difficulties of anachronism, at the same time as admitting that its answers may not, in fact, be the right ones.

G. WILSON KNIGHT

To some extent, both Bradley and Eliot remain caught within the development of literary criticism that saw Romanticism reacting against and seeking to replace neoclassical assumptions about how drama works. Bradley tried to reconcile these two strands in his ideas of 'character in action' and 'action from character' whilst Eliot's discussion of the play's artistic failure, as he judged it, saw the action of the play as inadequate to the delineation of Hamlet's character. Dover Wilson, whilst objecting quite strongly to what he saw as anachronisms in the Romantic interpretation of the play and the character, nevertheless sought to produce a coherent inner life for the hero, albeit to be discovered in the hitherto uncharted waters of historical context and the expectations of a contemporary audience. G. Wilson Knight (1897–1985), writing during the early 1930s, and then revisiting his discussion of *Hamlet* after the

Second World War, sought a different route away from the paradigms of traditional criticism. He initially explains this, in *The Wheel of Fire* (1930), as a move away from a strictly linear and temporal appreciation of the plays, which should be supplemented by what he calls a 'spatial' understanding of the play's dynamics.

■ But to receive the whole Shakespearian vision into the intellectual consciousness demands a certain and very definite act of mind. One must be prepared to see the whole play in space as well as in time. It is natural in analysis to pursue the steps of the tale in sequence, noticing the logic that connects them, regarding those essentials that Aristotle noted: the beginning, middle and end. But by giving supreme attention to this temporal nature of drama we omit what, in Shakespeare, is at least of equivalent importance. A Shakespearian tragedy is set spatially as well as temporally in the mind. By this I mean that there are throughout the play a set of correspondences which relate to each other independently of the time sequence which is the story; such are the intuition–intelligence opposition in *Troilus and Cressida*, the death-theme in *Hamlet*, the nightmare evil of *Macbeth*. This I have sometimes called the play's 'atmosphere'.[21] □

Knight's approach to Shakespeare, then, involves identifying a set of correspondences within the poetry of the play that moves beyond a simple understanding of its linear progression. If this approach is taken very reductively, it could indeed reveal nothing more banal than an inventory of the play's 'themes'; it is clear, for example, that *Hamlet must* in some way be about 'death'. However, Knight traces these correspondences or 'themes' throughout the language of the play in a way that deepens his readers' insights into the particular concerns of any given drama. In order to break away from the traditional assertions of *Hamlet* criticism, though, Knight deliberately has to distance himself from past judgements on the play. He does this by refusing to 'sentimentalise' Hamlet. Knight's version of Hamlet is cruel and immoral instead.

■ We have done ill to sentimentalise his [Hamlet's] personality. We have paid for it – by failing to understand him; and, failing to understand, we have been unable to sympathise with the demon of cynicism, and its logical result of callous cruelty, that has Hamlet's soul in its remorseless grip. Sentiment is an easy road to an unprofitable and unreal sympathy. Hamlet is cruel. He murders Polonius in error:

Thou wretched, rash, intruding fool, farewell.
I took thee for thy better: take thy fortune:
Thou find'st to be too busy is some danger.
[3.4.31–3]

He proceeds from this to the vile abuse of his own mother:

Hamlet: Nay, but to live
In the rank sweat of an enseamed bed,
Stew'd in corruption, honeying and making love
Over the nasty sty!
Queen: O, speak to me no more;
These words like daggers enter in mine ears;
No more, sweet Hamlet.
[3.4.91–6]

At the end of his scene with his mother there is one beautiful moment when Hamlet gains possession of his soul:

For this same lord
I do repent; but heaven hath pleas'd it so,
To punish me with this, and this with me.
[3.4.174–6]

And his filial love wells up in:

So, again, good-night.
I must be cruel only to be kind.
Thus bad begins, and worse remains behind.
[3.4.179–81]

But it is short-lived. Next comes a speech of the most withering, brutal and unnecessary sarcasm:

Let the bloat king tempt you again to bed,
Pinch wanton on your cheeks, call you his mouse ...
[3.4.184–5]

Even more horrible are his disgusting words about Polonius, whom he has unjustly killed, to the King:

King: Now, Hamlet, where's Polonius?
Hamlet: At supper.
King: At supper? where?
Hamlet: Not where he eats, but where a is eaten. A certain convocation of politic worms are e'en at him. Your worm is your only emperor for diet: we fat all creatures else to fat us, and we fat ourselves for maggots. Your fat king and your lean beggar is but variable service – two dishes, but to one table. That's the end.

King: Alas, alas!

Hamlet: A man may fish with the worm that hath eat of a king, and eat of the fish that hath fed of that worm.

King: What dost thou mean by this?

Hamlet: Nothing but to show you how a king may go a progress through the guts of a beggar.

King: Where is Polonius?

Hamlet: In heaven. Send thither to see. If your messenger find him not there, seek him i'the other place yourself. But indeed if you find him not within this month, you shall nose him as you go up the stairs into the lobby.

[4.3.16–37]

A long and unpleasant quotation, I know. But it is necessary. The horror of humanity doomed to death and decay has disintegrated Hamlet's mind. From the first scene to the last the shadow of death broods over this play. In the exquisite prose threnody [A song of lamentation on the occasion of someone's death] [...] of the Graveyard scene the thought of physical death is again given utterance. There its pathos, its inevitability, its moral, are emphasized; but also its hideousness. Death is indeed the theme of this play, for Hamlet's disease is mental and spiritual death. So Hamlet, in his most famous soliloquy, concentrates on the terrors of an afterlife. The uninspired devitalised intellect of a Hamlet thinks pre-eminently in terms of time. To him, the body disintegrates in time; the soul persists in time too; and both are horrible. His consciousness, functioning in terms of evil and negation, sees Hell but not Heaven. But the intuitive faith, or love, or purpose, by which we must live if we are to remain sane, of these things, which are drawn from a timeless reality within the soul, Hamlet is unmercifully bereft. Therefore he dwells on the foul appearances of sex, the hideous decay of flesh, the deceit of beauty either of the spirit or of the body, the torments of eternity if eternity exist. The universe is an 'unweeded garden', or a 'prison', the canopy of the sky but a 'pestilent contagion of vapours', and man but a 'quintessence of dust', waiting for the worms of death. □ (G. Wilson Knight, *The Wheel of Fire*, 1945)[22]

It has to be said that Knight is very selective in his extracts in making up this new Hamlet, a Hamlet who is cynical, cruel and bitter. He also, it seems to me, misreads the tone of the play at this point or, rather, does not admit the possibility of another kind of atmosphere – one that is playfully cynical rather than bitter, a Hamlet who is playing with different roles rather than being trapped in the one role of avenging agent of death. Knight is, I think, right to point out the morbidity of some of Hamlet's dialogue, and, indeed of some of the play, and this insight is something that has been missing from previous interpretations of

Hamlet. However, this morbidity might more properly be interpreted either as one of Hamlet's many changing roles and, therefore, not necessarily the defining one, or as a product of late Elizabethan /Jacobean culture rather than something that is peculiar to Hamlet, the man, or *Hamlet,* the play. When Knight does move on to illustrate his main point – that in *Hamlet,* 'Death is over the whole play'[23] – he sees, though, that it is through Hamlet that the play somehow gets 'infected' by death.

■ The general thought of death, intimately related to the predominating human theme, the pain in Hamlet's mind, is thus suffused through the whole play. And yet the play, as a whole, scarcely gives us that sense of blackness and the abysms of spiritual evil which we find in *Macbeth*; nor is there the universal gloom of *King Lear.* [...] in *Macbeth* and *King Lear* the predominating imaginative atmospheres are used not to contrast with the mental universe of the hero, but to aid and support it, as it were, with similarity, to render realistic the extravagant and daring effects of volcanic passion to which the poet allows his protagonist to give voice. We are forced by the attendant personification, the verbal colour, the symbolism and events of the play as a whole, to feel the hero's suffering, to see with his eyes. But in *Hamlet* this is not so. We need not see through Hamlet's eyes. Though the idea of death is recurrent through the play, it is not implanted in the minds of other persons as is the consciousness of evil throughout *Macbeth* and the consciousness of suffering throughout *King Lear.* Except for the original murder of Hamlet's father, the *Hamlet* universe is one of healthy and robust life, good-nature, humour, romantic strength and welfare: against this background is the figure of Hamlet pale with the consciousness of death. He is the ambassador of death walking amid life. The effect is at first primarily one of separation. But it is to be noted that the consciousness of death, and consequently bitterness, cruelty, and inaction, in Hamlet not only grows in his own mind disintegrating as we watch, but also spreads its effects outward among the other persons like a blighting disease, and, as the play progresses, by its very passivity and negation of purpose, insidiously undermines the health of the state, and adds victim to victim until at the end the stage is filled with corpses. It is, as it were, a nihilistic birth in the consciousness of Hamlet that spreads its deadly venom around.[24] □

Knight then traces the effects of Hamlet's confrontation with death in his actions during the play.

■ But Hamlet is not of flesh or blood, he is a spirit of penetrating intellect and cynicism and misery without faith in himself or anyone else, murdering his love of Ophelia, on the brink on insanity, taking delight in cruelty, torturing Claudius, wringing his mother's heart, a poison in the midst of the healthy bustle of the court. He is a superman among men. And he is a superman because he has walked and held converse with death, and his consciousness works in terms of death and the negation of cynicism. He has seen the truth, not only of Denmark, but of humanity, of the universe: and the truth is evil. Thus Hamlet is an element of evil in the state of Denmark. The poison of his mental existence spreads outwards among things of flesh and blood, like acid eating into metal. They are helpless before his very inactivity and fall one after the other, like victims of an infectious disease. They are strong with the strength of health – but the demon of Hamlet's mind is stronger thing than they. Futilely they try to get him out of their country; anything to get rid of him, he is not safe. But he goes with a cynical smile, and is no sooner gone than he is back again in their midst, meditating in graveyards, at home with death. Not till it has slain all, is the demon that grips Hamlet satisfied. And last it slays Hamlet himself:

> The spirit that I have seen
> May be a devil ...

> [2.2.594–5]

It was. ☐   (G. Wilson Knight, *The Wheel of Fire*, 1945)[25]

In reality, when Knight gets down to analysing the play, he does not move so very far away from post-Romanticism in his criticism as he might wish. In fact, his Hamlet seems more Coleridgean than Coleridge: isolated from the world because of his greater insight into its truths.

■ In the universe of this play – whatever may have happened in the past – he is the only discordant element, the only hindrance to happiness, health and prosperity: a living death in the midst of life.[26] ☐

What separates Knight from other post-Romantic critics, besides his professed attempt to examine the poetry of the play, rather than its action, is the underlying Christian message of his conception of tragedy. In the following passage, in which Knight attempts to isolate the solitary Hamlet of the soliloquies from the cruel, bitterly vengeful Hamlet that he has portrayed elsewhere in the essay, Hamlet eventually emerges as a kind of Christian sage. Although, Knight never makes it explicit, the insight afforded Hamlet – that it is in death that we are most alive – is clearly Christian in origin.

■ The lesson of the play as a whole is something like this – Had Hamlet forgotten both the Ghost's commands, it would have been well, since Claudius is a good king, and the Ghost but a minor spirit; had he remembered both it would have been still better – Hamlet would probably have felt his fetters drop from his soul, he would have stepped free, then – but not till then – have been a better king than Claudius, and, finally, the unrestful spirit would know peace. But, remembering only the Ghost's command to remember, he is paralysed, he lives in death, in pity of hideous death, in loathing of the life that breeds it. His acts, like Macbeth's, are a commentary on his negative consciousness: he murders all the wrong people, exults in cruelty, grows more and more dangerous. At the end, fate steps in, forces him to perform the act of creative assassination he has been, by reason of his inner disintegration, unable to perform. Not Hamlet, but a greater principle than he or the surly Ghost, puts an end to this continual slaughter.

But we properly know Hamlet himself only when he is alone with death: then he is lovable and gentle, then he is beautiful and noble, and, there being no trivial things of life to blur our mortal vision, our minds are tuned to the exquisite music of his soul. We know the real Hamlet only in his address to the Ghost, in his, 'To be or not to be ... ' soliloquy, in the lyric prose of the Graveyard scene:

Here hung those lips that I have kissed I know not how oft ...
[5.1.182–3]

These touch a melody that holds no bitterness. Here, and when he is dying, we glimpse, perhaps, a thought wherein death, not life, holds deeper assurance for humanity. Then we will understand why Hamlet knows death to be felicity:

Absent thee from felicity awhile,
And in this harsh world draw thy breath in pain
To tell my story ...
[5.2.351–3]

The story of a 'sweet prince' (5.2.373) wrenched from life and dedicate to death alone. □ (G. Wilson Knight, *The Wheel of Fire*, 1945)[27]

By the end of this account of Hamlet, Knight has changed him from the bitter revenge hero, trawling through the detritus of life, into an almost Christ-like figure, his dedication to death transformed from morbidity to martyrdom.

L.C. KNIGHTS

L.C. Knights should, perhaps, be thought of as a critic who really does break away from some of the post-Romantic concerns of criticism in the earlier twentieth century. His famous essay, 'How Many Children had

Lady Macbeth?' is a witty denouncement of the excesses of 'character criticism' as sometimes exhibited by A.C. Bradley.[28] His name, therefore, has come to be associated with the rejection of 'Bradleyan' frames of reference in approaching Shakespeare's plays. Even Dover Wilson's more 'scientific' speculations would be dismissed as just that – speculative. However, his essay, 'An Approach to *Hamlet*' (1960) is, in some ways an exception to his usual approach, and its concerns will be familiar to anyone who has any experience of *Hamlet* criticism after Coleridge.

■ Hamlet, in his denunciations [of his mother], is never free of himself, never centres entirely on the matter in hand or the person before him.

Hamlet, in short, is fascinated by what he condemns. His emotions circle endlessly, but find no direction. And it is because of the impurity and indiscriminateness of his rejections that, brief moments of friendship and respite apart, he takes refuge in postures. There is a further point to be made here. I do not remember seeing the question asked, but why on the success of the Gonzago play, does Hamlet call for the recorders?

> Ah ha! Come, some music; come, the recorders.
> For if the King like not the comedy,
> Why then, belike he likes it not, perdie.
> Come, some music.
>
> [3.2.285–8]

True, Shakespeare knew that recorders would be needed for the scene with Rosencrantz and Guildenstern, but this can hardly affect the reason imputed to Hamlet. The answer surely can only be that Hamlet intends the players to finish off the evening with a concert which Claudius will hear, thus keeping him in suspense and leaving the initiative of action to him: it will be one more *arranged scene*, and thus in line with Hamlet's habitual tendency to make everything, even what he deeply feels, into a matter of play-acting. Again and again, intrinsic values, direct relations, are neglected whilst he tries out various roles before a real or imagined audience. He dramatizes his melancholy – for he insists on his suit of inky black even while denying its importance – just as he dramatizes his love and his very grief at Ophelia's death; his jests and asides imply an approving audience 'in the know' and ready to take the point; he is fascinated by the business of acting (and highly intelligent about it), and he falls naturally into figures of speech suggested by the theatre – 'make mouths at the invisible event', 'Who calls me villain? Breaks my pate across?' etc. Before the last scene the note of sincerity is found in few places except some of the soliloquies and the intimate exchanges with Horatio.

Now to say that Hamlet adopts histrionic, even at times melodramatic postures is to bring into view another matter of central importance – that is, the static quality of Hamlet's consciousness. It is not for nothing that the popular conception is that this is a play about delay. Delay in the action, that is in the carrying out of Hamlet's strategy against the King, can of course be explained: he had to find out if the Ghost was telling the truth about the murder, and so on. But the fact remains that one of the most powerful imaginative effects is of a sense of paralysis. Hamlet feels, and we are made to feel, that he is 'stuck', as we say on more homely occasions.

> Sure he that made us with such large discourse,
> Looking before and after, gave us not
> That capability and godlike reason
> To fust in us unus'd. Now, whether it be
> Bestial oblivion, or some craven scruple
> Of thinking too precisely on th'event –
> A thought which, quarter'd, hath but one part wisdom
> And ever three parts coward, – I do not know
> Why yet I live to say this thing's to do,
> Sith I have cause, and will, and strength, and means
> To do't.

[4.4.36–46]

Hamlet is here of course referring to the specific action of revenge, and commentators have been quick to point out that in regard to outward action he is neither slow nor a coward. But there is another and more important sense in which his self-accusation here is entirely justified, in that he is indeed 'lapsed in time and passion' [3.4.108] – that is, as Dover Wilson explains, arrested or taken prisoner ('lapsed') by circumstances and passion [referring to Wilson's argument in his edition of *Hamlet* (2nd edition) (Cambridge University Press, Cambridge 1936), p. lxiv]. Hamlet, as everyone says, is an intellectual, but he does little enough effective thinking on the moral and metaphysical problems that beset him: his god-like reason is clogged and impeded by the emotions of disgust, revulsion, and self-contempt that bring him back, again and again, to the isolation of his obsession. Effective thinking, in the regions that most concern Hamlet, implies a capacity for self-forgetfulness and a capacity for true relationship.

With this, I think, we reach the heart of the play. If [...] in the world of the play there is, on the one hand death, on the other, life lived with a peculiarly crude vigour of self-assertion, in such a world where are values to be found? If we are true to our direct impressions we must admit that *that* is Hamlet's problem, and questions concerning the authenticity of the Ghost or the means whereby Claudius may be trapped are subordinate to it. Hamlet's question, the question that he is continually asking himself, is, How can I live? What shall I do to rid myself of this numbing sense of meaninglessness brought by the knowledge of corruption? But behind this, and implicit in the play as a whole, is the question of being, of the activated consciousness. Hamlet comes close to putting this question directly in the great central soliloquy, but he glides away from it. And no wonder, for the problem is insoluble in the state of unresolved emotion in which he delivers himself of his thoughts; as Coleridge was never tired of insisting, thinking at the higher levels is an activity of the personality as a whole. □

(L.C. Knights, 'An Approach to *Hamlet*', 1960)[29]

If much of this comes across as fairly standard analysis of Hamlet's 'character' as a man isolated from the social world around him, there are also hints at a new direction that will become increasingly important in the coming decades of the twentieth century – Hamlet as performer. L.C. Knights understands this as a note of insincerity, before the final scene, and different from the 'note of sincerity' that is sounded in the soliloquies. This is perhaps already prefigured, for Knights, in Dover Wilson's eventual discovery of Hamlet's mystery as illusion. Later critics, like Francis Barker (1952–99) and Catherine Belsey, will see it rather as characteristic of a Hamlet who *has* no 'real' identity but whose fractured subjectivity is realised in a series of different performances. Knights goes so far as to suggest that 'the play is [a] radical examination of the problem of consciousness, of self-identity,' and that, because of this, the line that everyone thinks of in connexion with this play – though we all quarrel about its meaning – is, 'To be or not to be, that is the question … '[30]; but he does not pursue the idea that the play is somehow *about* the notion of identity and of subjectivity as critics from the 1980s onwards will. In the following chapter, the traditional concerns of literary criticism – 'character' and narrative – will come to be looked at differently. Assumptions about the play's realism will be pushed aside and in place of this, *Hamlet* will be seen as being about the formation of identity, or even as taking part in the formation of modern subjectivity itself.

CHAPTER FIVE

Contemporary Interpretations: Historicist *Hamlet*

In the early 1980s, the study of Renaissance literature undertook a radical review of its own assumptions and practices. Under a variety of social pressures, including the radicalisation of the academy in the 1960s and 1970s, the advent of feminism and, perhaps especially, the arrival of a new generation of younger academics in University departments, new ways of working and new ways of talking about literature were developed. Two major critical developments in this period included an American school of criticism that came to be called the 'new historicism' and an English form of this development – 'cultural materialism'. As the names of both of these suggest, this kind of criticism moved away from what was perceived as the narrow Formalism that had dominated the study of literature in the earlier part of the twentieth century. Instead, literary texts were analysed for the ways in which they emerged within specific historical and cultural circumstances. Subjectivity and self-consciousness, the central concern of much of the *Hamlet* criticism that we have looked at so far, came to be viewed very differently. Under the influence of the French writer, Michel Foucault (1926–84), literary critics in the 1980s came to see subjectivity as an effect of power, as a cultural construction rather than something which might be considered as pre-cultural. Whilst many of the insights of earlier criticism, into how the drama worked, and into its chief concerns, were not discarded, they were, instead, situated within wider cultural fields than the play itself. Within *Hamlet* criticism particularly, the most important of these has come to be what has been seen as the study of the birth of modern subjectivity in the early seventeenth century.

In his book, *Renaissance Self-Fashioning* (1980), Stephen Greenblatt (born 1943) does not look specifically at *Hamlet*, but he does set the scene for much of this kind of criticism. In this book, he matches Foucault's post-structuralist insight that subjectivity is not self-determining, with an analysis of Renaissance selfhood which insists on the performativity of early modern subjectivity. In his introduction to the book, Greenblatt maintains that the Renaissance sense of self is something that occurs at a specific moment in time.

■ Perhaps the simplest observation we can make is that in the sixteenth century there appears to be an increased self-consciousness about the fashioning of human identity as a manipulable, artful process. Such self-consciousness had been widespread in the classical world, but Christianity brought a growing suspicion of man's power to shape identity: 'Hands off yourself', Augustine declared. 'Try to build up yourself and you build a ruin.' This view was not the only one in succeeding centuries, but it was influential, and a powerful alternative began to be fully articulated only in the early modern period.[1] □

Taking his cue from a line in the letter to Sir Walter Ralegh (1554–1618) that Edmund Spenser (?1552–99) appends to the 1589 edition of *The Faerie Queene*, in which Spenser claims that his purpose in writing his epic poem was to 'fashion a gentleman', Greenblatt adopts the word 'fashioning' to describe this new self-conscious attitude towards the 'artful' manipulation of identity.

■ As a term for the action or process of making, for particular features or appearance, for a distinct style or pattern, the word had long been in use, but it is in the sixteenth century that *fashion* seems to come into wide currency as a way of designating the forming of a self. This forming may be understood quite literally as the imposition upon a person of physical form – 'Did not one fashion us in the womb?' Job asks in the King James Bible, while, following the frequent injunctions to 'fashion' children, midwives in the period attempted to mould the skulls of the newborn into the proper shape. But, more significantly for our purposes, fashioning may suggest the achievement of a less tangible shape: a distinctive personality, a characteristic address to the world, a consistent mode of perceiving and behaving.[2] □

One of the reasons for the popularity of and high level of interest shown in Greenblatt's book may well have been that his notion of self-fashioning deliberately cuts across the generic boundaries of the literary and non-literary. For Greenblatt, literature is one of the arenas in which this newly self-conscious fashioning of the self can take place.

■ ... self-fashioning acquires a new range of meanings: it describes the practice of parents and teachers; it is linked to manners or demeanor, particularly that of the elite; it may suggest hypocrisy or deception, an adherence to mere outward ceremony; it suggests representation of one's nature or intention in speech or actions. And with representation we return to literature, or rather we may grasp that self-fashioning derives its interest precisely from the fact that it functions without regard for a sharp distinction between literature and social life. It invariably crosses the boundaries between the creation of literary characters, the shaping of one's own identity, the experience of being moulded by forces outside one's control, the attempt to fashion other selves. Such boundaries may, to be sure, be strictly observed in criticism, just as we may distinguish between literary and behavioural styles, but in doing so we pay a high price, for we begin to lose a sense of the complex interactions of meaning in a given culture.[3] □

In stressing the artful nature of self-fashioning in the Renaissance, Greenblatt opened up the possibilities for other critics to move away from the kind of 'character criticism' inaugurated by A.C. Bradley, and from the more formalist 'organic' approaches of critics like G. Wilson Knight or T.S. Eliot. Those critics who followed Greenblatt, but who turned their attention to *Hamlet*, saw a new kind of play and a new kind of central figure. Previous criticism that had focussed on Hamlet's 'character' had sought to find in it a unifying motive for the action of the play. In contrast, critics like Francis Barker and Catherine Belsey saw subjectivity in the play as constructed and as discontinuous. Jonathan Goldberg, influenced as much by Jacques Derrida (born 1930) and deconstruction as by the kinds of materialism on which Greenblatt, Belsey and Barker drew, is able to contextualise the category of 'character' itself. Patricia Parker, also influenced by deconstruction and materialism, situates the language of *Hamlet* within larger social and cultural contexts, unearthing hidden resonances in its infamous word play. What unites much recent work on early modern drama is that the critics do not look for a unifying argument that would explain what had previously been seen as a play's inconsistencies – in the case of *Hamlet*, a character ill at ease with the world in which he had been placed or an artistic failure – but rather regard inconsistency as part of the way in which subjectivity is revealed as *performed* rather than *essential*.

FRANCIS BARKER

In his short, but remarkable, fascinating and original book, *The Tremulous Private Body: Essays on Subjection* (1984), Francis Barker mounted an investigation into the birth of modern subjectivity. The way that we think of ourselves as subjects, within commonsense notions of the self, is based on an idea of interiority, an awareness that we are, essentially, not completely identical to our exterior selves. Barker sees the play, *Hamlet*, and the way in which the character, Hamlet, is presented in the play as representative of a crucial moment in the early development of this particularly modern form of subjectivity. *Hamlet* charts a moment in which modern subjectivity learns to reject corporeality in favour of a certain 'inwardness', but Barker suggests that 'inwardness' in *Hamlet* remains anachronistic and is merely gestured at, a foretaste of things to come. This anachronism in the play manifests itself as the character, Hamlet's, difference from the others and from the world in which he is situated. The world of *Hamlet*, according to Barker, is one of total visibility and appearance, of surface, whereas Hamlet, himself, is imagined as having a mysterious interiority. It is interesting to note that even in rejecting Romantic and post–Romantic versions of the play in which Hamlet's character is celebrated as the driving force and centre of interest in the play, Barker still has Hamlet at odds with the world of the play around him. This is not to deny, though, the radical force of Barker's argument.

■ Hamlet's world is riddled with difficulties: its alienation on the other side of naturalism, its own internal seeming, and, as we shall see, an incipient modernity. But in achieving its most explicit character in an interplay of visibilities, is this world not also one of relentless surfaces, without depth or mystery? The question formulates a crucial problem. For the moment it can be answered provisionally if enigmatically by remarking that it has only one modern depth because only one individual inhabits it, and even he is putative. For now it is enough to define the kind of obscurity, of difficulty, that is truly this world's and not his. Although the play, by turns ghostly and conspiratorial, is not lacking in the promise of mystery, it is of a very qualified kind, for all the conspiracies of the night are revealed, finally, and the whispered conversations overheard. There is little that remains ultimately opaque. Even Ophelia's madness moves in this world as the emblem of an indelible grief, but not as a diagnostic problem. Its typical figure is not Hamlet, but Polonius behind the arras. A thin veil hangs between him and the action that destroys him, a tapestry that conceals his presence but does not transform it. He learns nothing there. He dies because he is hidden, but his slaughter is one of the casual ones which Horatio survives to narrate in a place conservatively simplified again by Hamlet's *necessary* death. In no essential way do Polonius and his destiny encounter each other in the passage of the prince's blade through the fibres of the arras; his mistake, if such it is, is to be momentarily out of sight, not to be worthy or even desirous of such a death.[4] □

If there is a depth to this world which seems to thrive on surfaces and on visibility, then it is the depth of a proliferation of different surfaces:

■ This world achieves its depth not in the figure of interiority by which the concealed inside is of another quality from what is external, but by a *doubling of the surface*. Just as *The Mousetrap* layers a spectacle within the spectacle, so the sheet of the action may be folded over until an unexpected contact is made and a sudden discharge of violence touched off.

But the meaning of the action is generated in the productivity of the figures inscribed on the planar surfaces of the body of the text. *The Mousetrap* does not function to discover a truth (except in the most literal sense of discovery), for this is one of the few murder stories where the identity of the killer is revealed on the first page – and even if ghosts cannot be trusted, this operates as a vehicle of Hamlet's delay rather than as a real epistemological problem – but serves to organize in transit the necessary anxiety which must flow from and around the incestuous usurpation. It acts as a bridge between nodes of the extremely attenuated action (not much actually happens at Elsinore) rather than as an instrument of the revelation of a hidden mystery. This accounts for its curious, frustrated lack of consequence. Hamlet does not sweep to his revenge impelled by the proof of Claudius's guilt which the play within the play provides, because it isn't a *proof* of anything that was in doubt. *The Mousetrap* draws a line across the surface, an articulation in the diagram of the action. It functions to extend time rather than to excavate a hidden level of reality. Apart from the one great exception to the rule of this theatre's space, the reality of this world is utterly single, however it may be folded over on itself.[5] □

It is in Hamlet himself, though, that the play moves away from a reliance on surface, from extensions in time towards a kind of 'depth'.

■ In what are almost the first words we hear him speak, a claim is made for modern depth, for qualitative distinction from the corporeal order of the spectacle:

> Seems, madam? Nay it is. I know not 'seems'.
> 'Tis not alone my inky cloak, good mother,
> Nor customary suits of solemn black,
> Nor windy suspuration of forc'd breath,
> No, nor the fruitful river in the eye,
> Nor the dejected haviour of the visage,
> Together with all forms, modes, shapes of grief,
> That can denote me truly. These indeed seem,
> For they are actions that a man might play;
> But I have that within which passes show,
> These but the trappings and the suits of woe.
> [1.2.76–86]

Hamlet asserts against the devices of the world an essential interiority. If the 'forms, modes, shapes' fail to denote him truly it is because in him a separation has already opened up between the inner reality of the subject, living itself, as 'that within which passes show', and an inauthentic exterior: and in that opening there begins to insist, however prematurely, the figure that is to dominate and organize bourgeois culture. Seen from the viewpoint of this speech, the narrative of *Hamlet* is nothing but the prince's evasion of a series of personalities offered to him by the social setting. From the moment when the ghost of his father lays on him the burden of vengeance, his passage through the drama is the refusal of – or, at most, the parodic and uncommitted participation in – the roles of courtier, lover, son, politician, swordsman, and so on. Even the central task of revenge provides, in its deferral, no more than a major axis of the play's duration. But in dismissing these modes or 'actions' as he calls them, Hamlet utters, against the substance of the spectacular plenum which is now reduced in his eyes to a factitious artificiality 'that a man might play', a first demand for the modern subject. In the name now, not of the reign of body but of the secular soul, an interior subjectivity begins to speak here – an I which, if it encounters the world in anything more than a quizzical and contemplative manner, must alienate itself into an environment which inevitably traduces the richness of the subject by its mute and resistant externality. An early embarrassment for bourgeois ideology, and one of which Hamlet is in part an early victim, was that even as it had to legitimise the active appropriation of the world, it also had to encode its subject as an individual, privatised and largely passive 'consciousness' systematically detached from a world which is thus beyond its grasp: for all its insistence on the world as tractable raw object it none the less constructs a subjectivity whose form is that of the unique and intransitive soul, centred in meanings which are apparently its alone.

But this interiority remains, in *Hamlet*, gestural. 'The heart of my mystery' (3.2.368–9), as he describes it to Guildernstern in another place, is the real opacity of the text. Unlike those other obscurities of seeming which are *proper* to the spectacle, the truth and density of *this* mystery can never be apprehended. The deceptions of the plenum which surrounds Hamlet are always ultimately identifiable as such, and therefore only obscure for a few or within some tactical situation of the drama as it unfolds: they are never beyond the reach of its epistemology. But Hamlet's inner mystery is not of this order. Neither those who seek it out within the play, who try to discover whether he is mad in reality or 'in craft', nor the audience who overhear so many examples of the rhetorical form proper to this isolated subjectivity, the soliloquy, are ever placed by the text in a position from which it can be grasped. It perdures as a central obscurity which cannot be dramatized. The historical prematurity of this subjectivity places it outside the limits of the text-world in which it is as yet emergent only in a promissory form. The text continually offers to fulfil the claim of that first speech, but whenever it appears that the claimed core of that within which passes the show of the spectacle will be substantially articulated, Hamlet's riddling, antic language shifts its ground and the text slides away from the essence into a further deferral of the mystery. But if the text cannot dramatize this subjectivity, it can at least display its impossibility, when Hamlet offers a metaphor of himself, of his self, to Guildenstern who is an instrument, purely, of the king, and signally lacking any form of interiority. Challenging Guildenstern to 'pluck out the heart' of his mystery – in language sufficiently corporeal to point the failure – Hamlet gives him the recorder which he cannot play, although he would, in Hamlet's conceit, 'sound' the 'compass' of the prince. The hollow pipe is the refutation of the metaphysic of soul which the play signals but cannot realize. For Hamlet, in a sense doubtless unknown to him, is truly this hollow reed which will 'discourse most eloquent music' but is none the less vacuous for that. At the centre of Hamlet, in the interior of his mystery, there is, in short, nothing. The promised essence remains beyond the scope of the text's signification: or rather, signals the limit of the signification of this world by marking out the site of an absence it cannot fill. It gestures towards a place for subjectivity, but both are anachronistic and belong to a historical order whose outline has so far only been sketched out. □ (Francis Barker, *The Tremulous Private Body*, 1984)[6]

Barker sees *Hamlet*, then, as a forward-looking text where the idea of a modern (and, for Barker, this means 'bourgeois') subjectivity is gestured at in Hamlet's soliloquies but where that gesture is never met with a truly fully formed modern subject.

■ *Hamlet* is a contradictory, transitional text, and one not yet fully assimilated into the discursive order which has claimed it: the promise of essential subjectivity remains unfulfilled. From its point of vantage on the threshold of the modern but not yet within it, the text scandalously reveals the emptiness at the heart of that bourgeois trope. Rather than the plenitude of an individual presence, the text dramatizes its impossibility.[7] □

It is because of this 'impossibility', the yet-to-be-fulfilled promise of a fully formed subject position, that, Barker argues, a particular form of Romantic and post-Romantic criticism has found *Hamlet* to be particularly fruitful hunting ground.

■ It is into this breach in Hamlet that successive generations of criticism – especially Romantic and post-Romantic variants – have stepped in order to fill the vacuum and, in explaining Hamlet, to explain him away.[8] □

It is the project of cultural materialist criticism like that of Barker and Catherine Belsey to investigate that 'breach' – between Hamlet and the modern world – as precisely that: a breach. In place of Coleridge merely seeing himself reflected in the character of Hamlet, more recent criticism has sought to explore the differences between us and Hamlet as well as the resemblances.

CATHERINE BELSEY

In her book, *The Subject of Tragedy* (1985), Catherine Belsey takes up this idea that the modern 'subject' is something that is born in the early modern period, and that early modern tragedy is one form in which this birth can be witnessed. Like many of the critics based in the United Kingdom, and associated with the school of criticism termed 'cultural materialism', Belsey saw an explicitly political function in her writing. This is how she described the three aims of her influential book.

■ This book has three main aims. The first is to contribute to the construction of a history of the subject in the sixteenth and seventeenth centuries. The human subject, the self, is the central figure in the drama which is liberal humanism, the consensual orthodoxy of the west. The subject is to be found at the heart of our political institutions, the economic system and the family, voting, exercising rights, working, consuming, falling in love, marrying and becoming a parent. And yet the subject has conventionally no history, perhaps because liberal humanism depends upon the belief that in its essence the subject does not change, that liberal humanism itself expresses a human nature which, despite its diversity, is always at the most basic, the most intimate level, the same. I do not share this belief or the conservatism it implies.

The second aim is to demonstrate, by placing woman side by side with man, that at the moment when the modern subject was in the process of construction, the 'common-gender noun' largely failed to include women in the range of its meanings. Man is the subject of liberal humanism. Woman has meaning in relation to man. And yet the instability which is the result of this asymmetry is the ground of protest, resistance, feminism. The history of women since the seventeenth century has been the history of a struggle to secure for woman the rights and benefits man has awarded himself. At a more fundamental level it is also the history of an effort to redefine the terms of liberal humanism itself, to challenge the meanings and values which give rise to the asymmetry.

Thirdly, I have tried to bring together history and literature (or fiction, since 'literature' implies a value judgment which is irrelevant to my argument). It is true that historians frequently dip into fiction in quest of evidence, and that literary critics often feel it necessary to take account of the background to the text. But the relationship I propose between fiction and history is not one of foreground and background, text and context. The project is to construct a history of the meanings which delimit at a specific moment what it is possible to say, to understand and consequently to be. People make history under determinate conditions. One of these conditions is subjectivity itself, and this is in turn an effect of discourse. To be a subject is to be able to speak, to give meaning. But the range of meanings it is possible to give at a particular historical moment is determined outside the subject. The subject is not the origin of meanings, not even the meaning of subjectivity itself. Fiction, especially in the period from the sixteenth century to the present, is about what it is to be a subject – in the process of making decisions, taking action, falling in love, being a parent ... . Fictional texts also address themselves to readers or audiences, offering them specific subject-positions from which the texts most readily make sense. In that it both defines subjectivity and addresses the subject, fiction is a primary location of the production of meanings of and for the subject. The fiction of the past, intelligible in its period to the extent that it participates in the meanings in circulation in that period, constitutes, therefore, a starting-point for the construction of a history of the subject. □

(Catherine Belsey, *The Subject of Tragedy*, 1985)[9]

Belsey chooses the genre of tragedy for this project, partly because it seems, as a genre and in its reception, to have concentrated on the figure of 'man'. This allows her to develop her thesis, illustrating the constructed, rather than essential, nature of 'subjectivity'.

Belsey's argument is also helped by the fact that she sees, in early modern drama, and especially in tragedy, a development from earlier forms of theatre, such as medieval mystery plays. The 'Everyman' character in these plays, such as *Everyman* (*c.*1509–19) and *The Castle of Perseverance* (*c.*1400–25), does not possess his own 'agency'. That is, his actions cannot be understood as proceeding from his particular identity. Rather, his actions are caught up within a predetermined story. Early modern tragedy both emerges from and transcends these kinds of plays. It retains the sense of a subject caught up within a fateful universe, but in conflict with this, there is now a subject with a measure of agency who resists that fateful universe.

It can, of course, be seen that *Hamlet* would play a key role in this discussion. Like Barker, Belsey sees 'subjectivity' in *Hamlet* as conflicted; Hamlet is part modern subject-agent and part constructed out of the remnants of past traditions, theatrical and philosophical.

■ It is generally agreed that when Hamlet, speaking in the Globe, defines the earth as a promontory beneath the canopy of the o'erhanging firmament, he is invoking the familiar metaphor of the world as a theatre, and identifying the apron stage itself and the roof which protected it, the 'heavens' from which divinities were lowered to the stage when the play required them.

this goodly frame the earth seems to me a sterile promontory, this most excellent canopy the air, look you, this brave o'erhanging firmament, this majestical roof fretted with golden fire, why, it appeareth nothing to me but a foul and pestilent congregation of vapours. What a piece of work is a man, how noble in reason, how infinite in faculties, in form and moving, how express and admirable, in action how like an angel, in apprehension how like a god: the beauty of the world, the paragon of animals – and yet, to me, what is this quintessence of dust? Man delights not me – nor woman neither, though by your smiling you seem to say so. [2.2.298–310]

Man is present in the speech, and his other, woman, uneasily there in the concluding joke which draws attention to the way that then, as now, the term 'man' both includes ('embraces', they say, inviting us to laugh) and simultaneously excludes women. Anatomy is made both difference and destiny, comedy and oppression. Man, meanwhile, is another paradox: like a god and at the same time a quintessence of dust. Which half of the paradox is vindicated by the fiction? Which case does the play as a whole support? And who is speaking? Is the audience invited to see Hamlet expressing his deepest feelings, displaying the subjectivity, complex and contradictory, of the sensitive prince? Or, since he is talking to Rosencrantz and Guildenstern here, is this a pose, an antic disposition designed to delude them, an assumed melancholy? Or, if the world is a stage, what is Hamlet but an actor, expressing and concealing nothing, but offering a performance, a form which does not imply an anterior substance? Or, since conversely the stage must be a world, does this fiction, this conceit, lay claim to a kind of truth? But which of the possible truths?

The plurality of the speech depends on the multiple meanings of this play performed on this stage. The promontory which represents the earth is also Elsinore; Hamlet is a concrete individual with a particular history; the autonomous world of the fiction is geographically and chronologically specific, and separate from the world of the audience. At the same time, the promontory is between 'the heavens' and 'hell', the space below the stage from which infernal figures appeared through a trapdoor as necessary, and where old Hamlet's Ghost cries in the cellarage. (1.5.151) □

(Catherine Belsey, *The Subject of* Tragedy, 1985)[10]

Hamlet, for Belsey, draws on its position in theatrical history as a descendant of miracle plays and yet, at the same time, is part of a new kind of theatre that depends on specific characters, locations and narratives rather than the universals of the older theatre. Belsey shows this by drawing on a specific model of the early modern public stage (like 'The Globe') which understands it both as allegorical /universal and as having an ability to depict specific locations. This is something that is particular to this kind of stage. Related to this kind of transitional staging, the plays of the late sixteenth and early seventeenth centuries are, she argues, also poised between two forms of subjectivity in their depiction of character.

■ It is difficult ... to read these plays simply as humanist texts, endorsing the unified human subject or affirming a continuous and inviolable interiority as the essence of each person. This does not, of course, imply that nothing had changed since the fifteenth century. Patently what it meant to be human had altered radically since *The Castle of Perseverance* displayed its fragmented protagonist. But it was to change again before a fully-fledged humanism came to assert the inalienable identity of the individual.

None the less, there are in the plays of the late sixteenth and early seventeenth centuries intimations of the construction of a place which notions of personal identity were later to come to fill. [...]

The classic case is, of course, *Hamlet*. Francis Barker has written of Hamlet's assertion of an authentic inner reality defined by its difference from an inauthentic exterior.

> 'Tis not alone my inky cloak, good mother,
> Nor customary suits of solemn black,
> Nor windy suspuration of forc'd breath,
> No, nor the fruitful river in the eye,
> Nor the dejected haviour of the visage,
> Together with all forms, modes, shapes of grief,
> That can denote me truly. These indeed seem,
> For they are actions that a man might play;
> But I have that within which passes show,
> These but the trappings and the suits of woe.
>   [1.2.77–86]

'That within' is here distinguished from 'actions that a man might play', and this interiority, this essence, the heart of Hamlet's mystery, has been the quarry not only of Rosencrantz and Guildenstern, agents of the king's surveillance, but of liberal-humanist criticism of the nineteenth and twentieth centuries. Hamlet's irresolution, his melancholy, his relations with Ophelia, his career at Wittenberg and his Oedipal tendencies have all been thoroughly investigated and documented in the attempt to find the truth of Hamlet's subjectivity, the reason why he says what he says, and acts, or fails to act, as he does. ☐ (Catherine Belsey, *The Subject of Tragedy*, 1985)[11]

Belsey then goes on to agree with Barker that this interiority is not, in fact, there to find in Hamlet who is, she says, 'the most discontinuous of Shakespeare's heroes'.[12] Belsey also locates her discussion of the autonomy of the early modern subject within a political, as well as a philosophical, context. She situates *Hamlet*, as a revenge tragedy, within an early modern debate about the possibilities of resistance under absolutist monarchies. Revenge tragedies were particularly popular in the early seventeenth century and, in an argument that resembles that of her contemporary Jonathan Dollimore in his book *Radical Tragedy* (1984), Belsey links this popularity to a breakdown in traditional systems of justice and authority.[13]

■ In the revenge plays in the half-century before the civil war it is the sovereign's failure to administer justice which inaugurates the subject's quest for vengeance. Hieronimo rips the bowels of the earth with his dagger, calling for 'Justice, O justice, justice, gentle king' (*The Spanish Tragedy* [first published 1592, written by Thomas Kyd], 3.xii.63). Titus Andronicus urges his kinsmen to dig a passage to Pluto's region, with a petition for 'justice and for aid' (*Titus Andronicus*, 4.3.15). The Duchess Rosaura [from *The Cardinal* (1641) by James Shirley (1596–1666)] appeals direct to the monarch:

> Let me have swift and such exemplar justice
> As shall become this great assassinate.
> You will take off our faith else, and if here
> Such innocence must bleed and you look on,
> Poor men that you call gods of the earth will doubt
> To obey your laws.
>
> (*The Cardinal*, 3.2.104–9)

In each case, however, the sovereign fails to enforce the law. Indeed, in *Antonio's Revenge* [about 1600 by John Marsden (about 1575–1634)], *The Revenger's Tragedy* [(published 1608), authorship unproven, though almost certainly by Thomas Middleton (1580–1627)] and *Hamlet* the ruler is the criminal. In the absence of justice the doubt Rosaura defines propels the revenger to take in the interests of justice action which is itself unjust.

Revenge is not justice. Titus is a man 'so just that he will not revenge'. (*Titus Andronicus*, 4.1.29). Acting outside the legal institution and in defiance of legitimate authority, individuals have no right to arrogate to themselves the role of the state in the administration of justice: 'never private cause / Shuld take on it the part of public laws' (*The Revenge of Bussy d'Ambois* [(published 1613), by George Chapman (*c*.1530–1634)], 3.2.115–16). Conscience, which permits passive disobedience, forbids murder, and this makes cowards of some revengers (*Hamlet*, 3.1.83–5). Others, more resolute, like Laertes are deaf to its promptings:

> To hell, allegiance! Vows to the blackest devil!
> Conscience and grace, to the profoundest pit!
> I dare damnation. To this point I stand,
> That both the worlds I give to negligence,
> Let come what comes, only I'll be revenged
> Most thoroughly for my father.
>
> [*Hamlet*, 4.5.131–6]

When Hamlet differentiates revenge from hire and salary (3.3.79), he specifies the gap between vengeance and justice. Revenge is always in excess of justice. Its execution calls for a 'stratagem of ... horror' (*Antonio's Revenge*, 3.1.48–50). Titus serves the heads of Chiron and Demetrius to their mother and the Emperor in a pastry coffin. Antonio massacres the innocent Julio and offers him in a dish to his father, after cutting out the tyrant's tongue. Vindice prepares for the Duke a liaison with the skull of the murdered Gloriana, and the 'bony lady' poisons him with a kiss (*The Revenger's Tragedy*, 3.5.121). Hippolito holds down his tongue and compels him to witness his wife's adultery while he dies.

The discourse of revenge reproduces the violence and the excess of its practice: 'Look how I smoke in blood, reeking the steam of foaming vengeance' (*Antonio's Revenge*, 3.5.17–18); 'Then will I rent and tear them thus and thus, / Shivering their limbs in pieces with my teeth' (*The Spanish Tragedy*, 3.xiii.122–3); 'Now could I drink hot blood, / And do such bitter business as the day / Would quake to look on' (*Hamlet*, 3.2.380–2); 'I should 'a fatted all the region kites / With this slave's offal' (*Hamlet*, 2.2.574–5). As Claudius assures Laertes, it is in the nature of revenge to 'have no bounds' (*Hamlet*, 4.vii.128). The rugged Pyrrhus – avenging *his* father's death, 'roasted in wrath and fire, / And thus o'er-sized with coagulate gore' (*Hamlet*, 2.2.455–6) – is not, after all, entirely a caricature of the stage revenger.

And yet the act of vengeance, in excess of justice, a repudiation of conscience, hellish in its mode of operation, seems to the revenger (and to the audience?) an overriding imperative. Not to act is to leave crime unpunished, murder triumphant or tyranny in unfettered control. The orthodox Christian remedy is patience: 'Vengeance is mine; I will repay, saith the Lord' (Rom. 12:19).   (Catherine Belsey, *The Subject of Tragedy*, 1985)[14]

[...]

Whatever the requirements of Christian patience, the imperatives of fiction demand that heaven delays the execution of justice, and in the interim the crime continues. [...] In *Hamlet* Claudius is still in possession of the crown and Gertrude, and is planning the death of the hero in addition. [...] In these circumstances revenge is a political as well as a moral issue. Thus Hamlet asks,

Does it not, think thee, stand me now upon –
He that hath kill'd my king and whor'd my mother;
Popp'd in between th'election and my hopes,
Thrown out his angle for my proper life,
And with such coz'nage – is't not perfect conscience
To quit him with this arm? And is't not to be damn'd
To let this canker of our nature come
In further evil?

[5.2.63–70]

The question, like most of the questions raised in *Hamlet*, is not answered. [...]

Revenge exists in the margin between justice and crime. An act of injustice on behalf of justice, it deconstructs the antithesis which fixes the meanings of good and evil, right and wrong. Hamlet invokes the conventional polarities in addressing the Ghost, only to abandon them as inadequate or irrelevant:

Be thou a spirit of health or goblin damn'd,
Bring with thee airs from heaven or blasts from hell,

> Be thy intents wicked or charitable,
> Thou com'st in such a questionable shape
> That I will speak to thee.
>
> [1.4.40–4]

The Ghosts in revenge plays consistently resist unequivocal identifications, are always 'questionable' in one of the senses of that word. Dead, and yet living, visitant at midnight (the marginal hour) from a prison-house which is neither heaven nor hell, visible to some figures on the stage but not to others and so neither real nor unreal, they inaugurate a course of action which is both mad and sane, correct and criminal. To uphold the law revengers are compelled to break it. The moral uncertainty persists to the end. [...] Hamlet dies a revenger, a poisoner, but also a soldier and a prince. (*Hamlet*, 5.2.387–95) [...]

The question whether it is nobler to suffer in Christian patience or to take arms against secular injustice is not resolved in the plays. It is ultimately a question about authority – God's, the sovereign's or the subject's. To the extent that the plays condemn revenge, they stay within an orthodoxy which permits only passive disobedience and prescribes no remedy for the subject when the sovereign breaks the law. But in order to be revenge plays at all, they are compelled to throw into relief the social and political weaknesses of the ethical and political position. To the extent that they consequently endorse revenge, they participate in the installation of the sovereign subject, entitled to take action in accordance with conscience and on behalf of law. □ (Catherine Belsey, *The Subject of Tragedy*, 1985)[15]

The generality of Belsey's approach to early modern drama in *The Subject of Tragedy* is something that later critics have picked up on. As criticism of early modern literature has moved on from the first flush of excitement generated by the new historicism and cultural materialism of the 1980s, it has rejected what it has seen as a lingering formalism in the repeated patterns that it tended to find in the literature and developed a more nuanced approach to the relationship between literature and history, the literary and the non-literary, the political and the philosophical. Whilst maintaining an interest in the way that ideas might have circulated between apparently disparate areas of cultural production, recent work will tend to be more specific about the circumstances of those circulations. As illustration of this approach in relation to *Hamlet*, we can look at an essay from 1999 by Ronald Knowles (born 1940), '*Hamlet* and Counter-Humanism', in which he positions Belsey's and Barker's discussion of Hamlet as an incipient humanist 'subject' within a specific set of texts that negotiate between medieval and Renaissance notions of what it meant to be human, and particularly the sceptical tradition, often thought of as embodied by the sixteenth-century French essayist, Montaigne (1533–92). It is also the case that the more language-aware criticism of people like Jonathan Goldberg and Patricia Parker, influenced by, though moving away from, Derrida and American deconstruction, are particularly persuasive in their analyses of the play's position within the changing cultural circumstances of late sixteenth- and early seventeenth-century England, given the amount of attention they pay to the precise meaning of Shakespeare's language.

Before that, though, I would like to look at another important strand in the criticism of the 1980s and after – its concern for the political contexts of early modern drama. *Hamlet* was never an obvious choice for this kind of attention as it is not easy to link it, other than in a fairly general way, to the political concerns of Elizabethan and Jacobean London. The following two critics – Leonard Tennenhouse (born 1942) and Alan Sinfield – attempt just such an accommodation, however, between *Hamlet* and its possible political contexts. Tennenhouse examines ways in which the monarchy is represented, on and off the stage, and Sinfield sees the play operating in the 'intersection' between two powerful developments of the English Renaissance – Senecan Stoicism and Calvinist theology, necessarily politicised through Calvinism being the official position of the Elizabethan Church.

LEONARD TENNENHOUSE

In looking at the connections between text and history, early new historicism developed a particular fascination with the fictions of power. Much of this fascination stemmed from a reading of the work of Michel Foucault, particularly the opening chapter of *Discipline and Punish* (1975) which describes the public execution of a traitor in Renaissance France as a 'spectacle of power'. In the work of writers like Leonard Tennenhouse, this perspective resulted in seeing some aspects of early modern drama as an extension of the Renaissance monarch's controlling fictions, as spectacles which embodied the authorising power of the monarchical state. In his book, *Power on Display: the Politics of Shakespeare's Forms* (1986), Tennenhouse attempts to modify traditional literary configurations of genre and reconfigure the groupings of the Shakespeare canon in relation to the strategies of power that they share with each other, even when this crosses over traditional generic boundaries. To this end, he discusses *Hamlet* with the Elizabethan chronicle plays rather than with the later Jacobean tragedies with which it is more ordinarily grouped, and where Belsey continued to group it even as she elucidated some of its political implications. Tennenhouse does this in the belief that *Hamlet* and the chronicle plays share certain 'strategies of representation'.[16] In the chapter on the Elizabethan chronicle plays and *Hamlet*, Tennenhouse argues that the legitimacy of the monarch is underlined in the Henriad (*Richard II, Henry IV* parts one and two and *Henry V*) through the monarch's ability to contain potentially disruptive elements within his own representational strategies, with the ultimate monarch proving to be Henry V. This he relates to a particularly Elizabethan situation in which Elizabeth derived her power from two potentially contradictory sources – her right to the throne through her royal blood, and her right to it through the will (legacy) of her father, Henry VIII, which treated the throne as private property. While Elizabeth was on the throne, she was able to deflect attention from the problems that this dual legitimacy might entail but as she got older, it became increasingly clear that she might not be able to sustain this for much longer as the two different sources for her legitimacy potentially resulted in two different lines of succession. Henry, in his will, had insisted on his younger sister's children coming to the throne in the event of his line dying out, as it was going to do with Elizabeth, rather than the line of his older sister from whom the eventual successor, James I, gained his right to accede to the English throne. It is in this anxious situation that Tennenhouse locates *Hamlet*'s representations of the strategies of power.

■ *Hamlet* marks the moment when the Elizabethan strategies for authorizing monarchy became problematic. While he still thinks in terms of Elizabethan figures for power, Shakespeare appears to question their adequacy in representing the transfer of power from one monarch to another. History plays could not be written after *Hamlet*, I will argue, because this whole matter of transferring power from one monarch to another had to be rethought in view of the aging body of the queen, Elizabeth. That body was, as I have said, a political figure in its own right. Its decay without an apparent heir precipitated serious speculation about the transfer of power, and such speculation gave rise to narrative strategies to figure out how the continuity of the metaphysical body [of the monarch] might be preserved.[17] □

Tennenhouse, then, relates the strategies of power that are depicted in the play, *Hamlet*, to the particular time of the play's inception – in the very last years of Elizabeth's reign.

■ Elizabeth's physical condition seemed at regular intervals to open a gap between the two notions of kingship her physical presence had successfully mediated for some forty years. We might be tempted to say this is also true of chronicle plays which pit the claims of blood against the effective use of force. But Shakespeare invokes the possibility of such a threat to the body politic only to demonstrate that the monarch's two bodies [alluding to the theory that the monarch is situated in two separate bodies – the body natural (the physical body) and the body politic (the state)] cannot exist as separate entities. It is significant, then, when we find that the very presupposition allowing Shakespeare to play out a dialectics of power in the earlier plays was regularly called into question between 1699 and 1601, the years when it is most likely that *Hamlet* was being written.[18]

[...]

Hamlet rehearses this dilemma of a state torn between two competitors, neither of whom can embody the mystical power of blood and land associated with the natural body. Hamlet's claim to power derives from his position as son in a patrilinear system as well as from 'popular support'. It is this support which Claudius consistently lacks and which, at the same time, prevents him from moving openly against Hamlet. Following the murder of Polonius, for example, Claudius says of Hamlet, 'Yet must we not put the strong law on him / He's lov'd of the distracted multitude ... ' (4.3.3–4). But this alone does not guarantee authority. Hamlet is not by nature capable of exercising force. To signal this lack, Shakespeare has given him the speech of Stoical writing, which shifts all action onto a mental plane where any show of force becomes self-inflicted aggression. We find this identification of force with self-assault made explicit in Hamlet's speeches on suicide as well as those in which he berates himself for his inability to act.

In contrast with Hamlet, Claudius's authority comes by way of his marriage to Gertrude. Where he would be second to Hamlet and Hamlet's line in a patrilineal system, the queen's husband and uncle of the king's son occupies the privileged male position in a matrilineal system. Like one of the successful figures from a history play, Claudius overthrew the reigning patriarch. Like one of the successful courtiers in a romantic comedy, he married into the aristocratic community. What is perhaps more important, he has taken the position through the effective use of force. Thus Shakespeare sets in opposition the two claims to authority – the exercise of force and the magic of blood – by means of these two members of the royal family. Because each has a claim, neither Hamlet nor Claudius achieves legitimate control over Denmark. Each one consequently assaults the aristocratic body in attempting to acquire the crown. It is to be expected that Claudius could not legally possess the crown, the matrilinear succession having the weaker claim on British political thinking. Thus the tragedy resides not in his failure but in the impossibility of Hamlet's rising according to Elizabethan strategies of state. This calls the relationship between the metaphysics of patriarchy and the force of law into question.

Claudius's criminality is never the problem. What more heinous crime could be committed against the aristocratic body than a fratricide that is also a regicide? Add to this that both Hamlet and his father's ghost consider this crime incestuous in that it allows one member of the king's family to marry another. But even when they acquired state power by the most questionable means, and even when the magic of blood seemed to locate power elsewhere, the monarchs of the chronicle histories could authorize force and sanction their blood by certain displays of power. Thus we see them incorporating popular energy in the processions of state. In particular, we find them including alienated members of the aristocracy. We may observe this in such rituals of forgiveness as Bullingbroke uses to forgive Aumerle, for example, or Henry's vow to banish Falstaff while promising to those that do reform themselves, 'We will, according to your strengths and qualities, / Give you advancement' (5.5.69–70).

Henry V concludes in comic fashion with courtship and promises of marriage, much as *Richard III* ends with Richmond's prayer, 'O now let his Richmond and Elizabeth, / The true succeeders of each royal house, / By God's fair ordinance conjoin together' (5.5.29–31). All these gestures stress the patron's generosity rather than his power to subordinate. It is important, then, that Claudius cannot seize hold of these signs and symbols of power that would authorize his reign. If Hamlet cannot translate the claims of blood into the exercise of force, it is also true that Claudius cannot command the symbolic elements of his culture which testify to the magic of blood. This is especially apparent in the contrast Shakespeare draws between the patron's feast and the revels Claudius attempts to stage. Significantly, Hamlet must explain to a startled Horatio that the sudden noise of trumpet and cannon does not signal a military invasion but rather announce Claudius's revels:

> The King doth wake tonight and takes his rouse,
> Keeps wassail, and the swagg'ring up-spring reels;
> And as he drains his draughts of Rhenish down,
> The kettle-drum and trumpet thus bray out
> The triumph of his pledge.
>
> [1.4.8–12]

Add to this the fact that Shakespeare has Hamlet describe Claudius to Gertrude in terms that specifically invoke the figure of misrule:

> A murtherer and a villain,
> A slave that is not the twentieth part the tithe
> Of your precedent lord, a vice of kings,
> A cutpurse of the empire and the rule,
> That from a shelf the precious diadem stole,
> And put it in his pocket ...
> A king of shreds and patches ...
>
> [3.4.96–103]

As he leaves, he urges his mother not to let 'The bloat king tempt you again to bed ... ' (182). To call Claudius a 'bloat king', a 'lecherous' man, 'a cutpurse of the empire', 'a vice of kings', is for Shakespeare to cut this usurper out of the same cloth he used in fabricating Falstaff. Thus Claudius acquires the features of illicit power which the history plays subordinate, if not purge, in sanctifying power. □

(Leonard Tennenhouse, *Power on Display: the Politics of Shakespeare's Forms*, 1986)[19]

What I think is strongest about Tennenhouse's analysis of *Hamlet* is the way in which it succeeds in making the play strange to us again. By reading it alongside the chronicle, or history plays, as a play which is about the transfer of power, certain elements are drawn out which are inaccessible to a criticism that continues to focus on Hamlet as a central figure, whether as Romantic 'character' or as postmodern constructed 'self'. Of course, the danger of this approach is that, for all its lipservice to the particular nature of *Hamlet*'s political contexts, it tends to elide the politics of various plays. By reading *Hamlet* alongside *Henry V* rather than, say, *King Lear*, Tennenhouse does reveal some things about the politics of the play that he might not otherwise, but there is also a strange formalism about these politics, with characters from the plays, in this case Claudius and Hamlet, representing in a relatively straight-forward and formulaic way the options for monarchical power available in late Elizabethan / early Jacobean England. It is not the case, however, that Tennenhouse ignores completely the 'literariness' of *Hamlet*, linking it to Senecan tragedy as well as to Shakespeare's own history plays. The Roman writer Seneca (about 4 BC–AD 65) was the most popular ancient writer of tragedies in the Renaissance, and was much imitated on the English stage. This imitation produced a variety of tragedy that was frequently spectacular in its use of extreme violence and often centred around a figure intent on a bloodthirsty revenge.

■ That Hamlet's act of vengeance against his uncle constitutes a crime against the state is dramatized ... in the language that Hamlet speaks. Where he spoke a Stoic discourse (e.g. 'To be or not to be ... ') before staging his play, afterwards Hamlet speaks in the contrasting terms of Senecan tragedy:

'Tis now the very witching time of night,
When churchyards yawn and hell itself breathes out
Contagion to this world. Now could I drink hot blood,
And do such bitter business as the day
Would quake to look on.
(3.2.379–83)

This is the language which [Thomas] Nashe (1567–1601) identified a decade earlier as that of the 'English Seneca' which characterized earlier productions of 'whole Hamlets'. [from his preface to *Menaphon* (1589) by Robert Greene (1558–92)]. By giving him this familiar stage speech, Shakespeare distinguishes Hamlet's exercise of authority from the rituals and processionals concluding the chronicle history plays. At the same time, such speech identifies Hamlet with Claudius whose exercise of force turns into Senecan tragedy, first, in the murder of Hamlet's father which initiated the action of the play, and then in the murder of Hamlet with which the play concludes. Thus Hamlet's play figures out the power of the state on a symbolic plane in the very terms that Claudius uses to enact his authority. Neither can act in a way that establishes the family line according to the strategies of state governing the chronicle history plays.

One might be tempted to declare a generic difference between *Hamlet*, as a tragedy, and the history plays on just those grounds, but I will argue against the wisdom of doing so for those who want to understand Shakespeare's genres as political strategies. Even as he raises questions concerning the iconic relationship between the queen's two bodies, Shakespeare cannot imagine legitimate power in any other way. Given the fact that neither Claudius nor Hamlet could embody the state in a way that effectively hierarchized power – this, chiefly because each had equal claims to power – neither one could become the legitimate sovereign of Denmark. In light of their failure, the arrival of Fortinbras marks *Hamlet* as an Elizabethan play. Nowhere to be found in the sources, his name implies a natural ability to exercise force. Shakespeare also endows Fortinbras with aristocratic blood, though not that of the Danish line. In this, he obviously resembles the figure who emerges at the end of all the major history plays as the product of human history and providence as well. Most perfectly realized in *Henry V*, this figure acquires authority not only through material conflicts which display that effective exercise of force, but also through the metaphysics of blood which he embodies. □

(Leonard Tennenhouse, *Power on Display: the Politics of Shakespeare's Forms*, 1986)[20]

I find the way that Tennenhouse links generic form with forms of authority highly suggestive and, whilst it has become commonplace in discussions of Shakespeare's history plays to look at the strategies of theatricality in relation to the exercise of power, this avenue has, so far, proved rather a dead end in studies of *Hamlet* which continue to mine the rich vein of material concerned with ideas of subjectivity.

ALAN SINFIELD

In many ways, Tennenhouse is a primary example of the more conservative kind of criticism that is sometimes offered by new historicism. Its reliance on Foucauldian models of power has been seen by some as offering small scope for resistance to dominant modes of power and control. Alan Sinfield, instead, with his brand of cultural materialism, comes from a British school of criticism that borrows much more from the Marxist theories of the literary critic, Raymond Williams (1921–88), and is much more likely to identify ideological shifts operating within the literary text. In his account of *Hamlet*, Sinfield sees the play as existing at the crossroads between two different ways of seeing the world and human suffering – a Senecan Stoical and deeply sceptical way of approaching suffering and the Calvinist approach to suffering through the explanatory framework of God's providence. If it is assumed that the Calvinist discourse, which Sinfield argues is present at certain moments in *Hamlet*, is in some ways 'official', in that Calvinism was the dominant doctrine in the Elizabethan church, then its proximity to an alternative kind of fatalism – Senecan Stoicism – in the play is at least potentially subversive.

In the earlier acts of the play, before Hamlet's return from England initiates the sequence of events that lead up to the play's devastating climaxes, Sinfield sees Hamlet identifying with a kind of Stoicism, inspired by Seneca. It is Seneca that is the inspiration behind the tradition of revenge drama to which *Hamlet* belongs. Sinfield argues that, in the first four acts of the play it is a 'Stoic tranquillity of mind' which Hamlet is searching for.[21]

■ For Hamlet, Stoicism is an ideal he hopes to see achieved. He values Horatio because he perceives in him 'a man that Fortune's buffets and rewards / Hast ta'en with equal thanks; ... not a pipe for Fortune's finger / To sound what stop she please ... not passion's slave' (3.2.67–72). By subduing his emotions, Horatio is said to free himself from the effects of fortune and become the Stoics' wise and happy man. If Hamlet could do that then revenge might not be a problem.[22] □

What is at stake here is the attitude of the play and of Hamlet towards the ideas of providence and fate. Sinfield points out that in embracing God's providence, Calvinism explicitly rejects Stoical self-sufficiency. There is a shift in the play, though, at the start of Act Five.

■ Upon his return from England, Hamlet seems to have abandoned his Stoic aspirations and become a believer in providence. Now sermon tags roll off his tongue – 'There's a divinity that shapes our ends, / Rough-hew then how we will'; 'even in that was heaven ordinant' (i.e., 'directing, controlling; 5.2.10–11, 48); 'there is a special providence in the fall of a sparrow'. This is very strong phrasing. In fact, in the first quarto Hamlet says, 'there's a predestinate providence in the fall of a sparrow'. Even if that is no more than a faulty memorial reconstruction, it shows how one well-placed contemporary read the prince's thought: it is Calvinist.

Hamlet seems to have changed. To say this is to *expect* (but not necessarily to find) some continuity in his character. [...] This is not to suppose, in a Bradleyan or essentialist-humanist manner, that these dramatic personae are unified subjects, or independent of the multiple discursive practices of the culture. Indeed, I have tried to locate Hamlet at the intersection point of Senecan and Calvinist discourses, and it is in their terms that I perceive a break upon his return from England. [...] It is recognizing cues that some continuity in the character of Hamlet is to be expected that makes it possible to allege a break (as, for instance, Francis Barker does).

At such a breaking point, readers and audiences may either declare the play incoherent or attempt to intuit an appropriate linking factor. If we do the former, we may either complain about artistic quality (as did T.S. Eliot) or triumphantly discover once more (with some poststructuralists) the twin instabilities of subjectivity and textuality. Wishing to push further than either of these, I try instead to envisage a linking factor through which an audience might (having in mind Hamlet's changed mode of utterance and the play so far) plausibly renew the sense of Hamlet as a continuous subjectivity. This, again, sounds Bradleyan but is in fact only a specially determined application of the process through which any story is understood. The mistake would be to efface the work required, and to imagine that one is uncovering the inner truth of Hamlet's character. I am observing that, as well as producing a breaking point, the text does suggest at least one plausible link.

This is Hamlet's awareness, which is in the dialogue, of the extraordinary turn events have taken – the appearance of the Ghost when Claudius seemed secure, the arrival of the Players prompting the test of the king, Hamlet's inspired discovery on the boat of the plot against his life, and then his amazing delivery from the pirates. The latter is so improbable, and unnecessary to the plot, as to suggest the specially intricate quality of divine intervention wherein even a sparrow's death is purposive. It is when explaining how he found Claudius' letter and changed it that Hamlet attributes events to 'a divinity that shapes our ends'; and when describing how he was able to seal the altered instructions that he says heaven was 'ordinant'. The sequence seems to require the providential explanation; so the prince recognizes the folly and pretension of humanistic aspiration and the controlling power of God.

For so much strenuous narration to be necessary, and with such sudden consequences for character and theme, the play must be labouring at a particularly awkward ideological moment. The strain, it appears, is getting Hamlet to the point where he can express belief in a special providence. This could produce a Christian moral such as [Sir Philip] Sidney (1554–86) might have approved. The 'carnal, bloody and unnatural acts' and 'purposes mistook/ Fall'n on th' inventors' heads' (5.2.386. 389–90) are quite compatible with a violent and punitive deity. In Calvin's view, both believers and the wicked must expect such afflictions. [...] So we may envisage an Elizabethan audience not finding *Hamlet* sad and bleak (or even strangely uplifting in its sense of wasted human potential), but being satisfied by the working out of events in the providential manner described in the sermons they had heard. The same might be true of other tragedies. Yet all texts, I have said, produce meaning in excess of any ostensible ideological project. In *Hamlet* the difficulties emanate from the concept of special providence. ☐

(Alan Sinfield, *Faultlines: Cultural Materialism and the Politics of Dissident Reading*, 1992)[23]

It can be seen from the passage above that Sinfield borrows from the understanding of critics like Francis Barker, who stress the discontinuity of Hamlet's 'character' and argue that subjectivity in *Hamlet* is the product of discourse. However, Sinfield goes a step beyond this insight by seeking to trace links between the different apparent Hamlets. What he sees operating in the production of Hamlet's subjectivity is a debate between Stoicism and Calvinism, and this is problematic for Calvinism's rejection of Stoicism, because it reveals a proximity between the two attitudes.

■ Hamlet believes that providence wants Claudius removed, and that he should do it. He rehearses the king's manifold crimes and asks:

> is't not perfect conscience
> To quit him with this arm? And is't not to be damn'd
> To let this canker of our nature come
> In further evil?
>
> [5.2.67–70]

However, when he says, 'The readiness is all', he means not for action but for death. He is not making a reverent general statement about the rightness of God's control of the world, but dismissing Horatio's very reasonable suspicion about the duel.

[...]

He acknowledges divine determination, but without enthusiasm. At this point the play turns back upon itself, retrieving the Stoicism that it has seemed to dismiss, for the tone and the context of the speech and Hamlet's subsequent inactivity are more in keeping with Seneca's *De Providentia* [...]: 'It was settled at the first hour of our birth what length of time remains for each ... Therefore everything should be endured with fortitude, since things do not, as we suppose, simply happen – they all come.' So Hamlet: 'If it be now, 'tis not to come; if it be not to come, it will be now; if it be not now, yet it will come. The readiness is all ... Let be.' Hamlet falls back upon the fatalism that often underlies the Stoic ideal of rational self-sufficiency.

There is no speech saying that Hamlet feels thus because he feels alienated from the protestant deity; probably that could have been said on a stage only by a manifest villain. But as members of an audience try to make sense of events in the play and Hamlet's responses to them, it may appear that the divine system revealed in the action is not as comfortable and delightful as protestants proclaimed. It makes Hamlet wonder and admire; temporarily, when he is sending Rosencrantz and Guildenstern to their deaths, it exhilarates him; but ultimately it does not command his respect. The issue in Stoicism, for Hamlet, is how the mind might free itself, for to him Denmark and the world are a prison. ☐

(Alan Sinfield, *Faultlines: Cultural Materialism and the Politics of Dissident Reading*, 1992)[24]

Although Sinfield does not outline this very clearly in his chapter on *Hamlet*, the impact of Calvinist eschatology (beliefs about the afterlife) on a formerly Catholic community, was potentially devastating, and certainly had a big impact on attitudes towards death from the sixteenth century onwards. Where Catholicism might have believed in the ability of humanity to control their own fate through the efficacy of prayer etc. Calvinist dogma insisted on the concept of predestination where God has determined the fate of everybody and man can have no effect on his own end. The standard reaction to this potentially devastating shift in official doctrine was a mild acceptance of God's benevolence. Sinfield argues that *Hamlet* may well draw an early modern audience's attention to what he calls the 'faultlines' in this system. By 'faultlines' Sinfield means moments in works of literature where it becomes possible to see divisions in society's beliefs about itself.

■ ... members of an audience watching *Hamlet* may come to feel that this [Calvinist] Christianity cannot separate itself satisfactorily from a Stoic paganism that claims no divine revelation and no divine beneficence; that insofar as the protestant deity is distinguished by an intricate determination of human affairs, it is intrusive and coercive; and that such a tyrannical deity need inspire no more than passive acquiescence.[25] □

The play's revelation of 'faultlines' in the ideological project of Calvinisn *may*, then, reveal itself as a dissatisfaction with authority in general. In contrast to the way Tennenhouse situates the play within political contexts, Sinfield does not see *Hamlet* merely reproducing the representational strategies of authority. The theatrical event, rather, works to reveal the precarious nature of *any* ideological representation.

HAROLD BLOOM

Although the mainstream of literary criticism in the later part of the twentieth century has embraced the kind of cultural relativism exemplified in the work of Barker, Belsey, Sinfield and Tennenhouse, there have been some lingering objections to its apparently counter-literary standpoint. One of the most vociferous of these reactionary voices has been the American humanist critic, Harold Bloom (born 1930). He objects to what he sees as the philistinism of a literary criticism that appears, to him, to deny the literary as effective in its own right, and to locate meaning elsewhere – in power structures, in language systems, in cultural change. Superficially though, Bloom's position on *Hamlet* may seem to coincide with some of the work of the cultural materialists. He, like them, sees Hamlet's subjectivity, his apparent interiority, as new and as a fictional creation. He even goes further, insisting that Western concepts of the individual originate in Shakespeare's work and in the character of Hamlet in particular, that Shakespeare 'invented the human'. So far, it might be said that he would have much to agree with in the work of Barker and Belsey. However, the difference is that even though he sees subjectivity as a literary creation, he also regards it as a kind of discovery of something that pre-existed Hamlet and Shakespeare. As a humanist, Bloom places the human experience of individuation at the heart of his criticism and sees the investigation of the social and cultural construction of individuality as, therefore, necessarily wrong-headed. Man had an inner life; Shakespeare discovered this in writing *Hamlet*; *our* inner life is, therefore, structured like Hamlet's. Allied to this, in Bloom's sometimes confusing account of the play, is his theory about the origins of *Hamlet* as we have it. He argues that Shakespeare, in writing the *Hamlet* play that we have today, was revising a much earlier attempt at writing a play based on the same story. It is by way of Shakespeare's own revisionary mode, as well as that of his hero, Hamlet, that the 'human' is invented.

■ Hamlet appears too immense a consciousness for *Hamlet*, a revenge tragedy does not afford the scope for the leading Western representation of an intellectual. But *Hamlet* is scarcely the revenge tragedy that it only pretends to be. It is theater of the world, like *The Divine Comedy* [(date uncertain) by Dante Alighieri (1265–1321)] or *Paradise Lost* [(1667), by John Milton (1608–74)] or *Faust* [(1808–32), by Goethe], or *Ulysses* [(1922), by James Joyce (1882–1941)] , or *In Search of Lost Time* [*A la recherche du temps perdu* (1913–27), by Marcel Proust (1871–1922)]. Shakespeare's previous tragedies only partly foreshadow it, and his later works, though they echo it, are very different from *Hamlet*, in spirit and in tonality. No other single character in the plays, not even Falstaff or Cleopatra, matches Hamlet's infinite reverberations.[26]

We hardly can think of ourselves as separate selves without thinking about Hamlet, whether or not we are aware that we are recalling him. His is not primarily a world of social alienation, or of the absence (or presence) of God. Rather, his world is the growing inner self, which he sometimes attempts to reject, but which nevertheless he celebrates almost continuously, though implicitly. His difference from his legatees, ourselves, is scarcely historical, because here too he is out ahead of us, always about to be. Tentativeness is the peculiar mark of his endlessly burgeoning consciousness; if he cannot know himself, wholly, that is because he is a breaking wave of sensibility, of thought and feeling pulsating onward.[27] □

This is not wholly dissimilar to the ways in which Belsey and Barker see the character, Hamlet, although Bloom would undoubtedly deny the connection. Here, however, the resemblance stops. Although Bloom agrees that Hamlet is a modern individual in the making, he does not see that individuality as something that is wholly constructed, wholly material, but rather he regards humanity as somehow transcendent.

■ When we attend a performance of *Hamlet*, or read the play for our-selves, it does not take us long to discover that the prince transcends his play. Transcendence is a difficult notion for most of us, particularly when it refers to a wholly secular context, such as Shakespearean drama. Something in and of Hamlet strikes us as demanding (and providing) evidence from some sphere beyond the scope of our senses. Hamlet's desires, his ideals or aspirations, are almost absurdly out of joint with the rancid atmosphere of Elsinore. 'Shuffle', to Hamlet, is a verb for thrusting off 'this mortal coil', where 'coil' means 'noise' or 'tumult'. [You might want to compare this with Avi Erlich's discussion of the word 'coil' in chap-ter three of this Guide.] 'Shuffling', for Claudius is a verb for mortal trick-ery; 'with a little shuffling', he tells Laertes, you can switch blades and destroy Hamlet. 'There is not shuffling' there, Claudius yearningly says of a heaven in which he neither believes nor disbelieves. Claudius, the shuffler, is hardly Hamlet's 'mighty opposite', as Hamlet calls him; the wretched usurper is hopelessly outclassed by is nephew.[28] □

For Bloom, Hamlet hints at a transcendence that is denied both implicitly and explicitly in the materialist criticisms of the later twentieth century. Where they offer political, cultural and historical explanations for the emergence of the Western subject, Bloom offers an explanation of how Shakespeare discovered this development for us, in the process granting Hamlet the status of a kind of fictional and secular Messiah. His discussion centres on an assertion that it was Shakespeare himself who provided the original version of the play, of which the extant *Hamlet* is a revision. For Bloom, Shakespeare's revisionary process, in which he seems dissatisfied with a putative early attempt at a straightforward revenge tragedy, is linked to the character Hamlet's own revisionary processes.

■ Revisionism, in *Hamlet*, can be viewed very differently if Shakespeare is revising not the mythical play, Kyd's *Hamlet* [alluding to the theory that Kyd wrote an earlier version of Hamlet, of which the text under discussion is an adaptation.], but Shakespeare's own earlier *Hamlet*. Self-revision is Hamlet's mode; was it imposed upon him by Shakespeare's highly self-conscious confrontation with his own botched beginnings as a tragic dramatist?[29]

The inner drama of *Hamlet* is revisionary: Shakespeare returns to what was beyond his initial powers, and grants himself a protagonist who, by Act 5, has a relation to the Hamlet of Act 1 that is an exact parallel to the play-wright's relation to the *Ur-Hamlet* [the supposed original of *Hamlet*]. For Hamlet, revisioning the self replaces the project of revenge. The only valid revenge in this play is what [Friedrich] Nietzsche (1844–1900), theorist of revision, called the will's revenge against time, and against time's 'It was.' 'Thus I willed it,' Shakespeare is able to imply, even as *Hamlet* becomes an implicit model for Nietzsche's *Towards a Genealogy of Morals* (1887).

Nietzsche's most Shakespearean realization is pure Hamlet: we can find words only for what already is dead in our hearts, so that necessarily there is a kind of contempt in every act of speaking. The rest is silence; speech is agitation, betrayal, restlessness, torment of self and of others. Shakespeare, with *Hamlet*, arrives at an impasse still operative in the high comedy of *Twelfth Night*, where Hamlet's inheritor is Feste.

There is no 'real' Hamlet as there is no 'real' Shakespeare: the character, like the writer, is a reflecting pool, a spacious mirror in which we must needs see ourselves. Permit this dramatist a concourse of contraries, and he will show us everybody and nobody, all at once. We have no choice but to permit Shakespeare, and his Hamlet, everything, because neither has a rival. □

(Harold Bloom, *Shakespeare: The Invention of the Human*, 1999)[30]

As Shakespeare rejects the idea of a straightforward revenge drama, with a straightforward revenge hero, so Hamlet revises his attitude towards his task. In these questioning revisions, both Shakespeare and Hamlet together forge an interior space that we are all to inhabit.

■ I suspect that Shakespeare wrote in response not only to [Christopher] Marlowe (1564–93) and Kyd, but also to his own sympathy for his first Hamlet, a presumably wily avenger. Part of the definitive Hamlet's mystery is why the audience and readership, rather like the common people of Denmark in the play, should love him. Until Act 5, Hamlet loves his dead father (or rather, his image) but does not persuade us that he loves (or ever loved) anyone else. The prince has no remorse for his manslaughter of Polonius, or for his vicious badgering of Ophelia into madness and suicide, or for his gratuitous dispatch of Rosencrantz and Guildenstern to their undeserved deaths. We do not believe Hamlet when he blusters to Laertes that he loved Ophelia, since the charismatic nature seems to exclude remorse, except for what has not yet been done. The skull of poor Yorick evokes not grief, but disgust, and the son's farewell to the dead mother is the heartless 'Wretched Queen, adieu'. There is the outsize tribute to the faithful and loving Horatio, but it is subverted when Hamlet angrily restrains his grieving follower from suicide, not out of affection but so as to assign him the task of telling the prince's story, lest Hamlet bear forever a wounded name. There is indeed a considerable 'case against Hamlet', urged most recently by Alistair Fowler, but even if Hamlet is a hero-villain, he remains the Western hero of consciousness.

[Bloom is referring to Alistair Fowler's article, 'The Case Against Hamlet' from the *Times Literary Supplement* (22 December 1995)]

The internalisation of the self is one of Shakespeare's greatest inventions, particularly because it came before anyone else was ready for it. There is a growing inner self in Protestantism, but nothing in Luther prepares us for Hamlet's mystery; his real interiority will abide: 'But I have that within which passes show.' Perhaps learning from his first *Hamlet*, Shakespeare never directly dramatizes Hamlet's quintessence. Instead, we are given the seven extraordinary soliloquies, which are anything but hackneyed; they are merely badly directed, badly played, badly read. The greatest, the 'To be or not to be' monologue, so embarrassed director and actor in the most recent *Hamlet* I've attended, Ralph Fiennes's travesty, that Fiennes mumbled much of it offstage and came on only to mouth the rest of it as quickly as possible. Nevertheless, this soliloquy is the center of Hamlet, at once everything and nothing, a fullness and an emptiness playing off against each other. It is the foundation for nearly everything he will say in Act 5, and can be called his death-speech-in-advance, the pro-lepsis [anticipation] of his transcendence. □

(Harold Bloom, *Shakespeare: The Invention of the Human*, 1999)[31]

When this transcendence is indicated in an interiority, Bloom insists not on its being culturally determined, but rather on its social, cultural and moral necessity if the categories of 'literature' and 'human' are to mean anything at all. 'Life must be true to Shakespeare if personality is to have value, or is to *be* value.'[32]

RONALD KNOWLES

In his essay, '*Hamlet* and Counter-Humanism' Ronald Knowles picks up on and develops what he sees, not only as a central concern in the criticism that has been dedicated to *Hamlet*, but also a chief concern in the historiography of the Renaissance more generally. He takes it upon himself to investigate the cultural, and specifically the written, origins of Hamlet's apparent modern subjectivity.

■ In the study of the development of Western culture the question of sub-jectivity is a much debated issue which is often directed to the Renaissance in general, and to *Hamlet* in particular.[33] □

What Knowles does is to situate, perhaps more precisely than the cultural materialist critics of the 1980s, the cultural contexts of the birth of an interior subjectivity in *Hamlet*. However, the specific aspect of this development which he talks about is limited to the intellectual inheri-tance that both Shakespeare and *Hamlet* draw upon. Nevertheless, his account does mark an attempt at a detailed explanation of why it is at this moment in cultural history that we begin to see something like a modern subjectivity appear. He does this by looking at the play as part of the movement of European humanism. *Hamlet*, for Knowles, both draws on, and resists, the optimism of Renaissance humanism. In the conventions of Renaissance humanism, Knowles argues, human sub-jectivity was understood within the conventions of rhetoric. Hamlet's melancholy, he explains, is the result of his alienation within that system. He is caught within the conventions of rhetorical expression, but is dissatisfied with them, feeling that they are inadequate to his discovery of an interior subjectivity.

■ [on 5.1.191 ff: the Yorick speech and the meditation on Alexander's posthumous progress]:Hamlet's cast of mind here gives expression to an individually felt pessimism, but the personal experience that gives rise to this is to some extent depersonalised by the external public modality of logic and rhetoric working through a commonplace. [i.e. even though Hamlet is seen to be personally motivated in his speech, he is using language which is part of a widespread rhetorical system and even a little hackneyed.] The argument presented by Hamlet is part of the pessimism that culminates at this point in the play, a pessimism influenced by the philosophical scepticism of what Hiram Haydn called the sixteenth-century 'counter-Renaissance', which severely challenged the optimism of Renaissance humanism. [The reference is to Hiram Haydn, *The Counter-Renaissance*, New York: Harcourt, Brace and World, 1950.] At one point Hamlet specifically parallels the two, echoing a cultural context that needs re-examining in the light of modern scholarship. Hamlet's pessimism in part derives from his discovery of subjectivity. Renaissance ontology [ideas about the nature of being] is closely linked to the philosophy of rhetoric whereby something like grief is understood in a specific conventionalised way, which Hamlet reacts against but ultimately has to capitulate to, to evade the pain of his alienation. Hamlet's tragedy becomes the site of a cultural struggle between the Western tradition of Stoic rationalism and an affective individualism. As Hamlet traces the dust of Alexander, so we may trace these elements in the play, beginning indeed with that 'dust'.[34] □

Knowles, then, sees Hamlet as reacting against the conventions of his time, and yet unable to escape them. This is not so far removed from the versions of Hamlet given us by Barker and Belsey, but what Knowles provides is a specific intellectual context for their generalised analyses.

■ For Hamlet man is the 'quintessence of dust' (2.2.308), and the slain body of Polonius is 'compounded ... with dust whereto 'tis kin' (4.2.5). According to the queen, Hamlet had sought 'with ... vailed lids' his 'noble father in the dust' (1.2.70–1). This last image is important since it suggests the reversal of a commonplace of Renaissance humanism, that of *homo erectus* [upright man]. As will be shown, Renaissance celebrations of man took up the Patristic echo of this biblical theme of man's uniqueness in creation, for he was the only one of God's creatures to be created erect in order to worship the heavens, the source of his origin and end. Thomas Wilson in his *The Rule of Reason* (1551) included this as an example of the predicable *proprium* or property of man, 'To go upright is proper to a man, and only to a man, and to none other living creature' (sig. C1r) [some old books do not contain page numbers and so are identified with what are called signature numbers]. Hamlet's eyes and mind are fixed on earth, death and bodily corruption. Earlier, Hamlet's sardonically chosen diction had anticipated this: 'What should such fellows as I do crawling between earth and heaven?' (3.1.128–9). 'Crawling' that is, like one of the brute creation on all fours. This conscious rejection of Renaissance humanism had been systematically worked through earlier before Rosencrantz and Guildenstern: the passage needs to be quoted in full:

... this goodly frame the earth seems to me a sterile promontory, this most excellent canopy the air, look you, this brave o'erhanging firmament, this majestical roof fretted with golden fire, why, it appeareth to me but a foul and pestilent congregation of vapours. What piece of work is a man, how noble in reason, how infinite in faculties, in form and moving how express and admirable, in action how like an angel, in apprehension how like a god: the beauty of the world, the paragon of animals – and yet, to me, what is this quintessence of dust? (2.2.298–308)

The complementary parallelism of macrocosm and microcosm is turned into the antithesis of optimism and pessimism, humanism and scepticism. The fact of the speech itself is the first evidence that man is something more than a mere 'quintessence of dust', yet Hamlet is removed from the irony since the speech is a kind of mock-philosophical exercise worked up by the intellectual student from Wittenberg, seemingly to entertain Rosencrantz and Guildenstern who are, in fact, amused. Yet the similarity of this language to that used on other occasions implies that Hamlet means every word. Hamlet knows that the philosophical impersonation will amuse his auditors while at the same time this guise actually reveals what he thinks to the audience of the play. □

(Ronald Knowles, '*Hamlet* and Counter Humanism', 1999)[35]

Knowles situates the speech within a contemporary debate on the relative dignity and misery of human kind, stressing the dualism of Western culture and the way in which these two views of mankind develop alongside each other and are, to an extent, mutually dependant.

■ ... it can be seen that Hamlet's speech derives from someone who has read both sides of the debate, abstracted quintessential elements from each, and starkly juxtaposed one against the other in an alternating litany of pessimism.[36] □

This contextualisation also provides us with a more properly historicised background to the sense of isolation that critics have been discovering in Hamlet since the late eighteenth century; it is because of his distance from socialised forms of language. Knowles calls this an 'alienated subjectivity' and, though he gives it fairly conventional origins – 'brought about by grief and sexual loathing' – he succeeds in tying this alienation into the language of the play, and its particular rhetorical lines of attack.

■ Formal rhetoric and its affiliated modes were thought to equip the individual with ample resources for public discourse. Rhetoric provided a massive compilation of human truths inherited from the past. Human experience became a moral taxonomy of precepts. Given an ahistorical assumption of the universality of human nature, any individual experience was a minor reflection of the collective experience embodied, for instance, in that part of rhetoric called the commonplace. W.S. Howell speaks of a 'society that is satisfied with the traditional wisdom and knows where to find it.' [from Howell's *Logic and Rhetoric in* England (New York 1950)] But Hamlet's anguish is as far as one could possibly get from that 'satisfaction'. 'What is a man', Hamlet asks, 'If his chief good and market of his time / Be but to sleep and feed?' (4.4.33–5). The conditional question invites an automatic rebuttal in the form of the most commonplace of them all – man is a rational animal. Hamlet's mind and discourse divide around the two factors of reason and animality:

> Sure he that made us with such large discourse,
> Looking before and after, gave us not
> That capability and godlike reason
> To fust in us unus'd. Now whether it be
> Bestial oblivion, or some craven scruple
> Of thinking too precisely on th'event –
> A thought which, quarter'd, hath but one part wisdom
> And ever three parts coward – I do not know
> Why yet I live to say this thing's to do,
> Sith I have cause, and will, and strength, and means
> To do't ...
>
> [4.4.36–46]

Hamlet thinks rhetorically; 'cause', 'will', 'strength', and 'means' are topics or places or arguments for a deliberative oration on 'Should I act?' Public forms of discourse encroach upon Hamlet's subjectivity, his personal experience. In act 1, scene 2, we see Hamlet isolated by his black clothes refusing to accept the consolation of Gertrude and Claudius. He refuses to regard his subjective personal experience of grief in objectified general terms. He hears 'all that lives must die', and agrees 'Ay madam, it is common', yet will not accept this universally held 'truth' as at all meaningful for his personal experience. Conventional wisdom teaches that such anguish is an aberration. For Gertrude it is a wayward singularity, 'Why seems it so particular with thee?' (1.2.75).

Hamlet's sense of being, of alienated subjectivity brought about by grief and sexual loathing, is suspended in time from the moral imperatives of socially oriented action according to codes of honor and revenge, which is why being physically 'bounded in a nutshell' for such a mind could paradoxically be ruling 'infinite space' (2.2.254–5). Yet the 'space' of Denmark proves to be 'a prison ... A goodly one, in which there are many confines, wards and dungeons' (2.2.243, 245–6) – one of which is language. 'Words, words, words' are Hamlet's jailers, and rhetoric his prison. In the words, 'To be, or not to be' (3.1.56ff), Hamlet's dilemma finds perfect expression, yet their significance is beyond his grasp. Here, with the dramatically most introspective of perhaps all soliloquies, Hamlet's personal experience yields to the rhetorical disposition of the thesis. We have the opening exordium; 'To die, to sleep' adds a confirmatory argument; 'To sleep, perchance to dream' offers a rebuttal; 'For who would bear the whips and scorns of time' opens an extensive dilation, followed by the epilogue, 'Thus conscience does make cowards of us all ... .' The particular locution, 'To be, or not to be', forces upon us, but not Hamlet, the awareness that the question he asks, and the speech which seemingly considers it, neutralize the suffering being between words and action; like Pyrrhus, '*a neutral to his will and matter*' who '*Did nothing*' (2.2.477–8). However the antithesis reveals Hamlet's mind or being, although this and what follows in the famous soliloquy, the likeness of sleep and death, largely derives from [the *Tusculan* Disputations by Cicero (106–43BC)] by way of those sententiae or 'saws' Hamlet claims to have wiped from 'the table of [his] memory' (1.5.98). Cicero's first disputation at Tusculum was the *locus classicus* [best known or most authoritative passage on any given subject], and any educated auditor would have recognized it and the rhetorical mode of Hamlet's speech. As they would have recalled the situation of Hecuba as a recommended topic in rhetorical handbooks, and her speech as given by the Player as a good example of *copi verborum*, or copiousness of language, highly favoured for any situation (grief, lamentation, etc.) needing expressive amplifications. [...]

The social exchange of words seemingly implies the parity of public meaning – a common language reflecting the sameness of individual experience. The use of the word 'grief', for example, inevitably assumes that the word has the same meaning for different individual experiences of bereavement. This essentialist aspect of language use lends itself to logic and its syllogistic basis, but in actual existence, we cannot experience each other's experience per se [in itself]. Only Hamlet feels Hamlet's grief. To maintain his being Hamlet refuses the public language of rhetoric and adopts a counter-rhetoric; yet, as we have seen, the humanist culture which enthroned the arts of language shapes his mind. Hamlet's existential defences are scepticism, pessimism and seeming madness. □

(Ronald Knowles, '*Hamlet* and Counter Humanism', 1999)[37]

One of the particular strengths of Knowles' analysis is that it allows him to unpick the density of some of *Hamlet*'s language.

■ In refusing to resign his private grief to the public world of debased value masked by rhetoric, Hamlet refuses to communicate meaningfully, but is meaningful to himself. His understanding is so intense that he is not understood. His awareness of modes of being finds a correlative in modes of meaning. The intensity of his preoccupation with being, its origin and end, finds expression in concentrated language, particularly in the pun and the paradox. Consider the following exchange:

> *Hamlet*: For if the sun breed maggots in a dead dog, being a good kissing carrion – Have you a daughter?
>
> *Polonius*: I have, my lord.
>
> *Hamlet*: Let her not walk i' th' sun. Conception is a blessing, but as your daughter may conceive – friend, look to't.
>
> [2.2.181–6]

Editors annotate these words variously, but perhaps it would be just as well to dwell first on their difficulty, which is that their immediate obliquity renders them largely meaningless. That is, language does not communicate, at least to Polonius (and us?). Yet Hamlet appears to be in control of the situation since he baffles Polonius wilfully. And yet he cannot be said to baffle Polonius completely since Polonius thinks that he is mad anyway, and Hamlet is confirming his belief with his 'antic disposition' (1.5.180). Upon re-examination of the passage we can begin to unravel its meaning. The sun is the source of decay, yet in the form of life – the sun breeds (maggots) in what is already dead (a dog). In considering the process of fleshly corruption by lewd association of the physiological with the moral, Hamlet thinks of Ophelia ('have you a daughter?') and of human conception and birth. When he recommends 'Let her not walk i' th' sun,' he puns on the sun as a source of procreative life; the *sun* and *son*, namely Hamlet as possible procreator; and the sun as emblem of kingship. In sum, keep her out of court where the procreative act, sex, is corrupt, 'but as your daughter may conceive, friend look to't.' In this brief exchange, as with the micro-macrocosm speech and as with the 'Alexander ... dust' speech, we see Hamlet's preoccupation with the antithetical nature of existence in corruption and generation, life and death. ☐ (Ronald Knowles, '*Hamlet* and Counter Humanism', 1999)[38]

Knowles understands Hamlet's speeches as rhetorical events. This extends to his understanding of the performativity of his character. That is, like Barker and Belsey, he sees disunity in Hamlet, and that he is formed from the rags of various different kinds of rhetorical positions; his character is the by-product of a sequence of different performances. This is profoundly different from the humanist tradition, of which Bloom is a late descendant, in that there is not, necessarily, anything *behind* the rhetoric. Jonathan Goldberg's essay on *Hamlet* illustrates this still more, as will be seen. For Knowles, even the stuff of psychoanalysis' deepest indication of burgeoning individuality, a horror at parental sexuality, is one more rhetorical position amongst others.

■ Hamlet's father's death, his mother's concupiscence and hasty marriage to her husband's murderer produce a grief and loathing of such a profound degree that a sense of being created by emotion estranges him from
the previous identity of a princely role. Hamlet anticipates this in his
response to the revelations of the ghost:

> Remember thee?
> Yea, from the table of my memory
> I'll wipe all trivial fond records,
> All saws of books, all forms, all pressures past
> That youth and observation copied there,
> And thy commandment all alone shall live
> Within the book and volume of my brain,
> Unmix'd with baser matter.
>   (1.5.97–104)

Hamlet does not realise that this is impossible. He cannot replace a mind
shaped by rhetoric with unalloyed feeling. Rhetoric provided not just knowledge,
but *how* knowledge was assimilated and understood; it provided a cognitive
structure which enforced the Western censure of emotion. Consequently, in
desperation, Hamlet ponders on dissolution of mind and body: 'O that this too
too sullied flesh would melt' (1.2.129). But Hamlet's body actually undergoes a
kind of reification [a process in which an abstract idea is made more manifest
or in which a person is imagined as being transformed into an object] when we
hear, 'whilst this machine is to him' (2.2.122–3), the first recorded use of the
word in this way (*OED* 4.c). Hamlet is imprisoned by rhetoric, the enemy within.
He is self-policed by the inescapable guardians of rationalism and sin who sup-
press the radical threat of passion. His only options are loss of selfhood in real
madness or to reassume a role which travesties his truth. He hides his 'mystery' within the conventions of love's madness. Then Hamlet, the former
courtier, soldier, and scholar, seizes the opportunity to become actor-manager,
and then the philosopher roles of sceptic and stoic, until he finally capitulates
to the most evasive of all roles, the return of 'Hamlet the Dane' (5.1.251). It is
the most evasive because it completely confounds social and private, past and
present, illusion and authenticity, in its conformity with the world of public values where seeming cannot be differentiated from being. Only the audience is
fully aware of the existential disjunction between subjective being and public self-
presentation. □   (Ronald Knowles, '*Hamlet* and Counter Humanism', 1999)[39]

JONATHAN GOLDBERG

Twentieth-century accounts of *Hamlet* which discuss the play as the
birthplace of modern subjectivity tend to see character as a form of
performance. This is even the case in Knowles's account in which it is

during the performance of the play that the audience is made aware of an ironic distance between role and reality. Jonathan Goldberg has also looked at the play as being at a turning point in our understanding of what constitutes subjectivity and ideas of individuation. Goldberg's work, despite being in some ways part of the American movement of new historicism, was also influenced by the French theorist, Jacques Derrida, particularly his work on writing in *On Grammatology* (1967). In his 1988 essay, 'Hamlet's Hand' and his later book, *Writing Matter: From the Hands of the English Renaissance* (1990), Goldberg responds to Derrida's demand for a 'culture of graphology'.[40] As part of Derrida's project to resist metaphysical explanatory frameworks, and particularly what he calls 'logocentrism', the privileging of the unique voice in imposing meaning on the world, he has reversed the traditional understanding of the priority of voice over the written word. In his 'cultural graphology' Goldberg follows this project by unearthing early modern histories of 'character' where 'character' is understood as *written*, rather than as coming before writing. This project, whilst clearly linked to deconstruction, is also tied to the new historicism through its concern for the position of material practice (in this case, writing and printing) in the production of meaning in the literary text. In Goldberg's essay, he argues that Hamlet's 'subjectivity', his status as a character, is formed from precisely that – 'character' – but here understood instead as the characters of the written word.

■ *Hamlet* offers numerous instances of the literal embodiment of character, the socially scriptive formation that produces Hamlet's letter as the mark of character. Hamlet, burdened by memory, encounters a ghost, stages a play, both haunted by the memory of earlier scripts; and although the highly theatrical Senecan Ghost speaks only to him, Hamlet receives the Ghost's *words* as a scriptive command, one that re-marks his haunted memory as a locus of inscription, erasure, and reinscription:

> Remember thee?
> Yea, from the table of my memory
> I'll wipe away all trivial fond records,
> All saws of books, all forms, all pressures past
> That youth and observation copied there,
> And thy commandment all alone shall live
> Within the book and volume of my brain,
> Unmixed with baser metal.
> [1.5.97–104]

In these lines, subjectivity is a scene of writing. Hamlet proceeds to write in his copy-book what is inscribed in his brain, initiating a career continually invested in scriptive gestures. His instructions to the actors repeat the

Ghost's commands; they are to hold 'the mirror up to nature', to produce an 'image' that will give 'the very age and body of the time his form and pressure' (3.2.20–3). The actor's body – Hamlet's body – thus stands as a letter, 'form and pressure' here echoing the ghostly copy-book command: the body as the locus of inscription, to be read rather than heard, acting as dumb show, inscrutable as the private letter that assures privacy. Hamlet has no sooner written, and had produced, a script for the play within the play (scripting the oral world of theatrical performance) than the Ghost returns, now seen only by Hamlet; the Ghost has entered the performance of Hamlet's scriptive world. Yet from the start the Ghost exists within a scriptive order, and not merely that of the Senecan tragedy in which his lines are written. For when Horatio offers to vouch for the Ghost, he tells Hamlet, ' I knew your father, / These hands are not more like' (1.2.211–12). The identity of the Ghost is confirmed by the identity of the hand. This is not surprising; the Ghost exists only within similitude, appearing 'in the same figure like the king that's dead,' 'Most like', 'Mark it, Horatio' (1.1.41, 44, 43). And Horatio marks it by likening the likeness to the hand that marks.

Not surprisingly, then, when Hamlet returns to Denmark, he arrives in letters, first to Horatio (in 4.vi) and then to Claudius.

> Laertes: Know you the hand?
> King: 'Tis Hamlet's character. 'Naked'!
> And in a postscript here, he says 'alone.'
> Can you devise me?
>
> [4.vii.50–2]

That letter presents Hamlet as mere body, unclothed with social trappings, solitary, Hamlet as the private individual produced by script; the naked, solitary body is a character, a scriptive formation that Claudius literally finds baffling and opaque. 'What should this mean? ... Is it some abuse, and no such thing? ... Can you devise me?' A letter the messenger says he has from someone named Claudio (l. 40), and to which Laertes answers, 'I am lost in it, my lord' (l. 53). 'I beg leave to see your kingly eyes', the letter says (ll. 44–5); but in this letter scene, seeing is reading, and being does not go beyond the letter, copies observed, a circuit from Claudio to Claudius where all characters are lost in the letter; as Hamlet was from the first, in his 'inky cloak' (1.2.77), like Rosaline in *Love's Labours Lost*, 'Beauteous as ink ... /Fair as a text B in a copy-book' (5.2.41–2). □

(Jonathan Goldberg, 'Hamlet's Hand', 1988)[41]

The contexts in which Goldberg is placing this scriptive forming of 'character' are those of Renaissance humanist education. In the Renaissance, the ability to master different kinds of written script – italic and secretary – was of the utmost importance to those who wished to gain access to centres of power, and particularly to be of service to the

Renaissance prince or other aristocrats. Different kinds of script carried with them different social implications. The workaday hand of 'secretary' was reserved for workmanlike activities, whereas italic afforded a more elevated social standing, associated with aristocrats. However, with the expansion of humanist education, the supposedly aristocratic skill of writing was, more often than not, performed by a functionary of the prince rather than by the prince himself. The supposed sign of authenticity – the hand, the character – was, in fact, always replicable. The man, the prince, is both present in and absent from the sign that produces him in his individuality – his signature.[42]

■ At the end of the play, Hamlet, with all the urgency of the Ghost, asks Horatio if he remembers: 'You do remember all the circumstance?' 'Remember it, my lord!' (5.2.2–3), Horatio replies; and then, like Prospero with Ariel, Hamlet proceeds to recount what has been remembered. Handing the king's commission over to Horatio (5.2.26), Hamlet proceeds to the story of the substitution of the letter already enacted before our eyes:

Being thus benetted round with villainies,
Or I could make a prologue to my brains,
They had begun the play. I sat me down,
Devised a new commission, wrote it fair.
I once did hold it, as our statists do,
A baseness to write fair, and labored much
How to forget that learning, but, sir, now
It did me yeoman's service. Wilt thou know
Th' effect of what I wrote?
[5.2.29–37]

The text is already within his head, a play in progress to which he subscribes, literally: he descends to the base matter, the materiality of the letter, a social descent to the yeoman's secretarial skill, manual labor that nonetheless produces the royal word; not only are literate skills suborned, Hamlet also has to hand the royal seal (the proprietary mark of oral culture) to falsify and ratify the document. His father's seal: Hamlet has turned the Ghost's words into the script that he has written.

Horatio: How was this sealed?
Hamlet: Why, even in that was heaven ordinant.
I had my father's signet in my purse,
Which was the model of that Danish seal,
Folded the writ up in the form of th' other,
Subscribed it, gave't th' impression, placed it safely,
The changeling never known. □
[5.2.47–53][43]

Goldberg continues to discuss the implications of this idea of character in signature through an analysis of the ways in which a letter by Hamlet is presented in the second quarto and first folio texts of the play. The signature is seen as a way of producing Hamlet as an individual character, but it also reveals that character cannot be individuated when letters can, in fact, be reproduced.

■ Hamlet's hand is inserted within social practices; the mark of 'character' becomes a characteristic mark (that is, a mark of class and social standing); it becomes the hand of power precisely because the hand is not individualized; the fair hand is legible, but its very legibility means that it cannot be owned as a mark of individuality. It represents transcendent authority and appears to be de-corporealized, moving in language but not through an individual's body. The hand replaces the seal as a mark of property and ownership. But the seal, the mark preferred by cultures that conduct their business orally, was, as Michael Clanchy has argued, a prototype for the disowned mark, since it could be used by anyone; for Clanchy, moveable type takes its cue from the seal [referring to Michael Clanchy, *From Memory to Written Record: England 1066–1307* (Camb., Mass.: Harvard University Press, 1979)].

And the handwritten signature, suspected from the first as capable of forgery, is no more secure a mark of ownership or of propriety. Hamlet's skilled hand insures the force of the document he inscribes; but it does not reveal the writer. The document written fair has the anonymity and inevitability of social practice. Hamlet writes a royal commission. Suborning his father's seal, making himself the image of Claudius, Hamlet achieves, momentarily, the form of power within the scriptive world which replaces (which has always already replaced) the oral in the course of the play. Claudius, recall, murders the old king by pouring poison in his ear. Hamlet dies by the hand – the poisoned tip of a sword. In the very scene in which Laertes witnesses the letter that Hamlet sends to Claudius, Claudius bears witness to Laertes's hand by recalling the praise of the master swordsman Lamord. Margaret Ferguson [in '*Hamlet*: Letter and Spirits', G. Hartmann and P. Parker (eds) *Shakespeare and the Question of Theory* (New York: Methuen, 1985)] has reminded us that the name is a pun on the order of death – and language – in which Hamlet moves to be incorpsed. Hamlet moves to occupy 'the place of the king as the play defines it', Ferguson writes, with some disapproval, 'a *role* associated ... with the power to kill'. That role, Hamlet's embodiment, we would add, rehearses the scriptive order; it also might be attached to the 'desp'rate hand' (5.1.207) of Ophelia that took her own life, grasping 'dead men's fingers' (4.vii.170).

Vives's writing master turns to the lads, having impressed upon them their need to write fair. 'Did you come here properly armed for your task?' he asks, and the young man first takes him literally and needs to be disabused: 'Come now! I'm not talking about the bloodthirsty arms of the soldier but those of the writer, which we need now. Have you your pencase and quills?' [quoted in A.J. Osley (ed.), *Scribes and Sources* (Boston: David R. Gordine, 1980), p. 41]. The violence of the letter: 'I will speak daggers to her, but use none', Hamlet says, as he proceeds to his mother's closet. (3.2.381). 'These words like daggers enter in mine ears' (3.4. 96), she testifies. The hand, as Claudius remarks, is 'instrumental to the mouth' (1.2.48), an instrumentality that produces the mouth as well as the hand within the scriptive order. Claudius sends dispatches throughout the play; and Hamlet writes the dead character, folding Rosencrantz and Guildenstern, Claudius and Laertes in his path. This is the writer's path: for 'many wearing rapiers are afraid of goosequills' (2.2.336). The pen, mightier than the sword, I a mortal instrument. 'The treacherous instrument is in thy hand' (5.2.305).

For the pen produces character, the letter and the person, and the etymology of character reveals the violence of this engendering. In Greek, to character means to brand or sharpen, and a character is as much the instrument that engraves or brands. Hamlet's place in the scriptive order, in the economy of death, is marked in his final utterances. Twice he says the impossible sentence upon which, as Derrida insists, writing rests. Hamlet says twice, 'I am dead' (5.2.322, 327).

Hamlet's character is – literally – the character. And so, we might turn to the letter (in the second-quarto and Folio texts of the play) that marks Hamlet's return to Denmark and the mark that authenticates the character *as character*. How is the letter to Horatio signed? In the second quarto (1604/5), the final line of the letter is printed in italics. It reads: '*So that thou knowest thine Hamlet*' (L3r). In the Folio (1623), the letter closes printing '*He that thou knowest thine*', in italics, with the name, 'Hamlet' printed in Roman [...]. Thus in the quarto text Hamlet's signature forms part of the closing line of the letter – the *only* line of the letter printed in italic type. The italic signature, *Hamlet*, is not produced simply as part of the line, for italic type is also used in the letter for the names *Horatio*, *Rosencrans*, *Guyldensterne*, and *England*. Italics may mark Hamlet's signature, but not in a typeface that distinguishes it from other proper names or from the hand that has produced the formula of subscription. Moreover, the rest of the letter is printed in the same typeface as the rest of the play. Nothing in the typography distinguishes it as Hamlet's writing.

In the Folio, on the other hand, Hamlet's signature is printed in the same type as the rest of the text of the play and the same type as the names 'Horatio', 'Rosincrance', and 'Guildensterne' that appear in the letter; save for them the entire body of the letter as well as the subscription is in italics. Do the italics therefore mark the letter as *not* part of the play, or not part of the script produced by the hand that wrote the rest of the text?

In posing these typographic questions of character, I mean to situate Hamlet's hand in the history of handwriting and printing, remembering, for instance, that increasingly in the sixteenth century, and invariably by the close of the period, English royalty wrote their private correspondence in an italic hand, but also that others, aspiring to this mark of privilege, signed their letters in italic, although the rest of their letter (whether written by themselves or by a secretary) usually remained in secretarial hand. Recalling, too, that manuscripts of Elizabethan plays are usually written in secretary hand – except for the names of characters, stage directions, and the like, which are written in italic. Italic serves to mark what is not part of the script, and in some scripts such matters are written in Latin, observing the propriety of script to text. The playscript thus marks the extratextual in the same way that the private letter marks the proper name; its propriety therefore lies in being written in a foreign hand that serves as a mark of class (or class aspiration). The signature marks *différance* [In Derrida's work, the word 'différance', an invented word in French, can also be translated into English as either 'difference' or 'deferral'. This is used as an indication of the play of meaning within all writing. That is, that all meaning is produced by the difference between linguistic signs rather than by reference to anything that is outside of language and that, as a result of this, all meaning is always deferred, located somewhere else.] I am assuming that the italic type used in the Folio and quarto texts of Hamlet's letter to Horatio corresponds to an italic hand, and I depend too on the fact that, whether in quarto or Folio (and not only in the case of *Hamlet*), the typefaces in letters and of proper names within them almost always play off the multiple scripts that characterize the handwritten letter; the letter – whether as a printed letter or as a printed playscript – marks Hamlet's name and signature as a textual property. In which case, it is perhaps worth returning to the letter to Claudius with which I began; in the Folio version of the letter, Hamlet's signature appears in the ordinary typeface of the rest of the play; the quarto letter, printed in the same type, has no signature at all. 'Hamlet's character' is produced without the proper name.

What *can* a signature authenticate, especially in a culture that does not seem to place any particular value on the spelling of the proper name or on the hand in which it is written? A pedagogue complains: 'our English proper names are written as it pleaseth the painter', he writes [quoting from David Cressy's *Literacy and the Social Order* (Cambridge: Cambridge University Press, 1980), p. 25]; the proper name might be the prime example of what Claudius calls the 'painted word\' (3.1.53). For all writing exists within the sphere of the visible, indeed defines that sphere and with it the sociality of sight. This is the counterfeit order in which the hand participates. Claudius notes it when he reflects upon his 'cursed hand', 'Offense's gilded hand' (3.3.43, 58). As emphatic as Hamlet's insistence on the pictures of his brothers is the Ghost's remorse at his dispatch 'by a brother's hand' (1.5.74). The brother's name we might suspect to be Cain, on whose brow, or so a writing master suggests, God wrote the first inscription [referring to David Browne, *The New Invention, Intituled Caligraphia* (St. Andrews: Edward Raban, 1622)], the mark that descends as the benefit of clergy; the hand that writes is mystified in that social order where literacy would seem to insure immortality, the order in which the individual is a mark like the signature. Is this why Claudius has a name that can only be read, but which no one in the play ever speaks? Guaranteeing the social order are two kings; Hamlet has the name of one, and the other withholds his name, or has it withheld, or has it in his hand. □

(Jonathan Goldberg, 'Hamlet's Hand', 1988)[44]

Goldberg's insistence on the constructed nature of individual 'character' is audaciously different from the main thrust of the readings of *Hamlet* that we have seen prior to the later twentieth century which have sought, rather, to produce a Hamlet who is the most fully realised 'individual' in literature. His particular brand of historicism inflected with deconstruction enables a thorough analysis of the ways in which such individuality is both produced and undermined by the same token, in the same signature.

As has been seen in this chapter, much of the recent work on Shakespeare's plays, and *Hamlet*, has concerned itself with the historical contexts of the writing. One of the ways that this has been done is through a discussion of the historical origins of character, or of the idea of what it means to be a modern man, as was the case in Barker, Belsey, Knowles, Bloom and Goldberg. Another route, illustrated here by the work of Sinfield and Tennenhouse, has been to uncover the more overt political contexts of a play that does, after all, begin and end with the murder of a head of state – old Hamlet and Claudius. The next chapter will look at ways in which this historicising project has been picked up on by those critics more interested in the gender implications of the play's apparent position within a history of Western subjectivity. We have already seen how, in the chapter on psychoanalysis, Janet Adelman sought to supplement previous psychoanalytic accounts of the play with an analysis more attuned to the women in the cast. The writers in the next chapter seek both to refute older gender-biased work and to add to the ways in which the play might be contextualised by situating it within histories of gender relations.

CHAPTER SIX

Contemporary Interpretations: Feminism

Another way in which the subjectivity in *Hamlet* has been analysed is through looking at gender differences in the play. From the neo-classical concern with the state of Ophelia's breath through to the family dramas of psychoanalysis, *Hamlet* has been a play in which the relationship of the male protagonist to the female characters has been fore-grounded. In *The Subject of Tragedy*, one of Catherine Belsey's aims was to reveal the constructedness of the term, 'man' through a juxtaposition with 'woman', and thus to reveal the potential gender bias of any discussion of subjectivity. We have already, in the chapter on psychoanalytic readings of the play, looked at a specifically feminist analysis of *Hamlet*. Janet Adelman refuted and rewrote the masculinist bias of traditional psychoanalytic approaches to the play by revaluing the position of the mother within the play and within Hamlet's development. In her now famous essay, '*Hamlet* – the Mona Lisa of Literature' (1986), Jacqueline Rose attempts to do much the same thing – providing her own reading of the play at the same time as revising previous approaches that she sees as blind to the questions of gender that they, nevertheless, introduce.

JACQUELINE ROSE

Although Rose's immediate target is, as mentioned in Chapter 4, T.S. Eliot, she, too, is responding to Ernest Jones and the conventional psychoanalytic approach to the play. She argues against the weight placed in these kinds of account of *Hamlet* on Gertrude's shoulders in particular, and on 'femininity' in general. She suggests that at the heart of Eliot's difficulties with what he perceives as the play's *artistic* failure is a problem with femininity. This, she claims, can be seen in his choice of the 'Mona Lisa' as an emblem for the play.

■ By choosing an image of a woman to embody the inexpressible and inscrutable content which he identified in Shakespeare's play, Eliot ties the enigma of femininity to the problem of interpretation itself.[1]

Hamlet poses a problem for Eliot ... at the level of both matter and form. Femininity is the image of that problem; it seems in fact to be the only image through which the problem can be conceptualised or thought. The principal danger – femininity – thus becomes the focus for a partly theorised recognition of the psychic and literary disintegration which can erupt at any moment into literary form.[2] ☐

Rose attempts in this essay to place femininity at the heart of aesthetic concerns related to *Hamlet*. If the play is in some ways viewed as excessive by its male critics, the name that they give for that excess, she insists, is 'woman'. Rose outlines these concerns in an essay from the previous year which links *Hamlet* with Shakespeare's 'problem' comedy, *Measure for Measure* (1604), a play whose themes centre on questions of sexual morality.

■ In both of these plays, the central woman character finds herself accused – Gertrude in *Hamlet* of too much sexuality, Isabella in *Measure for Measure* of not enough. In both cases, the same notion of excess or deficiency has appeared in the critical commentaries on the plays. *Hamlet* and *Measure for Measure* have each been described as aesthetic failures which ask too much of – or offer too little to – the act of interpretation itself. By focusing on the overlap of these two accusations, of the woman and of the play, we might be able to see how the question of aesthetic form and the question of sexuality are implicated in each other.[3] ☐

The problem that Rose has with this connection between sexuality and aesthetics is not that it is there in the play, but that critics like Eliot merely repeat the connection without asking why it is there in the first place.

■ What requires explanation, therefore, is not that Gertrude is an inadequate object for the emotions generated in the play, but the fact that she is expected to support them. Hamlet's horror at Gertrude (like the horror Eliot sees behind the play) makes her a focus for a set of ills which the drama shows as exceeding the woman *at the same time* as it makes of her their cause. It has often been pointed out that Hamlet's despondency seems to centre more on his mother's remarriage than it does on his father's death even after the revelation of his uncle's crime. Eliot does suggest that it is the nature of the sentiments dealt with in *Hamlet* – a son's feelings towards a guilty mother – that they are unmanageable by art. But he does not ask why it is, in the play as in his own commentary, that the woman bears the chief burden of the guilt.[4] ☐

Towards the end of this essay, Rose begins to suggest that the reason that criticism such as Eliot's has placed an unfair burden on the women in these plays is because of its need to maintain balance in artistic form. When it sees a work of art that resists interpretation, such as she suggests *Hamlet* to be, the blame for that resistance is placed squarely at the feet of femininity. Whilst this might be useful as a critique of literary criticism, there are other ways in which the questions posed by Rose can be answered. More recent materialist feminist criticism of Shakespeare has concentrated on the material conditions, pertaining to gender, sexuality and family life, that have produced the kinds of aesthetic problems identified in the Rose essays. Again, much of this has not looked at *Hamlet*, concentrating instead on more obviously fruitful areas of inquiry such as the comedies. However, in her chapter on *Hamlet* in the book, *Shakespeare and the Loss of Eden* (2001), Catherine Belsey looks at the uses made of the stories of the first family, Adam, Eve, Cain and Abel in order to situate the play's family relationships within a wider context of ideas about the family that were current in the late sixteenth century. On the other hand, Patricia Parker's essay on *Hamlet* and *Othello* concentrates on much smaller details in order to make connections between text and context, linking the material practices that underpin the position of women in *Hamlet* to the use of language in the play through close examination of the words in the play that deal with ideas relating to spying and secrecy.

PATRICIA PARKER

In '*Othello* and *Hamlet*: Dilation, Spying and the "Secret Place" of Woman', an essay from 1993, Parker employs a technique that has she has developed over the years in her penetrating interpretations of Shakespeare's social contexts through focussing on the resonances of particular words. She describes her project as a consideration of 'the implications of reading both Shakespeare and the texts of early modern culture with an awareness of the historical resonance of their terms, not just for the purposes of local interpretation but as a way of perceiving links between the plays and larger contemporary discursive networks'.[5] She explores the links between literary texts and their cultural, political and social contexts by picking up on key words that seem to provide a way into the structures of those contexts in the early modern period.

■ To approach a culture as important to and yet distant from us as that now termed the 'early modern' must be to take its own complexly developing language seriously. To read with care in this sense is not simply to add to the resources of cultural studies or cultural 'poetics' those of a cultural semantics or philology, but to begin to explore the network of terms that shaped politics, institutions, and laws, as well as discourses of the body and all that we have subsequently come to think of as 'literature'.[6] □

Parker begins the essay by outlining the various uses of the word 'dilation' in early modern texts, to refer not only to its current senses of the opening of bodily orifices or other kinds of enlargements, or to delays, but also to a kind of legal representation, taking Samuel Johnson's reading of *Othello*'s 'close dilations' from the Folio text of 3.3.123 as 'close delations', 'delations' meaning 'secret accusations'. Parker argues that the two words, 'dilation' and 'delation' are not only interchangeable in the early modern period in terms of spelling, but that their meanings are frequently linked when 'that which accuses' is also 'that which opens and amplifies'.[7] Although neither is a word used directly in *Hamlet*, the link is there with the senses employed in *Othello*, through *Hamlet*'s obsession with spying into things, with accusation and with revelation. As you will see, one of the virtues, but also one of the difficulties, of Parker's approach is her extensive use of punning as a means to access networks of meaning in the early modern texts she deals with – a virtue because it attends with seriousness to the language games that are a frequent part of early modern drama, but difficult because it means that she darts rapidly between different scenes and different texts in order to illustrate the semantic fields to which the puns relate.

■ Spying is everywhere in *Hamlet*, adding to the sense of claustrophobia that pervades the world of the play (and may be one of the resonances in the name of Claudius) and giving to it the sense at its end in the advent of Fortinbras, of the arrival on stage of something like the beginnings of a modern state. Claudius sends Polonius, and then Rosencrantz and Guildenstern, to 'pluck out the heart' of Hamlet's 'mystery', to spy into the causes of his 'antic disposition'. Polonius sends Reynaldo to spy on Laertes in Paris and extract a narrative from acquaintances in order to 'make inquire' (2.1.4) into the private life of his own son. He demands to know of his daughter what was 'between' her and Hamlet, reporting the results of this intelligence dutifully to the King and Queen ('This in obedience hath my daughter *shown* me, / And more above, hath his solicitings, / as they fell out by time, by means, and place, / All given to mine *ear*' 2.2.125–8). The play on *show* and *tell*, eye and ear, exploited in the Mousetrap Scene, echoes throughout in these dual modalities of 'informing'. Spying with the eye and feretting out a narrative are combined within the Closet Scene, where Polonius, come as a spy, hides behind the arras in order to 'hear' the 'process' (in early modern English, 'narrative') of what transpires. And the play ends by promising, beyond its own theatrical spectacle, the narrative of Horatio/*oratio* that is to report Hamlet's story faithfully to those who could not see or ocularly witness it.

'How all occasions do *inform* against me', laments Hamlet, using 'inform' in the sense of impeach or accuse, in a soliloquy (4.4.32–66) not long after the scene of players who 'tell all'. 'Who is't that can *inform* me?' asks Marcellus in the opening scene, opening the way to Horatio's exposition of a prior offstage history, the 'source of this our watch, and the chief head / Of this post-haste and romage in the land' (1.1.79–107). So much of the play is in the 'interrogative' mode – to invoke, but in a politically more resonant context, the familiar phrase of Maynard Mack. [Parker is referring to Maynard Mack's article, 'The World of Hamlet' from *The Yale Review* (1952)] The impulse that stands behind such questioning, as Hamlet's address to the Ghost ('Say *why* is this? wherefore? what should we do?') frequently verges on what elsewhere in Shakespeare are called 'interrogatories', forms of interrogation in a more aggressive sense, determination to bring a 'mystery' to light that involves the attempt to extract information or a narrative, to get a 'questionable shape' to 'speak' (1.4.43–4). Once again, the emphasis on questioning, espial, and informing crosses with an epistemological hunger to 'see' and 'know': the play is filled not just with spies but with what Polonius expresses as the desire to 'find / Where truth is hid, though it were hid indeed / Within the centre' (2.2.157–9), a hunger to ferret out mysteries shared, as with *Othello*, by the whole history of its criticism.

The sense of opening something of his to a 'show' that will 'tell all' links the play on 'show' and 'tell' around the Dumb Show with the iteration throughout *Hamlet* of the sense that secrets, or the hid, will finally out – from Hamlet's 'Foul deeds will rise, / Though all the earth o'erwhelm them, to men's eyes' (1.2.256–7), after Horatio tells him of the appearance of the Ghost, to his description of the 'purpose' of players and the play meant to 'catch the conscience of the King' (2.2.605):

> I have heard
> That guilty creatures sitting at a play
> Have, by the very cunning of the scene
> Been struck so to the soul, that presently
> They have proclaim'd their malefactions.
> For murder, though it have no tongue, will speak
> With most miraculous organ.
>
> [2.2.584–90]

The 'show' presented by players Hamlet predicts, when the 'Prologue' appears, 'cannot keep counsel' but will 'tell all' – publishing secrets to both onstage and offstage audiences – is one that is to bring out into the open this 'occulted guilt'. The collocation of the two – bringing to light a hidden guilt and a 'prologue' that indicates in brief what the 'show' will present 'at large' – sounds again in the lines in which Gertrude envisions the spilling of her secret 'guilt' ('To my sick soul, as sin's true nature is, / Each toy seems *prologue* to some great amiss'; 4.5.17–18). The sense that the 'secret' or 'occulted' will come finally to light is countered, however, within the play by a powerful contrary sense of opacity, of inability to penetrate to the 'show' beyond the 'show', of mysteries that cannot be uncovered or made visible to the eye. This is the language of the Ghost's 'But that I am forbid / To tell the *secrets* of my prison-house, / I could a tale *unfold* whose lightest word / Would harrow up thy soul' (1.5.13–16), or the soliloquy 'To be or not to be' with its evocation of death as an '*undiscover'd* country, from whose bourn / No traveller returns' (3.1.78–9). The Ghost, warning that 'this eternal blazon must not be / To ears of flesh and blood' (1.5.21–2), goes on to a narrative unfolding or blazon meant to counter the 'forged process' or lying narrative with which the 'ear of Denmark' is 'rankly abused' (36–8). But the play never offers any perspicacious or unambiguous sense of a revelation beyond 'forgery'. Not even in the player's oblique 'show' of a hidden scene its commissioner seeks to bring unambiguously to light. ☐

(Patricia Parker, '*Othello* and *Hamlet*: Dilation, Spying and the "Secret Place" of Woman', 1993)[8]

The interest in spying and surveillance that Parker sees as operating within the play has recently been echoed in two film versions – the version that Kenneth Branagh directed and starred in from 1996 and Michael Almereyda's updated *Hamlet*, starring Ethan Hawke in the lead role, from 2000. Much of the action of the Branagh film takes place in the great hall of a large country house, a hall that is lined with two-way mirrors and surrounded by small antechambers with secret passages between them. Especially good use of these is made during the 'To be or not to be' speech where Hamlet speaks the soliloquy to himself in front of a two-way mirror, seeing only himself, but behind which are the King and Polonius whom we are allowed to see from the reverse side of the mirror. Some ambiguity seems to be intended as to whether Hamlet knows that he is playing himself to a gallery, or whether he is ignorant of being under surveillance. This becomes especially loaded as he points the dagger at his own reflection, causing the two eavesdroppers to move back in fear. Surveillance and spying are also a key part of the Almereyda film which is set in contemporary New York, with the state of Denmark replaced by the Denmark corporation. The film is littered with reference to contemporary modes of surveillance – CCTVs, digital cameras and others producing an atmosphere of claustrophobic paranoia.

Having established *Hamlet*'s interest in spying and accusation, secrecy and revelation, Parker then relates this to the supposed secrets of women, a concern both of the play and of its critics, making the intriguing suggestion that traditional psychoanalytic interest in this kind of unveiling of secrets is not so much an analysis *of* the play as a continuation of its modes and obsessions.

Hamlet's fascination with seeing or uncovering the secrets of his mother has been the focus of much of the psychoanalytic criticism of the play – indeed, one of the founding texts of psychoanalysis itself. The Queen is the woman who betrays her son first, as a mother, a woman whose sexuality is something secret or withheld from him, and then in the opacity and ambiguities of her complicity with Claudius, the man who killed his father and lay with his mother, though in which order is unclear. It is this that produces the sense in *Hamlet* that the play turns on the pivot of an offstage primal scene beyond the reach of vision, a scene on which gazing is forbidden, even in the deflected re-presentation of the player's 'show' – the reason, perhaps, why this *dramatic* show includes its bitter double entendres on the 'o' or 'no-thing' that is woman. This desire to open up to 'shew' involves the sense of a crime that, at least as centrally as Claudius's, involves an offstage secret the entire play comes belatedly after and then attempts recursively to bring to light. In a pun on 'lap' and *lapsus* that joins the punning on 'fault' and 'fall' linked to the play's fallen Edenic imagery – the sin of origin in a frail and 'faulty' mother – the 'o' or 'lap' of woman in the Mousetrap Scene invokes the *lapsus* or falling off of woman more generally, the sexual cleft or 'fault' which is both the 'frailty' of woman and her crime. Critics of *Hamlet* have sensed the centrality of Gertrude and Ophelia to this play even when, as characters, they are marginalized by what appears to be taking center stage – the reliability of the Ghost or Hamlet and Claudius as 'mighty opposites'. Criticism informed by psychoanalysis has focussed especially on Gertrude. I want, however, to supplement the suggestive but necessarily universalising paradigms of psychoanalysis (which follow *from* as much as they provide interpretive paradigms *for* this play), with an historically more immediate model in which woman, and the mother in particular, represents a 'matter', 'lapse', or 'fault' that comes *between*, one related to the resonances of 'secretes' in the play, as well as of the contemporary world of agents and intermediaries, go-betweens and spies.

Hamlet swears his mother, in her 'closet', to secrecy against her husband, in lines that underscore the link between a female 'matter' and a 'close' or secret matter not to be revealed or 'ravelled out'. When Claudius presses her to disclose what has transpired in that private place ('There's matter in these sighs, these profound heaves, / You must translate' [4.1.1–2]), the terms of his questioning echo Hamlet's invocation in the Mousetrap Scene of the translator or 'interpreter' (3.2.246) the figure who goes between (*inter-pres*) in a different sense. The play draws repeated attention to something that is not just 'the matter' but the 'matter *between*', as in Polonius's 'What is the matter, my lord?' in act 2 and Hamlet's responding 'Between who?' (2.2.193–4). 'Matter' here is something that comes 'between', just as the play on 'country matters' and *matter/mater/mother* before the 'closet' scene is linked with female 'matter', the matrix of both sexuality and increase.

This female 'matter' also, however, comes 'between'. Hamlet's 'Now, *mother*, what's the *matter?*' comes just after Polonius counsels this mother to remind her son that she has 'stood between / Much heat and him' (3.4.3–7). There is an even more striking juxtaposition of 'woman' and a frail or 'baser matter' that might be interposed or come between in the commission delivered by Hamlet-father to Hamlet-son:

> thy commandment all alone shall live
> Within the book and volume of my brain,
> Unmix'd with baser matter. Yes, by heaven!
> O most pernicious woman!
> [1.5.102–5]

Beyond the generalized oedipal paradigms of a mother who 'comes between' a father and son as the object of rivalry (elicited more readily from Hamlet by the shift from brother to nephew as the murderer in the Mousetrap Scene), the reference here to mixture with a 'baser matter' summons the specific historical resonance of Aristotelian notions of female 'frailty' as a 'matter' or material that 'comes between' father and son in a different sense. In a generative context, this female 'matter' is the 'woman's part' in man (Cymbeline, 2.5.20) that undermines and adulterates the perfect copying or reproduction of parthenogenesis – a lapse in what might otherwise be the replication of Hamlet-father in Hamlet-son. In the influential tradition of woman as imperfect and secondary, a lapsus or falling off from the more perfect male, she is both 'baser matter' and adulterating mixture, a frail or 'weaker vessel' whose coming between involves an aberrant and translative detour, a creature whose status is also figured by sexual parts that are secret, 'occult', or hidden from the eye. In this historically contemporary model of the female matrix, the 'matter' of woman thus 'comes between' – as lapsus, error, detour, frailty – the generative reproduction of a paternal original in a son who might be a faithful copy or representative, perfect instrument of a father's will. □

(Patricia Parker, 'Othello and Hamlet: Dilation,
Spying and the "Secret Place" of Woman', 1993)[9]

In some ways, then, Parker repeats the idea, gained from psychoanalysis, that there is a kind of Oedipal conflict played out in Hamlet, between Hamlet, his father and his mother. Instead, though, of repeating this as a narrative to be taken as a natural story of childhood psychic development, however arrested in the case of Hamlet himself, Parker outlines the ways in which these narratives position women as both weak and dangerous, both unnatural and uncultured. Contained within Parker's puns is the important story of the Fall, as important, if not more so, than the Oedipal myth for the ways in which family relationships have been represented in Western culture. The Fall is central to Catherine Belsey's explanation of why the family is represented in the way that it is in Shakespeare's plays.

CATHERINE BELSEY 2

In her book, *Shakespeare and the Loss of Eden,* Catherine Belsey analyses Shakespeare's plays in relation to the development of the family in early modern England. From a starting point of wishing to undo the apparently 'natural' notion that family values are beneficial for the individual and to promote, instead, the idea that the modern family is a cultural construction rather than a natural state of affairs, Belsey traces a cultural history of the emergence, in the early modern period, of an idea of the family as the main social unit. Her analysis of *Hamlet* forms a part of this and she relates it to the story of the first murder, popular as a subject in both domestic and high art (tapestries as well as plays, woodcuts as well as poetry) in the period.

■ *Hamlet* originates in fratricide, and invokes the parallel with the death of Abel. 'O, my offence is rank', exclaims Claudius, 'it smells to heaven; / It hath the primal eldest curse upon't - / A brother's murder' (3.3.36–8). And the motive, he himself confesses in his effort to pray, was envy, though this time of his brother's power and his wife: after all, he still possesses

> those effects for which I did the murder –
> My crown, mine own ambition, and my queen.
> [3.3.54–5]

Attempting to reconcile Hamlet to his father's death, Claudius invokes 'the first corse' (1.2.105). Ironically, the first corpse was Abel's, and his blood cried out to God for vengeance (Genesis 4.10). Sibling rivalry leads to the death of old Hamlet, and inaugurates the sequence of killings which eventually destroy Rosencrantz and Guildenstern, Polonius, Ophelia and Laertes, as well as Gertrude, Claudius, and Hamlet himself. In consequence of family violence, the play opens on to a world of death both within the family unit and beyond it.[10] □

Belsey, then, introduces ways of thinking about the family unit right into the heart of the tragedy itself. This extends not only to Hamlet's living family but also to his dead father.

■ By speaking in the name of the father, the spirit lays claim to the authority of the paternal law. Fathers, who socialize and civilize their sons, who, by inculcating the proprieties of their culture, prepare little boys to take their own place in due course, are entitled to expect obedience. Filial piety consists in proper respect for the father and his surrogates, the tutor, the teacher. When Hamlet indicates, by promising to 'sweep' to his revenge, that he has duly internalised his lesson, the Ghost comments approvingly, 'I find thee apt' (1.5.31), for all the world as if it were delivering a school report. Eager to act, the pupil, we are invited to believe, is neither lazy nor stupid. On the contrary, but then

> duller shouldst thou be than the fat weed
> That roots itself in ease on Lethe wharf,
> Wouldst thou not stir in this.
>
> [1.5.32–4]

The educational authority of the father is reinforced by the love that is due within the family, and the Ghost invokes that emotion as well as Hamlet's duty: 'If thou didst ever thy dear father love ... ' (1.5.23). To this day, family values have not lost their rhetorical power. The Ghost of Hamlet's father can count on filial and familial feeling to motivate a son who has been brought up to recognize the authority of nature in allegedly creating a relation of love between parents and children, and between siblings who share their blood. Even now, despite any number of counter-examples, we continue to suppose that genetic inheritance must produce affection as well as obligation. Claudius contravenes the law of nature in repeating the sin of Cain: fratricide is 'foul and most unnatural murder' (1.5.25); he also breaks it by seducing his brother's wife. By contrast, the Ghost wants Hamlet to act in accordance with his natural impulses, in order to prevent the criminal's continued enjoyment of the fruits of his unnatural deeds:

> If thou hast nature in thee, bear it not,
> Let not the royal bed of Denmark be
> A couch for luxury and damned incest.
>
> [1.5.81–3]

Hamlet *has* nature in him, and passion too: 'O most pernicious woman! / O villain, villain, smiling damned villain!' (1.5.105–6). And as the Ghost darts back and forth, coming and going under the stage, the son 'dances' in response, skipping backwards and forwards across the acting space: 'Art thou there, truepenny?'; '*Hic et ubique*? Then we'll shift our ground. / Come hither, gentlemen'; 'Well said, old mole. Can'st work i'th'earth so fast? / O worthy pioneer! Once more remove, good friends' (1.5.158; 164–5; 170–1).

In the intensity of the moment, Hamlet responds eagerly to the Ghost's seduction and undertakes to 'sweep' to an act of vengeance which risks his own death (1.5.31). But the remainder of the play replicates the ambiguity of the Dance itself for the spectator: the living Hamlet hangs back after all, resists his own seduction, fears the death he also embraces. His soliloquies are preoccupied with what seems an unaccountable anxiety: 'Am I a coward?' he asks (2.2.566);

> it cannot be
> But I am pigeon-liver'd and lack gall

> To make oppression bitter, or ere this
> I should ha' fatted all the region kites
> With this slave's offal
>
> [2.2.572–6]

The play registers Hamlet's ambivalence in the imagery of the period, the effect of centuries of Christian iconography. What it withholds – both from the hero and from the audience – is the place of origin which would specify the moral identity of the Ghost. At its first appearance to Hamlet, he approaches it in the explicit recognition of this uncertainty:

> Be thou a spirit of health or goblin damn'd,
> Bring with thee airs from heaven or blasts from hell,
> Be thy intents wicked or charitable,
> Thou com'st in such a questionable shape
> That I will speak to thee.
>
> [1.4.40–44]

What is a 'questionable shape'? a shape, perhaps, which prompts a question, a signifier whose significance is unknown? Does the term 'shape' imply the possibility of alternatives, of other shapes? Has a shape no shape of its own, no proper shape? Or might this figure change its shape at will, on the basis that there is behind the appearance a substantial, if immaterial identity, whether angel or demon?

The Romantic critics, locating the cause of Hamlet's delay in the character of the sensitive prince – too imaginative, too intellectual, too 'poetic', as, indeed, they were themselves, to be capable of direct intervention in the affairs of a violent world [See Chapter 2 of this Guide.] – tended to disregard the questionable shape of a spectral figure from outside the frame of what it is possible to know. And Hamlet, caught up in the immediate intensity of filial propriety and family values, at the moment of the encounter, disregards it too, accepting the spectral father's injunction as precisely *un*questionable. But his first anxiety recurs throughout the play, as the hero repeatedly reopens the 'question' of an injunction from the Ghost of a loving father who, apparently, commands an action which might incur his son's damnation. 'The spirit that I have seen', he reflects,

> May be a devil, and the devil hath power
> T'assume a pleasing *shape*, yea, and perhaps,
> Out of my weakness and my melancholy,
> As he is very potent with such spirits,
> Abuses me to damn me. I'll have grounds
> More relative than this.
>
> [2.2.594–600]

What kind of father would expose his son to the possibility of damnation? Why Adam, of course, and in Adam all his descendants. As Thomas Peyton rhetorically asks,

> Adam, what made thee wilfully at first
> To leave thy offspring to this day accursed,
> So wicked, foul and overgrown with sin;
> And in thy person all of it begin?
> (*The Glasse of Time,*
> *in the first two ages* (1620))

The play reduplicates fathers who seem to risk their sons' immortal souls by demanding acts of violence as proof of love: Old Fortinbras; Achilles, whose blood incites the rugged Pyrrhus to kill Priam; and finally Hamlet's own victim, Polonius. Claudius, who speaks on Polonius's behalf, repeats the appeal of the Ghost: 'Laertes, was your father dear to you?' And he adds, as if he had learnt from Hamlet's affirmation of the difference between appearance and 'that within', 'Or are you like the painting of a sorrow, / A face without a heart?' (4.7.106–8) Challenged to demonstrate filial love, Laertes offer the most sacrilegious of murders: 'To cut his throat i'th' church' (4.7.125). Fortinbras, however, restrained by his uncle, relinquishes the attempt to recover the lands his father lost. And Hamlet, too, on reflection, withholds the blind, hectic and deadly obedience that filial love seems to require. He seeks 'grounds', and to know the 'nobler' course. Hamlet, in other words, wants to make up his own mind.

And analysis of the play as a record of Hamlet's quest for the grounds on which to base an ethical decision represents an alternative reading to the Romantic story of the sensitive, suicidal Prince. ☐

(Catherine Belsey, *Shakespeare and the Loss of Eden*, 2001)[11]

Even Belsey, in this account of the play feels the need to return to the old critical chestnut of *Hamlet* criticism – Hamlet's delay. She explicitly confronts the Romantic and post-Romantic assumptions about a Hamlet that is too good for this world, 'too imaginative, too intellectual, too poetic' and rejects them. Instead, she locates Hamlet's delay in a confrontation between two ethical or moral demands – the demand to obey your father and the demand that you do not murder. These twin demands, though, are at the heart of the story of the first family.

■ In *Hamlet*, as in the Book of Genesis, death is in the first instance a family affair. Fratricide, the primal sin, leads on to a world of death, where innocence is no longer an option. All intimate relationships are problematic, and the most problematic are named love. For love, Gertrude marries her husband's brother, who is also his murderer; the Ghost of Old Hamlet bitterly incites his son to murder in the name of love; the son who does his loving, pious, scrupulous best to make ethical sense of the Ghost's command, casually eliminates a succession of collaborators in a series of transferential repetitions, before finally killing his uncle with a poisoned sword.[12] □

The direction in which *Hamlet* criticism seems to be moving in the latter half of the twentieth century and the early years of the twenty-first is towards a greater elucidation of the play's contexts, in more and more careful detail. This can be seen in the way that Belsey positions the central dilemmas and conflicts of the play within the development of ideas to do with the family. This criticism is at its best when it continues to engage, as the Knowles article and the Belsey book both do, with the kinds of questions that engage an audience or a reader of *Hamlet* – why does the play seem to delay Hamlet's actions? Why does Hamlet have so many soliloquies in which he appears to reflect upon his own mortality? Why does he seem more worried by his mother's marriage than his father's death? – whilst at the same time providing a *Hamlet* that is new and excitingly alien.

The final chapter of the Guide will provide a brief survey of the history of criticism that has gone before in the earlier chapters, as well as looking at two radical views of the play that may provide readers of *Hamlet* with indications of new ways of reading the play in the future, ways that might, at last, prevent us from seeing ourselves in the character of Hamlet.

CHAPTER SEVEN

Derrida and Lévinas

C hapter 2 of this Guide, in presenting the Romantic developments in
the ways in which Hamlet was discussed, largely ignored one very
important thing – its revolutionary character. The *Hamlet* of Schlegel
and Coleridge was elucidated in relation to its position within the history of literary criticism – as a further move away from neoclassical concerns with decorum and as a presiding influence on much of the
criticism that has followed it. However, it must also be noted that the
Hamlet that they wrote about was of his time. The late eighteenth and
early nineteenth centuries were a period of important political change,
both in Europe and in America, with the American Revolutionary War
being followed closely by the French Revolution, both of which had an
massive impact on the culture and writing of the whole of Europe,
England included. It is no accident, then, that the Hamlet that emerges
from that period is, himself, at odds with the world that surrounds him,
the champion of a different way of viewing things from the old order,
here represented by his uncle and his mother. This political reading is
never overt, though, in these writings. In fact, Coleridge's reading of the
play could even be seen as rather conservative. Coleridge's Hamlet has a
mind kept 'in a state of abstraction, beholding the world as hieroglyphs'.
He 'delays action till action is of no use'.[1] This kind of virtuous indolence
might be seen as a reaction to the failures of the revolutionary period of
the American and French Revolutions. Hamlet is a man in retreat from
a world that is too unforgiving.

In recent years, a more overtly political use has been made of *Hamlet*,
emerging from another period of European revolution. Its implications
might help lead us out of the dominance of the Romantic view of the
prince. In the early 1990s, following the collapse of the Soviet Union
and of the communist regimes that had dominated Eastern Europe
since the Second World War, it appeared to some that history was over.
The theory that the great ideological clashes of the past were now
behind us and that the future was merely to bear witness to the steady
progress of capitalism and liberal democracy was advanced by Francis
Fukuyama in his book, *The End of History* (1992). The French writer,

Jacques Derrida, amongst others, mounted a challenge to this prevailing feeling and this emerged in his book, *Specters of Marx: The State of the Debt, the Work of Mourning, the New International* (1994). In this book, he outlines the continuing legacy of Marx and Marxism in contemporary Europe, despite its apparent disappearance. One of the figures that he uses to discuss this is the ghost as it appears in *Hamlet*. The conference at which he gave the initial paper from which the book developed was entitled, 'Whither Marxism?'.

■ So 'Whither Marxism?' That is question the title of this colloquium would ask us. In what way would it be signalling toward Hamlet and Denmark and England? Why does it whisper to us to *follow* a host? Where? Whither? What does it mean to follow a ghost? And what if this came down to being followed by it, always, persecuted perhaps by the very chase we are leading? Here again what seems to be our front, the future, comes back in advance: from the past, from the back. 'Something is rotten in the state of Denmark', declares Marcellus at the point at which Hamlet is preparing, precisely, to *follow* the ghost ('I'll follow thee' [1.4]). And he too will soon ask him 'Whither?': 'Where wilt thou lead me? Speak; I'll go no further. *Ghost*: Marke me ... I am thy Father's Spirit.'[2] □

Derrida analyses the meeting between Hamlet and his father's ghost as a way of talking about the working out of history within time, and of introducing the idea that history can never end. The figure of the spectre became increasingly important in some of his more political work at this point and it is used to talk about the sometimes uncanny return of the past into the present, but a movement from the past into the present that is not the same as linear history, progressive history.

For our purposes as students of *Hamlet* criticism, what might perhaps be most interesting about this is that Derrida provides an exciting reading of the relationship between father and son, past and present as it appears in the play. For Derrida, this relationship is played out in the questions that Hamlet has about the way in which his father's ghost appeared and the way in which he was costumed. It moves this relationship convincingly away from the psychoanalytic arena of the family unit and into the wider consequences of the past's impact on the present.

■ The armor, this 'costume' which no stage production will ever be able to leave out, we see it cover from head to foot, in Hamlet's eyes, the supposed body of his father. We do not know whether it is or is not part of the spectral apparition. This protection is rigorously *problematic* ... for it prevents perception from deciding on the identity that it wraps so solidly in its carapace. The armor may be the body of a real artifact, a kind of technical prosthesis, a body foreign to the spectral body that it dresses, dissimulates and protects, masking even its identity. The armor lets one see nothing of the spectral body, but at the level of the head and *beneath the visor*, it permits the so-called father to see and to speak. Some slits are cut into it and adjusted so as to permit him to see without being see, but to speak in order to be heard. The *helmet*, like the visor, did not merely offer protection: it topped off the coat of arms and indicated the chief's authority, like the blazon of his nobility.[3] □

Derrida goes on to elucidate the concern that Hamlet has for the appearance of his father when he questions Marcellus about his appearance on the ramparts – whether he was armed like him, whether his armour went from head to foot (*'cap a pe'*) and so on. This produces, I think, a Hamlet who is forced to respond to the past in circumstances of which he is only partly aware. Derrida's version of *Hamlet* is obviously very limited as this analysis of the play is far from the main thread of his book. However, its suggestive nature perhaps indicates a way forwards in *Hamlet* criticism, a way that responds to the narrative lapses in the play – the way that the demands made on the character come from an undecided past and have to be operated on in an uncertain present – and allies these to the demands made on the character of Hamlet.

As these demands are couched within the realm of European politics, it is also easier to understand them as ethical demands. What was sometimes missing from Romantic and post-Romantic versions of the play and of the character was the sense that the disjunctions in the play, and between the character and the narrative, were questions of ethics. We have seen how Romanticism's discovery of Hamlet's interior life came to dominate the criticism of the early twentieth century – either in psychoanalytic diagnoses of Hamlet's family relationships or in Bradleyan 'character criticism'. Hamlet's questioning – of his father, of himself, of his mother – was seen as solipsistic, narcissistic even. To see Hamlet's questions, the play's delays and its narrative lapses as part of the way that the play articulates a much wider concern with the impact of the past on the present is potentially to break the spell of the Romantic Hamlet. Romanticism rejected the neoclassical interest in the primacy of plot as an inappropriate tool for understanding Shakespearean drama, and they were of course right not to judge the playwright by anachronistic standards. However, in rejecting the importance of narrative, they produced a Hamlet who existed in a world of his own.

Contemporary criticism has, of course, started to redress this balance, seeking historical contexts for the development of Hamlet's peculiar individuality. Where Barker and Belsey identified the birth of modern man in the play's soliloquies, others, such as Goldberg and Knowles, have elaborated on the conditions which allowed for this to happen. Still others have built on these insights to elucidate the political fields within which the play operates. Sinfield's account of the play understands the lapses in Hamlet's story, his emergence as a divided modern subject, as part of wider divisions in the emerging modern state. Belsey, Rose and Parker seek, in different ways, to redress the gender imbalance in the stories of subjectivity that appear to be told, both within *Hamlet* and in the history of its criticism.

For all the careful elucidation of context that has dominated the field of literary studies in the last few decades, perhaps there is something missing. Derrida's brief reading of the play started to ask questions about what it means to have the past impinge on the present, perhaps about what it might mean for this play to be so much a part of *our* modernity. Another French philosopher, Emmanuel Lévinas (1906–95), has discussed the play in terms of the ethical demands that are placed on its lead character. Unlike Derrida, he is not concerned with the demands that are placed on Hamlet to *act*, but rather with the ethical situation that emerges from his confrontation with death. Where Lévinas might lead us in our reading of *Hamlet*, is not towards recognising ourselves as most critics have done, but towards an awareness of what it might mean to try not to recognise ourselves in someone else. This is what is meant by an ethical demand – a demand that you respond to something other than yourself. In his book, *Time and the Other* (1946–47, trans. 1987), Lévinas argues that it is in our experience of death that we become aware that other people might make demands upon us.

■ This approach of death indicates that we are in relation with something that is absolutely other, something bearing alterity not as a provisional determination we can assimilate through enjoyment, but as something whose very existence is made of alterity. My solitude is thus not confirmed by death but broken by it.[4] □

The confrontation with death that makes us experience the limit of our own being, our own ability to encompass the world within our experience, is then explained in terms of Hamlet's own ontological doubts in the 'To be or not to be ...' speech, where Hamlet contemplates suicide, although Lévinas is also concerned with *Macbeth*.

■ Does not the hero of tragedy assume death? [...]
Prior to death there is always a last chance; this is what heroes seize, not death. The hero is the one who always glimpses a last chance, the one who obstinately finds chances. Death is thus never assumed, it comes. Suicide is a contradictory concept. The eternal immanence of death is part of its essence. In the present, where the subject's mastery is affirmed, there is hope. Hope is not added to death by a sort of *salto mortale* [a 'somersault' or 'deadly jump'], by a sort of inconsequence; it is in the very margin that it is given, at the moment of death, to the subject who is going

to die. *Spiro/spero*. [(If) I breathe, I hope] *Hamlet* is precisely a lengthy testimony to this impossibility of assuming death. Nothingness is impossible. It is nothingness that would have left humankind the possibility of assuming death and snatching a supreme mastery from out of the servitude of existence. 'To be or not to be' is a sudden awareness of this impossibility of annihilating oneself.[5] □

That is, Hamlet cannot really kill himself, as at the moment of annihilation he could not be said to be 'assuming' death, but rather death, in all its impersonality, would be taking him. Lévinas' Hamlet, then, is a character whose ontological questions are less to do with an isolation within a harsh world, or with the lapses in the narrative structure of a tragedy, but rather illustrate an ongoing ethical confrontation with the absolute alterity of the other. Hamlet, at all points, confronts the limits of his existence and his inaction is the inaction of us all. He attempts to control his experience of the world, but the world cannot be assumed in that way.

In Lévinas's ethical framework, a confrontation with death is always a confrontation with the Other, and within this confrontation we realise the limits of our own experience's ability to define the world. As well as this being an interesting and illuminating reading of Hamlet's action / inaction, of what has been called his delay, it is at least potentially illuminating for the ways in which we might approach *Hamlet* more generally. Perhaps in place of Coleridge using the play as a mirror for himself, future critics of the play might engage instead with the ethical demands that the play puts on us to confront the different.

NOTES

NOTE ON TEXT

1 W. Shakespeare, *Hamlet*, ed. H. Jenkins (London: Methuen, 1982).

INTRODUCTION

1 Harold Bloom, *Shakespeare: The Invention of the Human* (London: Fourth Estate, 1999) p. 404.
2 Bloom would argue that all their readings have been proleptically provided for by the play itself, containing within itself the genesis of the entire Western tradition of thought.

CHAPTER ONE

1 Brian Vickers, *Shakespeare: The Critical Heritage*, 6 volumes (London: Routledge, 1979) I, p. 94 (Hereafter, 'Vickers I' etc.).
2 Paul Conklin, *A History of Hamlet Criticism* (London: Routledge, 1957) p. 24.
3 Jeremy Collier, *A Short View of the Immorality and Profaneness of the English Stage* [1698] (London: Scolar Press, 1971) pp. 7–9.
4 Collier (1971) pp. 9–10.
5 This is, of course, both a cliché and a generalisation, but, like all good clichéd generalisations, quite useful.
6 J.M. Levine, *Between the Ancients and the Moderns: Baroque Culture in Restoration England* (New Haven and London: Yale University Press, 1999) p. 39, quoting John Evelyn's diary from 26 November 1661.
7 E.S. de Beer (ed.) *The Diary of John Evelyn* (London: Oxford University Press, 1959) 18 October 1966.
8 Collier (1971) p. 7.
9 Vickers I (1979) pp. 99–101.
10 Aristotle, *Poetics* (ed. and tr. Malcolm Heath) (Harmondsworth: Penguin, 1996) p. 10.
11 Aristotle (1976) pp. 11–12.
12 Vickers I (1979) p. 100.
13 Vickers I (1979) p. 186. For an account of Rymer's objections and their critical contexts, see the volume on *Othello* in this series.
14 Aristotle (1976) pp. 20–1.
15 Vickers II (1979) pp. 79–80.
16 *The Yale Edition of the Works of Samuel Johnson*, Vol. VIII: 'Johnson on Shakespeare', ed. A. Sherbo (New Haven and London: Yale University Press, 1968) pp. 1010–11.
17 Johnson (1968) pp. 973–4.
18 Johnson (1968) p. 981.
19 Johnson (1968) p. 990.
20 Johnson (1968) p. 1010.
21 Vickers III (1979) pp. 40–3.
22 Vickers III (1979) pp. 61.
23 Vickers III (1979) p. 59.
24 Vickers III (1979) p. 58.

CHAPTER TWO

1 William Hazlitt, *Character's Of Shakespeare's Plays* (London: J. Templeman, 1838) p. 88.
2 Hazlitt (1838) p. xxxi; pp. xxxii–xxxiii.
3 William Richardson, *A Philosophical Analysis of Some of Shakespeare's Remarkable Characters* (London: J. Murray, 1774) pp. 97–8.
4 Richardson (1774) pp. 102–4.
5 Richardson (1774) pp. 105–6.
6 Richardson (1774) pp. 148–52.
7 Vickers III (1979) p. 150.
8 Vickers II (1979) p. 151.
9 Paul Conklin, *A History of* Hamlet *Criticism 1601–1821* (London: Routledge, 1957) p. 94.
10 Alexander Welsh, *Hamlet in His Modern Guises* (Princeton and Oxford: Princeton University Press, 2001) p. 72.
11 Wolfgang von Goethe, *Wilhelm Meister's Apprenticeship*, tr. T. Carlyle [1824], Volume 1 (London: J.M. Dent, 1912) pp. 211–12.
12 [*Schlegel's Note:*] *It has been censured as a contradiction, that Hamlet in the soliloquy on self-murder should say, 'The undiscover'd country, from whose bourn / No traveller returns ... '. For was not the Ghost a returned traveller? Shakespeare, however, purposely wished to show, that Hamlet could not fix himself in any conviction of any kind whatever.*
13 Augustus William Schlegel, 'Criticisms of Shakespeare's Tragedies: *Hamlet*' from *Lectures on Dramatic Art and Literature* (1808), tr. J. Black (London: Henry G. Bohn, 1846) pp. 66–8.
14 Reginald A. Foakes (ed.), *Coleridge's Criticism of Shakespeare: A Selection* (London: Athlone, 1989) p. 89.
15 Samuel T. Coleridge, *Biographia Literaria* [1817] vol. 1, ed. J. Shawcross (Oxford: Oxford Univerity Press, 1907) p. 202.
16 Foakes (1989) pp. 67–8.
17 Foakes (1989) pp. 69–70.
18 Foakes (1989) p. 72.
19 Foakes (1989) p. 75–6.
20 Hazlitt (1838) pp. 80–5.
21 Hazlitt (1838) pp. 85–7.
22 Hazlitt (1838) pp. 87–8.
23 *The Letters of John Keats 1814–21*, ed. H.E. Rollins (Cambridge, MA: Harvard University Press, 1958) Letter no. 166, pp. 114–16. 'Boyardo' is the fifteenth-century court poet, Matteo Maria Boiardo, writer of the romance *Orlando Innamorata*, and favourite at the Este court in Ferrara who was well rewarded for his literary efforts.
24 Keats (1958) Letter no. 277, pp. 312–13.

CHAPTER THREE

1 Sigmund Freud, 'Some Psychopathic Characters on the Stage' [1904] in James Strachey (ed.), *The Penguin Freud Library: Volume 14: Art and Literature* (Harmondsworth: Penguin, 1985) p. 126.
2 Peter S. Donaldson, 'Olivier, Hamlet and Freud' in R. Shaughnessy (ed.), *Shakespeare on Film: New Casebooks* (London: Macmillan, 1998) p. 103.
3 This is, of course, a more general complaint about Freud's psychoanalytic account of human development as a whole. He extrapolates general rules for human development from peculiar cases.
4 Sigmund Freud, *The Interpretation of Dreams*, tr. J. Crick (Oxford: Oxford University Press, 1999) pp. 201–3.
5 Freud (1999) p. 204, n. 23.
6 Ernest Jones, *Hamlet and Oedipus* (London: Victor and Gollancz, 1949) p. 45.
7 Jones (1949) pp. 50–1.

8 Jones (1949) pp. 60–1.
9 Jones (1949) pp. 69–70.
10 Jones (1949) p. 80.
11 Jones (1949) pp. 81–2.
12 Jones (1949) pp. 82–3.
13 Jones (1949) p. 88.
14 Avi Erlich, *Hamlet's Absent Father* (Pennsylvania: Pennsylvania University Press, 1977) p. 18.
15 Erlich (1977) p. 207.
16 Erlich (1977) p. 25.
17 Erlich (1977) p. 51.
18 Erlich (1977) pp. 260–1.
19 Erlich (1977) pp. 28–31.
20 Erlich (1977) pp. 32–3.
21 Erlich cites the Variorum edition.
22 Erlich (1977) pp. 192–8.
23 Erlich (1977) p. 208.
24 Erlich (1977) pp. 249–52.
25 Elizabeth Wright, *Psychoanalytic Criticism: A Reappraisal* (2nd edition) (Cambridge: Polity Press, 1998) p. 99.
26 See Philip Armstrong, *Shakespeare in Psychoanalysis* (London: Routledge, 2001), p. 63.
27 Jacques Lacan, 'Desire and the Interpretation of Desire in *Hamlet*' (tr. Jacques-Alain Miller and James Hulbert) in *Yale French Studies*, Volume 0, Issue 55/56, *Literature and Psychoanalysis: The Question of Reading: Otherwise* (1977) p. 12.
28 Lacan (1977) pp. 17–18.
29 Lacan (1977) p. 24.
30 Lacan (1977) p. 25.
31 Lacan (1977) pp. 40–1.
32 Janet Adelman, *Suffocating Mothers: Fantasies of Maternal Origin in Shakespeare's Plays*, Hamlet *to* The Tempest (London: Routledge, 1992) p. 10.
33 Adelman (1992) p. 11.
34 Adelman (1992) pp. 12–13.
35 See the relevant part of the following chapter of this Guide.
36 Adelman (1992) pp. 15–16.
37 Adelman (1992) p. 20.
38 Adelman (1992) p. 25.

CHAPTER FOUR

1 It will be seen in the next chapter that Alan Sinfield uses the adjective 'Bradleyan' in this pejorative sense.
2 A.C. Bradley, *Shakespearean Tragedy: Lectures on* Hamlet, Othello, King Lear *and* Macbeth [1904] (Harmondsworth: Penguin, 1991) p. 29.
3 Bradley (1991) pp. 29–30.
4 Bradley (1991) p. 35.
5 Bradley (1991) p. 19.
6 Bradley (1991) pp. 108–9.
7 Bradley (1991) p. 110.
8 Bradley (1991) pp. 117–18.
9 Bradley (1991) pp. 119–20.
10 T.S. Eliot, 'Hamlet and his Problems' in *The Sacred Wood: Essays on Poetry and Criticism* (London: Faber, 1920) pp. 98–9.

11 Eliot is referring to the prose piece, 'Hamlet or the Consequences of Filial Piety' (1886) by the French poet Jules Laforgue (1860–87).

12 An essay by the French writer Michel de Montaingne (1533–92) which tackles the controversial subject of suicide and attempts a justification.

13 Eliot (1920) pp. 100–3.

14 J. Dover Wilson, *What Happens in Hamlet* (3rd edition) (Cambridge University Press: Cambridge, 1959) p. 16.

15 Wilson (1959) p. 17.

16 Wilson (1959) p. 43.

17 Wilson (1959) p. 39.

18 Wilson (1959) pp. 46–7.

19 Wilson (1959) pp. 49–50.

20 Wilson (1959) pp. 228–9.

21 G. Wilson Knight, *The Wheel of Fire: Interpretations of Shakespearian Tragedy* (2nd edition) (London: Methuen, 1949) p. 3.

22 Knight (1949) pp. 27–8.

23 Knight (1949) p. 31.

24 Knight (1949) p. 32.

25 Knight (1949) pp. 38–9.

26 Knight (1949) p. 40.

27 Knight (1949) pp. 45–6.

28 L.C. Knights, 'How Many Children Had Lady Macbeth?' in his Hamlet *and Other Shakespearean Essays* (Cambridge: Cambridge University Press, 1979) pp. 270–308.

29 L.C. Knights, 'An Approach to *Hamlet*' [1960] in his Hamlet *and Other Shakespearean Essays* (Cambridge: Cambridge University Press, 1979) pp. 55–9.

30 Knights (1979) p. 34.

CHAPTER FIVE

1 Stephen Greenblatt, *Renaissance Self Fashioning: from More to Shakespeare* (Chicago and London: Chicago University Press, 1980) p. 1.

2 Greenblatt (1980) p. 2.

3 Greenblatt (1980) p. 3.

4 Francis Barker, *The Tremulous Private Body: Essays on Subjection* (London and New York: Methuen, 1984) pp. 27–8.

5 Barker (1984) pp. 28–9.

6 Barker (1984) pp. 35–7.

7 Barker (1984) p. 38.

8 Barker (1984) p. 37.

9 Catherine Belsey, *The Subject of Tragedy: Identity and Difference in Renaissance Drama* (London: Methuen, 1985) pp. ix–x.

10 Belsey (1985) pp. 27–8.

11 Belsey (1985) pp. 40–1.

12 Belsey (1985) p. 41.

13 See Jonathan Dollimore, *Radical Tragedy: Religion, Ideology and Power in the Drama of Shakespeare and his Contemporaries* (Brighton: Harvester, 1984).

14 Belsey (1985) pp. 111–13.

15 Belsey (1985) pp. 115–16.

16 Leonard Tennenhouse, *Power on Display: the Politics of Shakespeare's Forms* (New York and London: Methuen, 1986) p. 72.

17 Tennenhouse (1986) p. 85.

18 Tennenhouse (1986) p. 87.

19 Tennenhouse (1986) pp. 88–90.

20 Tennenhouse (1986) p. 93.

21 Alan Sinfield, *Faultlines: Cultural Materialism and the Politics of Dissident Reading* (Oxford: Oxford University Press, 1992) p. 222.

22 Sinfield (1992) pp. 222–3.

23 Sinfield (1992) pp. 227–8.

24 Sinfield (1992) pp. 228–9.

25 Sinfield (1992) p. 230.

26 Harold Bloom, *Shakespeare: The Invention of the Human* (Fourth Estate: London, 1998) pp. 383–4.

27 Bloom (1998) p. 405.

28 Bloom (1998) pp. 385–6.

29 Bloom (1998) p. 408.

30 Bloom (1998) pp. 400–1.

31 Bloom (1998) pp. 408–9.

32 Bloom (1998) p. 427.

33 Ronald Knowles, '*Hamlet* and Counter Humanism' *Renaissance Quarterly*, Volume 52, 1999, p. 1046.

34 Knowles (1999) p. 1048.

35 Knowles (1999) pp. 1048–9.

36 Knowles (1999) p. 1052.

37 Knowles (1999) pp. 1058–60.

38 Knowles (1999) pp. 1061–2.

39 Knowles (1999) pp. 1063–4.

40 Jonathan Goldberg, *Writing Matter: From the Hands of the English Renaissance* (Stanford University Press: Stanford, 1990) See also his collection of essays, *Shakespeare's Hand* (University of Minnesota Press: Minnesota, 2002).

41 Jonathan Goldberg, 'Hamlet's Hand' *Shakespeare Quarterly*, Volume 39, Issue 3 (Autumn 1988) pp. 311–13.

42 An essay by Derrida entitled, 'Signature, Event, Context' is of particular importance to Goldberg's understanding of 'signature-effect' at this point (J. Derrida, 'Signature, Event, Context' in *Margins of Philosophy*, tr. A. Bass (Brighton: Harvester Press, 1982)).

43 Goldberg (1988) pp. 321–2.

44 Goldberg (1988) pp. 323–6.

CHAPTER SIX

1 Jacqueline Rose, '*Hamlet* – the "Mona Lisa" of Literature' in *Critical Quarterly*, Volume 28, 1986, p. 38.

2 Rose (1986) p. 40.

3 Jacqueline Rose, 'Sexuality in the Reading of Shakespeare: *Hamlet* and *Measure for Measure*' in J. Drakakis (ed.), *Alternative Shakespeares* (London: Routledge, 1985) pp. 95–6.

4 Rose (1985) p. 101.

5 Patricia Parker, '*Othello* and *Hamlet*: Dilation, Spying and the "Secret Place" of Woman' in *Representations*, Issue 44 (Fall 1993) p. 60.

6 Parker (1993) p. 86.

7 Parker (1993) p. 60.

8 Parker (1993) pp. 76–8.

9 Parker (1993) pp. 79–81.

10 Catherine Belsey, *Shakespeare and Loss of Eden: the Construction of Family Values in Early Modern Culture* (London: Palgrave, 2001) p. 139.

11 Belsey (2001) pp. 158–61.

12 Belsey (2001) pp. 172–3.

CHAPTER SEVEN

1 Foakes 1989, p. 76. Also see Chapter 2 of this Guide.

2 Jacques Derrida, *Specters of Marx: The State of the Debt, the Work of Mourning, the New International*, tr. P. Kamuf (London: Routledge, 1994) p. 10.

3 Derrida (1994) p. 8.

4 Emmanuel Lévinas, from *Time and the Other* [1946–47], tr. Richard A. Cohen (1987) in *The Lévinas Reader*, ed. Seán Hand (Oxford: Blackwell, 1989) p. 43.

5 Lévinas (1987) pp. 41–2.

SELECTED BIBLIOGRAPHY

Janet Adelman, *Suffocating Mothers: Fantasies of Maternal Origin in Shakespeare's Plays*, Hamlet *to* The Tempest (London: Routledge, 1992).

Aristotle, *Poetics*, ed. and tr. Malcolm Heath (Harmondsworth: Penguin, 1996).

Philip Armstrong, *Shakespeare in Psychoanalysis* (London: Routledge, 2001).

——, 'Sexuality in the Reading of Shakespeare: *Hamlet* and *Measure for Measure*', in J. Drakakis (ed.), *Alternative Shakespeares* (London: Routledge, 1985).

Deborah E. Barker and Ivo Kamps (eds), *Shakespeare and Gender: A History* (London and New York: Verso, 1995).

Francis Barker, *The Tremulous Private Body: Essays on Subjection* (London and New York: Methuen, 1984).

Catherine Belsey, *Shakespeare and Loss of Eden: the Construction of Family Values in Early Modern Culture* (London: Palgrave, 2001).

Catherine Belsey, *The Subject of Tragedy: Identity and Difference in Renaissance Drama* (London: Methuen, 1985).

Harold Bloom, *Shakespeare: The Invention of the Human* (London: Fourth Estate, 1999).

A.C. Bradley, *Shakespearean Tragedy: Lectures on* Hamlet, Othello, King Lear *and* Macbeth [1904] (Harmondsworth: Penguin, 1991).

Samuel Taylor Coleridge, *Coleridge's Criticism of Shakespeare: A Selection*, ed. Reginald A. Foakes (London: Athlone, 1989) *Biographia Literaria* [1817] vol. 1, ed. J. Shawcross (Oxford: Oxford Univerity Press, 1907).

Jeremy Collier, *A Short View of the Immorality and Profaneness of the English Stage* [1698] (London: Scolar Press, 1971).

Paul Conklin, *A History of Hamlet Criticism* (London: Routledge, 1957).

Jacques Derrida, *Specters of Marx: The State of the Debt, the Work of Mourning, the New International*, tr. P. Kamuf (London: Routledge, 1994).

Peter S. Donaldson, 'Olivier, Hamlet and Freud', in R. Shaughnessy (ed.), *Shakespeare on Film: New Casebooks* (London: Macmillan, 1998).

T.S. Eliot, 'Hamlet and his Problems' in *The Sacred Wood: Essays on Poetry and Criticism* (London: Faber, 1920).

Avi Erlich, *Hamlet's Absent Father* (Pennsylvania: Pennsylvania University Press, 1977).

John Evelyn, *The Diary of John Evelyn*, ed. E.S. de Beer (London: Oxford University Press, 1959).

Sigmund Freud, 'Some Psychopathic Characters on the Stage' [1904] in James Strachey (ed.), *The Penguin Freud Library: Volume* 14: *Art and Literature* (Harmondsworth: Penguin, 1985).

——, *The Interpretation of Dreams*, tr. J. Crick (Oxford: Oxford University Press, 1999).

Wolfgang von Goethe, *Wilhelm Meister's Apprenticeship*, tr. T. Carlyle [1824] Volume 1 (London: J.M. Dent, 1912).

Jonathan Goldberg, 'Hamlet's Hand', *Shakespeare Quarterly*, Volume 39, Issue 3 (Autumn 1988), pp. 307–27.

Stephen Greenblatt, *Renaissance Self Fashioning: from More to Shakespeare* (Chicago and London: Chicago University Press, 1980).

William Hazlitt, *Character's Of Shakespeare's Plays* (London: J. Templeman, 1838).

Samuel Johnson, *The Yale Edition of the Works of Samuel Johnson*, Vol. VIII, 'Johnson on Shakespeare', ed. A. Sherbo (New Haven and London: Yale University Press, 1968).

Ernest Jones, *Hamlet and Oedipus* (London: Victor Gollancz, 1949).

John Keats, *The Letters of John Keats 1814-21* ed. H.E. Rollins (Cambridge, MA: Harvard University Press, 1958).

G. Wilson Knight, *The Wheel of Fire: Interpretations of Shakespearian Tragedy* (2nd edition) (London: Methuen, 1949).

L.C. Knights, Hamlet *and Other Shakespearean Essays* (Cambridge: Cambridge University Press, 1979).

Ronald Knowles, '*Hamlet* and Counter Humanism', *Renaissance Quarterly*, Volume 56 (1999), pp. 1046–69.

Emmanuel Lévinas, from *Time and the Other* [1946–47], tr. Richard A. Cohen (1987) in *The Lévinas Reader*, ed. Seán Hand (Oxford: Blackwell, 1989).

Jacques Lacan, 'Desire and the Interpretation of Desire in *Hamlet*', tr. Jacques-Alain Miller and James Hulbert, *Yale French Studies*, Issue 55/56, *Literature and Psychoanalysis: The Question of Reading: Otherwise* (1977).

J.M. Levine, *Between the Ancients and the Moderns: Baroque Culture in Restoration England* (New Haven and London: Yale University Press, 1999).

Patricia Parker, '*Othello* and *Hamlet*: Dilation, Spying and the "Secret Place" of Woman', *Representations*, Issue 44 (Fall 1993), pp. 60–95.

William Richardson, *A Philosophical Analysis of some of Shakespeare's Remarkable Characters* (London: J. Murray, 1774).

Jacqueline Rose, '*Hamlet* – the "Mona Lisa" of Literature', *Critical Quarterly*, Volume 28 (1986) [This is also available in some collections of feminist criticism, including Deborah E. Barker and Ivo Kamps (eds), *Shakespeare and Gender: A History* (London and New York: Verso, 1995).]

Augustus William Schlegel, 'Criticisms of Shakespeare's Tragedies: *Hamlet*' from *Lectures on Dramatic Art and Literature* [1808], tr. J. Black (London: Henry G. Bohn, 1846).

Alan Sinfield, *Faultlines: Cultural Materialism and the Politics of Dissident Reading* (Oxford University Press: Oxford, 1992).

Leonard Tennenhouse, *Power on Display: the Politics of Shakespeare's Forms* (New York and London: Methuen, 1986).

Brian Vickers, *Shakespeare: The Critical Heritage*, 6 volumes (London: Routledge, 1979).

Alexander Welsh, *Hamlet in His Modern Guises* (Princeton and Oxford: Princeton, University Press, 2001).

J. Dover Wilson, *What Happens in Hamlet* (3rd edition) (Cambridge: Cambridge University Press, 1959).

Elizabeth Wright, *Psychoanalytic Criticism: A Reappraisal* (2nd edition) (Cambridge: Polity Press, 1998).

SUGGESTIONS FOR FURTHER READING

The reading listed below does not contain anything that has already been cited in the text of the Guide, and listed in the bibliography above. Reading in the selected texts would be advisable as a first step for any students wishing to pursue the topics of the Guide. The reading lists below will enable further study.

EARLIER STUDIES

This also lists some more recent criticism that could be said to be more 'traditional' in its approach than that in the sections given below. The first port of call for any student wishing to read some pre twentieth-century criticism should be the collection, *Shakespeare: The Critical Heritage*, edited by Brian Vickers and listed in the 'Selected Bibliography'.

Nigel Alexander, *Poison, Play, and Duel: A Study in* Hamlet (London: Routledge, 1971).

John Bayley, *Shakespeare and Tragedy* (London: Routledge, 1981).

Roland Frye, *The Renaissance* Hamlet: *Issues and Responses in 1600* (Princeton: Princeton University Press, 1984).

Martin Holmes, *The Guns of Elsinore* (London: Chatto and Windus, 1964).

G.K. Hunter, *Dramatic Identities and Cultural Tradition* (Liverpool: Liverpool University Press, 1978).

Henry Levin, *The Question of* Hamlet (New York: Oxford University Press, 1959).

Arthur McGee, *The Elizabethan* Hamlet (New Haven and London: Yale University Press, 1987).

Maynard Mack, 'The World of *Hamlet*', *Yale Review*, Volume 42 (1952).

Eleanor Prosser, Hamlet *and Being* (Stanford and London: Stanford University Press, 1967).

Mark Rose, '*Hamlet* and the Shape of Revenge' in *English Literary Renaissance* 1 (1971).

Morris Weitz, Hamlet *and the Philosophy of Literary Criticism* (London: Faber, 1964).

PSYCHOANALYTIC CRITICISM

Philip Armstrong, *Shakespeare in Psychoanalysis* (London and New York: Routledge, 2001).

——, 'Watching *Hamlet* Watching: Lacan, Shakespeare and the Mirror / Stage', in T. Hawkes (ed.), *Alternative Shakespeares volume 2* (London and New York: Routledge, 1996).

Joel Fineman, 'Fratricide and Cuckoldry: Shakespeare's Doubles', in M. Schwartz and C. Kahn (eds), *Representing Shakespeare: New Psychoanalytic Essays* (Baltimore: Johns Hopkins University Press, 1980).

Norman Holland, *Psychoanalysis and Shakespeare* (New York: Octagon Press, 1989).

David Leverenz, 'The Woman in *Hamlet*: An Interpersonal View' in *Signs*, Volume 4 (1978).

John Russell, *Hamlet and Narcissus* (Newark: University of Delaware Press, 1995).

FEMINIST CRITICISM

Phillipa Berry, *Shakespeare's Feminine Endings: Disfiguring Death in the Tragedies* (London: Routledge, 1999).

Juliet Dusinberre, *Shakespeare and the Nature of Women* (London: Macmillan, 1975).

Peter Erickson, *Patriarchal Structures in Shakespeare's Drama* (Berkeley, CA: University of California Press, 1985).

Marilyn French, *Shakespeare's Division of Experience* (London: Jonathan Cape, 1982).

Lisa Jardine, *Still Harping on Daughters: Women and Drama in the Age of Shakespeare* (Brighton: Harvester, 1983).

Carol Thomas Neely, *Broken Nuptials in Shakespeare's Plays* (New Haven: Yale University Press, 1985).

Patricia Parker, *Literary Fat Ladies: Rhetoric, Gender, Property* (London: Methuen, 1987).

Elaine Showalter, 'Representing Ophelia: Women, Madness and the Responsibilities of Feminist Criticism', in P. Parker and G. Hartman (eds), *Shakespeare and the Question of Theory* (London: Methuen, 1985).

Juliana Schiesari, *The Gendering of Melancholia* (New York and London: Cornell University Press, 1986).

Kay Stanton, '*Hamlet*'s Whores', in M. Thornton Burnett and J. Manning (eds), *New Essays on* Hamlet (New York: AMS Press, 1994).

Valerie Traub, *Desire and Anxiety: Circulations of Sexuality in Shakespearean Drama* (New York and London: Routledge, 1996).

DECONSTRUCTION, NEW HISTORICISM AND CULTURAL MATERIALISM

New historicism was initially a way of breaking free from what had become the narrow formalism of much of American deconstruction, the dominant movement in criticism in the 1970s. However, in the criticism of the last twenty years or so, it is not always possible to differentiate between work that is under the influence of deconstruction, and that which is the product of new historicism's revolutionary impact on the study of Renaissance literature. The same might be said of the two lists above – psychoanalytic and feminist criticism, which inevitably overlap, both with each other and with other kinds of theoretically informed writing. However, they at least have two discernible aims – to respond to the work of Sigmund Freud in some way and to interrogate the position of women in the play and the work of its critics. We saw, however, the way in which historicist criticism has been inflected by poststructuralist concerns in, for example, the work of Jonathan Goldberg, as seen in Chapter 5. As a result, the list below contains a wide variety of contemporary *Hamlet* criticism that is all influenced, one way or the other, by the theoretical concerns that have been at the forefront of literary study in the last two decades. It ranges from the Marxism of Terry Eagleton through to the playful poststructuralism of Bill Readings. Whilst some of these pieces will have a clearer, more defined theoretical agenda than others, it would really be a misrepresentation of the current field to provide thoroughly demarcated reading lists.

Francis Barker, *The Culture of Violence: Essays on History and Tragedy* (Manchester: Manchester University Press, 1993).

Stephen Booth, 'On the Value of *Hamlet*', in N. Rabkin (ed.), *Reinterpretations of Elizabethan Drama* (New York and London: Columbia University Press, 1969). (This is an older but highly influential essay that makes some use of structuralist ideas.)

James L. Calderwood, *To Be and Not To Be: Negation and Metadrama in* Hamlet (New York: Columbia University Press, 1983).

Linda Charnes, 'We Were Never Early Modern' in John Joughin (ed.), *Philosophical Shakespeares* (London and New York: Routledge, 2000).

Maurice Charney, *Hamlet's Fictions* (London: Routledge, 1988).

Terry Eagleton, *Shakespeare and Society: Critical Studies in Shakespearean Drama* (London: Chatto and Windus, 1967). (This book is a very early work by Terry Eagleton, but one which bares the marks of his teacher, Raymond Williams, the great Marxist literary theorist.)

——, *William Shakespeare* (Rereading literature series) (Oxford: Blackwell, 1986) Margaret W. Ferguson, '*Hamlet*: Letters and Spirits', in P. Parker and G. Hartman (eds), *Shakespeare and the Question of Theory* (London: Methuen, 1985).

Ewan Fernie, *Shame in Shakespeare* (London and New York: Routledge, 2002).

Marjorie Garber, *Shakespeare's Ghost Writers: Literature and Uncanny Causality* (New York: Methuen, 1987).

Stephen Greenblatt, *Hamlet in Purgatory* (Princeton: Princeton University Press, 2001).

Terence Hawkes, 'Telmah' in his *That Shakespeheareran Rag: Essays on a Critical Process* (London: Methuen, 1986).

John Hunt, 'A Thing of Nothing: The Catastropic Body in *Hamlet*' in *Shakespeare Quarterly*, Volume 39, Issue 1 (Spring 1988).

Frank Kermode, *Forms of Attention* (Chicago and London: University of Chicago Press, 1985), Chapter Two, 'Cornelius and Voltemand: Doubles in *Hamlet*'.

Shakespeare's Language (Harmondsworth: Penguin, 2000). (Listed here as an exciting account of all the plays (and the chapter on *Hamlet* is particularly good) even though it is not of a piece with the author's previous 'theoretical' work. It is, rather, a reaction against this and an attempt at addressing a 'non-professional' audience.)

Bill Readings, '*Hamlet*'s Thing' in M. Thornton Burnett and J. Manning (eds), *New Essays on* Hamlet (New York: AMS Press, 1994).

Nicholas Royle, *After Derrida* (Manchester: Manchester University Press, 1995).

Mark Thornton Burnett, 'The "heart of my mystery": *Hamlet* and Secrets', in M. Thornton Burnett and J. Manning (eds), *New Essays on* Hamlet (New York: AMS Press, 1994).

Index